P9-DTT-292

THE BRENNER ASSIGNMENT

THE

BRENNER ASSIGNMENT

The Untold Story of the Most Daring Spy Mission of World War II

PATRICK K. O'DONNELL

A Member of the Perseus Books Group

Da Capo Press is a member of the Perseus Books Group

Text design by BackStory Design
Set in 11 point Fairfield

Cataloging-in-Publication Data is available from the Library of Congress.
ISBN 978-0-306-81577-5
First printing, September 2008
Visit us on the World Wide Web at http://www.perseusbooks.com

Da Capo Press books are available at special discounts for bulk purchases in the United States by corporations, institutions, and other organizations. For more information, please contact the Special Markets Department at the Perseus Books Group, 2300 Chestnut Street, Suite 200, Philadelphia, PA, 19103, or call (800) 255-1514, or e-mail special.markets@perseusbooks.com.

10 9 8 7 6 5 4 3 2 1

To Stephen Hall, Howard Chappell,
and Albert "The Brain" Materazzi

And to my "cute-osaurus," the Apple of My Eye,
and the greatest daughter in the world, Lily

CONTENTS

CONTENTS

LIST OF MAPS

PREFACE

The idea for *The Brenner Assignment* began nearly seven years ago, when I was looking through the dusty files of the Tacoma Mission—an OSS covert mission in northern Italy near the end of World War II. At one point, I read Tacoma team leader Howard Chappell's description of how he disarmed the SS soldier who had been detaining him, broke his neck, and escaped. Reading Chappell's straightforward report of this episode, and yet realizing how dramatic and heroic it was, convinced me that there was a story to be told about Howard Chappell and his team. But getting Chappell to talk was a problem. For over sixty-five years, in the style of a true operative, he had remained silent about his exploits behind the lines during World War II.

After completing my previous book, *We Were One: Shoulder to Shoulder with the Marines in the Battle for Fallujah*, in 2006, on a long train ride from Boston to my home near Washington, D.C., I began thinking about my next book. I remembered Chappell's exploits, but also knew that he probably wouldn't talk to me. On the train, I contacted a very dear friend for help: Albert Materazzi, aka "the Brain," the operations officer in charge of Chappell's mission. He was also Chappell's best friend.

During one of our subsequent conversations, I told Materazzi that I planned on returning to Iraq to research my next project. Fearing my return to the country for a third time would be unlucky, he told me he would help convince Chappell to talk to me. Materazzi, too, was convinced the story must be told. In a very real sense, my ninety-three-year-old friend may have saved my life.

For the next two years, I spent every month in Materazzi's basement, a treasure trove of thousands of secret documents outlining the covert missions he directed in World War II. Tuesdays with Morrie became, for me, Tuesdays with the Brain. Imparting a few lessons on life, he became a mentor to me and the guiding light for the book I began to write. While researching the OSS files, we broke bread countless times at numerous Italian cafés in Bethesda, Maryland; we even took a trip to Italy together in 2006 so that we could interview surviving partisans who worked with the Brain's special operations teams. This was combined with years of research at the National Archives studying thousands of archives. After a few months of research at the Brain's "Historical Document Boot Camp," and hours of oral history-taking, I was ready for Howard Chappell.

Nevertheless, visiting the Bond-like operative, who lived in California, and convincing him to talk proved an exceptionally challenging endeavor over a seven-year period. Each telephone interview merely unearthed one tantalizing nugget at a time. Much to my dismay, the conversations would always end abruptly with "Well, we'll talk about it one day when you come out here." Frustrated, I finally bought a plane ticket to California, without telling Chappell. Upon arriving, I picked up the phone, had a short chat, and was dismissively given his same stock response:

"We'll talk later when you come out here."

"Howard, I am here. Can I see you tomorrow?"

He paused and, much to my surprise, he agreed. I immediately called the Brain. I needed him to cement the deal. Thankfully the Brain called Chappell and "strongly encouraged" him to tell me his story.

Following his tour of duty, Chappell had spent the remainder of his career taking down drug kingpins and Mafia dons here at home as a narcotics agent. These experiences had embedded in him a sense of alertness and survival that did not fade with age.

I'll never forget his somewhat ornery response when I called him back:

"Meet me at the gas station at Spy Glass Drive at high noon, sharp."

I arrived five minutes early, called him, and waited. A large black Lincoln Towncar with tinted windows rolled up to the vacant lot. I recognized Chappell easily. As if casing the area for threats, he peered at me from the crack of a half-opened window.

"Follow me," he confidently barked from the black sedan.

Arriving at his house, we sat in the living room. For the next ten hours, Howard Chappell took me on a journey back in time to his war behind the lines. Even at ninety years of age, Chappell commanded respect, and even fear. At times, he would fiddle with his favorite wartime dagger, now relegated to the mundane duty of opening mail. Over the next few years, I had numerous other sessions with Chappell.

Thanks to the Brain, thousands of previously unseen documents were also made available to me during my years of research at the National Archives. Finally, the story began to take shape.

OSS veterans Nick Cangelosi and Charles "Chuck" Ciccone, who each fought behind the lines with Chappell, filled in details. Chuck graciously spent two full days along with countless hours on the telephone revealing hidden details of the mission.

During the waning days of summer 2006, I took the Brain back to Italy to meet many of the aging partisan heroes his mission worked with. I went from village to village, thanks to Roberto Testolini, whose mother fought behind the lines and whose uncle, "Brownie," was part of the drama of this book. Roberto took me everywhere, taking four days out of his busy schedule to escort me to all the drop zone sites and places where OSS operative Stephen Hall and Howard Chappell fought. He also arranged many interviews with the now aging partisan warriors who fought shoulder to shoulder with Hall and Chappell. I walked and hiked large portions of Hall's and Chappell's battlescape, enjoying some of the best natural scenery in the world.

I would also like to thank ISBREC (Istituto Storico Bellunese della Resistenza e dell'Età Contemporanea), a professional historical institute dedicated to the history of the Italian resistance, for their invaluable assistance. And I am most grateful to Carla at the Bolzano historical institute, for inviting me and Albert Materazzi to a conference on Italian covert operations.

I'm indebted to two Italians: Paride Brunetti, the fearless partisan commander (known as "Bruno" during the war), for answering my detailed questionnaire; and Judge Guiseppe Sorge for allowing me to see some of his research, specifically his interview with the countess's housekeeper.

I've spent over eight years researching the declassified files of the OSS at the National Archives. I would like to thank Larry McDonald and John Taylor for their archival assistance.

I would also like to thank my agent and friend, Andrew Zack, and my close friend Rajai Hakki, a hard-charging US Marine I met during the Battle of Fallujah. His editorial comments, advice, and ideas were invaluable to the manuscript. His keen sense of the story and flow helped me overcome numerous bouts of writer's block. He also provided me with the morale and encouragement necessary for a long project such as this. I would also like to thank Brian Fitzpatrick for his editorial suggestions and comments. I'm indebted to Madison Parker for timeless proofreading and her keen eyes.

I would like to thank the staff at Da Capo, specifically Ashley St. Thomas and the best publicist I have ever had, Lissa Warren.

Most importantly, I would like to thank my editor and friend, Robert Pigeon. Bob's vision and guidance were an integral part of the process, especially his understanding of the vast challenge of capturing the drama from a forgotten piece of history and his suggestion that the story of Chappell's team should begin, as it truly did, with Stephen Hall's "Brenner assignment." I benefited from Bob's peerless editorial skills and judgment.

PROLOGUE

MAY, 1945
ANDRICH, ITALY

A gray-green bottle glistened in the Alpine snow. A blackened cork protected its fragile content, a yellowed piece of paper. The bottle, part of a collection of bottles buried next to the wall of a little house in the tiny Italian mountain village of Andrich, held the written legacy of a bold young saboteur.

Peering at the bottles, Captain Howard Wheeler Chappell vaguely recalled a lesson from his days in grammar school. History tells the story of a Japanese captain stranded on a reef. The shipwrecked skipper recorded his plight on a thin plank of wood, placed it in a bottle, corked it, and set it adrift. Almost magically, the bottle made landfall at the captain's home port, finally delivering his message. Throughout the ages, messages have been transported in such small glass vessels.

These bottles, buried in the Italian snow, served the same purpose, preserving the story of Chappell's fellow officer. They contained the diary and letters of his brother in arms, Captain Roderick Stephen Goodspeed Hall.

As he stood above the bottles, Chappell was also standing in the middle of a journey into his recent past. The officer did not know the bottles would send him back to learn more about Hall's sojourn behind the lines, revisiting familiar places and familiar souls. No stranger to battle, Chappell had just survived one of the epic covert missions of World

War II. Bearded, wearing a dirty, ragged M-42 paratrooper jumpsuit, he was physically and mentally exhausted, but emotionally victorious.

A stale odor emerged as Chappell's powerful hand pulled out the cork. He unrolled the brittle yellow paper and scanned Hall's neat handwriting. The letter contained clues to one of the great, untold stories of World War II: the adventures of a young man fighting behind enemy lines, enduring great hardship on a solitary quest to cripple Nazi Germany.

Chappell focused on a single sentence embodying both men's missions:

"I perfected a plan for blowing out one of the tunnels on the railroad through the Brenner."

The Brenner—one of the most famous and important mountain passes in the world. Hall's life for the last two years had been aimed toward getting there, and the bottled messages he left in Andrich were a mere sixty miles away. As the crucial supply and communication corridor through the Alps, the pass had been fought over by rival armies since Roman times. When Adolf Hitler and Italian leader Benito Mussolini personally met there at the beginning of World War II, shaking hands to memorialize their infamous Pact of Steel, the pass connecting Italy and Austria gained symbolic importance—and Hall meant to strike at its heart. Chappell and a crack team of commandos had come to back him up.

The Brenner Pass was no less important to Nazi Germany than it was to ancient Rome. Through the Brenner's railroad tunnels and highways flowed the troops and supplies that sustained the German armies fighting the Allies farther to the south. Control of this vital throughway determined whether these armies would fight on or wither on the vine. The Brenner was a carotid artery of the Third Reich—and the point of convergence of Hall's and Chappell's lives.

1

Letter to Destiny

A PLUME OF MATTE-BLACK SMOKE billowed from the locomotive's stack, and gritty soot stippled the rolling mass of clouds that began to cover the star-filled night as the fifteen-car train sped down the steel tracks toward a rural army camp north of Corvallis, Oregon. An arc of white lightning signaled an imminent storm. During the wee hours before the northwestern dawn, a light in one of the passenger cars flickered as Lieutenant Roderick Stephen Hall put the final touches on a letter that would change his life. Writing to a deputy at the newly formed Office of Strategic Services (OSS), he was proposing to undertake one of the most audacious sabotage missions of World War II.

Dear Mr. Stebbins,

It seems to me, who knows nothing about your organization [OSS], that finding an agent with the necessary personal accoutrements to go to Cortina [on the southwest approaches of the Brenner Pass] and carry out missions of sabotage, political organization, reconnaissance, or whatever is desired would be difficult. Even if he was a European, he would encounter official questioning at every turn, with danger of exposure each time. And traveling by land, how could he carry sufficient explosives and tools to effect sabotage himself if all other plans failed?

These obstacles could, of course, be overcome one way or another: but here is my suggestion, based on the premise that sabotage is more important in the near future than political organization: Drop a man by parachute on the open country between Pocol and the Falzàrego Pass and drop enough Army "mountain rations" and personal equipment to sustain him indefinitely in the peaks, if necessary. Drop TNT and a tool kit. I believe one could get away with it, if the jump was made in the early dawn when mist rises profusely over the terrain or through a snowfall. This man, if he is a good rock and snow climber and skier would have no trouble moving about the valley unnoticed, even in the day time. The matter of tracks in the snow is of no consequence, paths and brooks could cover his movements and he could always take to the mountain rock. Operating even under adverse conditions, this man, I believe, could block the Ampezzo Highway and railroad beyond use during the winter within three days after he landed. It should be possible for him to blow out the Drava River roads within another ten days. Thereafter, he could work on any opportunities that presented themselves. I feel sure he would not have to search out anti-Nazi elements for laying the plans for continued sabotage, they would come to him. Of course, the problem of how he would get out and save his own skin is a matter of chance and circumstance. Perhaps, he would have to perch on the peak of Antelao nibbling concentrated chocolate until German capitulation.

I would be willing to do the job and I think I could. Here are my qualifications:

Trained in military demolitions.

Trained in mapping, reconnaissance, communications and similar subjects. (I am battalion S-2) Familiar with the Val Ampezzo. Particularly the well-known pass and minor terrain features from walks and skiing.

Skilled in rock and snow climbing with fifteen years experience on the cliffs and snow of N.E., in Wyoming (Grand Tetons) and Cortina. Expert rifle and pistol shot since 1930. National Rifle Association and Army.

Physically: Somewhat above average.

Endurance: Accustomed to living in the open under all conditions. No major operations, illnesses or frailties.

Twenty-eight years of age. Education: I am no linguist, but I have picked up enough Italian in five days at Cortina to get about conveniently. Personal situation: Unmarried, ready to go any time, under any circumstances that augur success.

Cordially yours,
R. S. G. Hall,
2nd Lt. 270th Engr. (C) Bn. Camp Adair, Oregon

The roads and valleys Hall cited all led to the great mountain pass that links Italy with Austria and the rest of western Europe: the Brenner. Specifically, Hall was proposing to cut off the small arteries that fed the major artery. The scheme was novel, innovative, and bordering on suicidal.

Roderick Stephen Goodspeed Hall, born in Peking, China, in 1915, came from a privileged background. His father Raymond was influential in the State Department, a wealthy international businessman with a PhD. His mother was a doctor. As a young man, he received his education at Phillips Academy Andover, one of the most prestigious prep schools in America. Known as "Monk," "Goodspeed," or "Rod," his charismatic nature earned him many friends at school. He scored high in drama, Latin, and history, but received a C– for neatness.

After graduating from Andover in 1933, the eighteen-year-old traveled the world embarking on a lifetime journey that would take him on numerous adventures in many exotic places. He began his sojourn as a sailor on a steamer traveling up and down the West Coast, and moved on to work in the oil fields of Texas. Like Theodore Roosevelt, he also became a committed outdoorsman. An avid skier and rock climber, he tested his mettle climbing the Grand Tetons of Wyoming.

After a few years experiencing life and the outdoors, Hall put his journey on hold to attend Harvard University. He earned mediocre grades, dropped out after a couple of semesters, and went to Italy for the 1937–38 winter on a ski trip. The experience changed his life.

Cortina d'Ampezzo is roughly a hundred and fifty miles northwest of Venice and sixty miles southwest of the Brenner Pass. The landscape is breathtaking; the dominant features are the gray-faced, snow-capped Dolomites, a mountain range forming part of the lower Alps, which run from Italy through Switzerland and Austria. Playing the part of the international playboy, Hall enjoyed the good life, staying at a famous Cortina resort known as the Hotel Argentina. Hiking, rock climbing, and cross-country skiing filled his days. Hall's firsthand experience with the Brenner area would later prove valuable for his clandestine mission in World War II.

After returning to the United States, Hall tried his hand again at academics, this time at Yale. Meanwhile, in Europe, Hitler and Mussolini were solidifying their Pact of Steel, planning to carve up most of western Europe. After Hitler invaded Poland in September 1939, the country fell quickly. By the summer of 1940 France had fallen, and likewise, once again, had Hall's academic standing.

In 1941, Hall had again dropped out of college and was searching once more for purpose, or another adventure. With the winds of war blowing toward America, Hall patriotically joined the US Army as a private—an enlisted man.

Army life suited him. Because he quickly grew bored, he eagerly took on new projects, and his energy and enthusiasm catapulted him rapidly through the ranks to staff sergeant. He impressed his commanding officer by taking on the task of writing a comprehensive history of his regiment from the Revolutionary War to 1941. Hall was realizing his potential.

Twenty-six years old, five foot ten, muscular, good-looking, intelligent, and with a flair for leadership, Hall was now in his prime. His commander recommended him for Officer Candidate School (OCS). While he was at OCS, he was fascinated by the war and came to believe that a single individual could make a difference. Hall had a messianic faith in himself, and he set out to conceive a plan he could execute personally that would alter the course of the war. During his spare time, Hall began devising his plan for the Brenner Pass, hoping that someday it would become his Brenner assignment. On paper, the scheme seemed workable, but would he ever have a chance to try his plan? As the circumstances unfolded, reality on the ground would eclipse even Hall's best-laid plans.

Sporting his brand-new lieutenant's gold bars, the Army assigned Hall to the 270th Engineer Battalion, a unit gearing up for war at Camp Adair, a former logging camp a few miles north of Corvallis, Oregon. Because of its fifty thousand acres of variable terrain, the War Department had chosen Camp Adair as the location to train four infantry divisions: the 91st, the 96th, the 104th, and the 70th. The 70th, known as the Trailblazer Division, ultimately gobbled up Hall's 270th Engineers. During the war, Corvallis became the second-largest city in Oregon. The hard-charging soldiers dubbed the camp "Swamp Adair" for the constant downpours.

Under these damp and rugged conditions, Hall learned the core skills of a combat engineer: how to build things and how to blow things up. Hall learned to erect bridges and fortifications and even lay minefields, but of greater importance to him, he became an expert in demolitions. The budding engineer also mastered the fundamental tools of the infantryman—the pistol and the rifle. As a soldier capable of fighting with his brain as well as brawn, Hall became his company's intelligence chief (known as "S-2"), assuming responsibility for collecting and analyzing information about what an enemy could do to thwart a unit's mission in the field. Hall's S-2 duties required him to develop a set of intelligence-handling skills that would come in handy for a behind-the-lines secret agent. During his time at Camp Adair, Hall was unwittingly preparing himself for the adventure of his life.

By the time of the invasion of Italy in 1943, Hall began to see that the hour for his Brenner plan was approaching. In the Allied effort to knock Italy out of the war, Lieutenant General Mark Clark's Fifth Army had carved out a small toehold on the beaches of Salerno in Italy. The Salerno campaign inspired Hall to flesh out his plans for the Brenner mission. On leave from his rigorous training schedule, Hall went home to see his family and friends in Connecticut. It was on his return journey that he put the finishing touches on the plan and wrote the letter that brought him to the attention of the Office of Strategic Services.

✳ ✳ ✳

The OSS was born in the summer of 1941. Initially called the Office of the Coordinator of Information (COI), it was America's first central intelligence organization. Before the OSS was created, multiple government departments gathered information in reports sent arbitrarily up the chain of command in the hope that the most crucial information would find its way to the White House. No clearinghouse existed to ensure the information was shared, funneled, or packaged for White House review and direction.

To lead the new agency, President Franklin Delano Roosevelt could not have chosen a more dynamic or qualified figure than Wall Street lawyer William J. Donovan. One of America's most highly decorated heroes of World War I and former Assistant Attorney General of the United States, he was a larger-than-life figure. Commanding a battalion of the 165th Infantry Regiment, better known as the "Fighting 69th," Donovan won the Medal of Honor, a Distinguished Service Cross, and two Purple Hearts, earning himself the nickname "Wild Bill."

After the war, Donovan traveled extensively, resuming his legal practice and serving as Assistant Attorney General under President Calvin Coolidge. In the late 1920s, he served as personal political advisor for President Herbert Hoover. His position of influence and power allowed Donovan to build relationships at all levels of American society and throughout the world.

In 1940, Donovan traveled overseas as an official emissary from President Roosevelt to report on Britain's staying power in the war. Hoping to win American support, Prime Minister Winston Churchill granted Donovan unprecedented access to Britain's greatest intelligence secrets. Churchill eventually recommended that FDR make Donovan America's intelligence chief.

Many of the techniques and strategies America has used to fight every clandestine war developed out of Wild Bill Donovan's vision. After his appointment as chief of the OSS, Bill Donovan formulated an integrated "combined arms" approach of shadow-war techniques: "persuasion, penetration, and intimidation . . . are the modern counterparts of sapping and mining in the siege warfare of former days." Propaganda represented the "arrow of initial penetration." Espionage, sabotage, and guerilla operations would then soften up an area before conventional forces invaded. The integration of shadow-war techniques was a groundbreaking approach to covert warfare.

Donovan considered his main competition the Germans, saying they were "big league professionals in shadow warfare, while America lagged behind as the bush league club." The only way to catch up with Germany, he told Roosevelt, was to "play a bush league game, stealing the ball and killing the umpire."

Making the best of his vast network of personal contacts, Donovan possessed a flair for picking the right people for the right job. Wild Bill threw together the OSS practically overnight from scratch. He organized the OSS into departments such as Research and Development, Counterintelligence, Secret Intelligence, and Special Operations. To fill these departments, Donovan tapped his high-society connections: Ivy League schools, law firms, and major corporations. The OSS may have been dubbed "Oh So Social" for its blue-blooded foundation, but in truth the OSS recruited anybody with useful skills. Safecrackers freshly sprung from prison would purloin documents from embassy safes and deliver them to Ivy League professors for analysis. Debutantes worked alongside army paratroopers. One study noted: "The OSS undertook and carried out more different types of enterprises, calling for more varied skills than any other single organization of its size in the history of our country." For work in the field, the OSS needed not only the best and the brightest intelligence analysts, but out-of-the-box thinkers and risk-takers. Stephen Hall was an archetypical example of this group.

Hall's Brenner proposal attracted the attention of the Special Operations (SO) branch of the OSS. According to a memorandum sent to the president on December 22, 1941, SO was responsible for "Sabotage, Fifth Column activities, and other forms of subversive action." SO also conducted guerrilla warfare: "the establishment and support of small bands of local origin under definite leaders and the formation in the United States of guerrilla forces military in nature."

To his surprise, Hall received a letter from the OSS ordering him to report to Washington, D.C., for training. After flying across the country,

Hall reported to 2430 E Street, a cluster of masonry buildings located on a bluff overlooking the Potomac River. The new headquarters for the OSS, known as the Q Building, was sandwiched between a turreted brewery and an abandoned gasworks. Hall confidently walked through the entrance to undergo a brief orientation. His next stop was Area B, a base near Washington, D.C., designated as an OSS training ground for operatives, spies, and saboteurs. Area B, nine hundred acres of mountainous terrain lying twenty miles north of Frederick, Maryland, had formerly been a recreational project of the National Park Service. One part of Area B is now the presidential retreat, Camp David.

SO's training regime had a number of goals in mind:

> Instruction of agent personnel recruited for infiltration into enemy-occupied territory, either as individual saboteurs and Fifth Columnists or to organize and direct locally recruited guerrilla bands or individual sub-agents. Or chains of individual sub-agents. The program was further designed to permit such agents to effect arrangement to supply local resistance groups.

Hall's training included sabotage and organization of guerrilla movements.

Before recruits entered the program, the OSS stripped them of their personal belongings and issued olive drab one-piece uniforms. The recruits received code names to hide their identities from their fellow trainees.

Hall's first instructor, dubbed "the Shanghai Buster" or "Fearless Dan," was in his fifties, thin and gray-haired—he looked more like "Toothless Dan." British Major William Ewart Fairbairn was, however, one of the world's most lethal hand-to-hand combat experts. Fearless Dan had reputedly been involved in hundreds of street fights. As assistant commissioner of the municipal police during the twenties and thirties in one of the toughest cities on earth—Shanghai, China—Fairbairn developed one of the deadliest systems of street fighting known to man. Fairbairn himself called it "gutter fighting": "You are interested in disabling or killing your enemy, that is why I teach what I call 'gutter fighting.' There is no fair play; no rules except to kill or be killed."

One recruit summed it up this way: "All of us who were taught by Major Fairbairn soon realized that he had an honest dislike for anything that smacked of decency in fighting, to him there were no rules in staying alive. He taught us to enter a fight with one idea: to kill an opponent quickly and efficiently."

The wiry master began by teaching the recruits how to handle the Fairbairn-Sykes, a razor-sharp stiletto of Fairbairn's personal design. Fairbairn taught the recruits the art of silent killing. "The knife is a silent, deadly weapon," the instructor would say. "It's great for sentries. Never mind the blood, just take care of it quickly." The OSS issued Fairbairn's stiletto to many of its recruits.

After learning how to hack and slash, the recruits went through Fairbairn's "House of Horrors," a darkened labyrinth of popup targets, to learn how to handle a pistol in close combat. As the recruits moved through the house, trainers simulated battle with flashing lights and resounding gunshots, as Nazi silhouettes popped out of darkened rooms. Fairbairn emphasized a technique known as "point shooting," getting off quick hits on the targets. Hall, already a crack shot, navigated the House of Horrors with ease.

Finally, Hall and the other recruits learned gutter fighting. Fairbairn explained:

[Gutter fighting] is for fools. You should never be without a pistol or a knife. However, in case you are caught unarmed, foolishly or otherwise, the tactics shown here will increase your chances of coming out alive.

One of Fairbairn's techniques, the "Tiger Claw," involved stabbing an opponent's eyes with clenched fingers:

Deceive your opponent. Make him think you are out on your feet, now bring your Tiger Claw up from the cellar and put force behind it. It will knock your opponent out. But you must attack with surprise.

Another weapon in Fairbairn's arsenal was a karate chop known as the "Axe Hand." A single blow to the Adam's apple with the bony edge of the hand can kill a man.

Fairbairn's advice on countering a bear hug was equally diabolical: "go limp . . . grab his testicles . . . ruin him."

Fairbairn also taught Hall and the other trainees how to roll a simple newspaper into a stiletto that can be driven lethally into the soft fleshy tissue under an opponent's chin.

While in hand-to-hand combat training, Hall met his closest friend, Second Lieutenant Joseph Lukitsch, a twenty-eight-year-old paratrooper of Austrian descent. At five foot ten, Lukitsch was the picture of health, possessing a keen wit and a basic command of German. The Clevelander, known for his silent presence, was a natural leader. He carried himself with the demeanor of Gregory Peck, a man of few words, often responding with a simple "Yep." He had a strong moral compass and loyalty to those around him. Like many leading men of his day, he was sentimental but reserved. As a result, his personality meshed perfectly with Hall's.

Hall and Lukitsch went through demolition school together, where they met the masters of destruction, Frank Gleason and Charlie Parkin. Formerly combat engineers, the two instructors, trained by the British Special Operations Executive (SOE), taught recruits how to use demolitions strategically and how to cripple a city. SOE training went beyond simple sabotage to destroying locomotives, power plants, bridges, tunnels, and communication systems. Gleason summed up their SOE-inspired training: "We learned how to make people sick by poisoning a city's water supply. We learned how to make explosives from sugar and basic household supplies. How to start a fire that could take out a city. Shitty stuff like that. We were taught how to fight dirty."

One of Gleason's "dirty tricks" was a novel explosive substance, developed by OSS scientists, known as "Aunt Jemima." The gritty substance looked like simple baking flour and could even be baked into muffins and bread. But after adding a blasting cap, Aunt Jemima was deadly. Gleason demonstrated Aunt Jemima to trainees by baking explosive muffins.

Like other recruits, after finishing basic sabotage school, Hall and Lukitsch were let loose by the OSS on the local Washington, D.C., area to execute mock sabotage missions on American targets as if they were enemy agents. One trainee infiltrated an armaments factory and planted a dummy bomb. Once safely out of the plant, he boldly called the police. The FBI was not informed. If the men were caught by the FBI, they would likely be roughed up, even tortured. For an added twist of reality, the OSS would deny their existence. It was all part of the OSS's realistic training.

After Hall and Lukitsch passed their final tests, they celebrated their graduation as secret operatives with a party at the opulent Statler Hotel, a stone's throw from the White House. The rooftop restaurant offered a fine view of the Washington skyline, a glittering panorama of evening lights. Lukitsch was accompanied by his future wife, Eleanor, a beautiful Broadway actress he fatefully met while on liberty in New York. Remembering her husband's friend's eyes, she saw "a strong, quiet, confident-looking man, a man with a mission." She sensed Hall was destined to do something important.

2

"Looking for Trouble"

Fort Benning's 250-foot jump towers loomed in the sky, four-armed Goliaths made of cold, painted steel. The angular monsters knifed into the clouds, their massive arms each supporting a fully deployed parachute. The looming towers stood like gatekeepers to America's newest elite soldiers—paratroopers. Many paratrooper wannabes washed out of the program when they failed to get past the jump towers.

At six feet two inches and 230 pounds, with arms that could rip through his shirt sleeves, twenty-four-year-old instructor Howard Chappell dominated the Fort Benning Jump School's towers during the summer of 1943. Chappell, one of America's first paratroopers, commanded the giant gatekeepers. He was a sight to see: his blond hair slicked back and glistening, his posture absolutely straight, his body muscled and sun bronzed. One of the recruits muttered to another, "Flash Gordon."

As the Georgia sun beat down on raw recruits, they confronted the special challenge faced by every paratrooper—learning how to jump out of a perfectly good airplane. And Chappell was there to guide the way.

"Move it! Are you strapped in?"

Chappell made sure the harness fit snugly on the recruit. One of them seemed to hesitate.

"Are you ready to jump?" Chappell barked.

The man nodded as Chappell strapped him into a harness. The winch in the tower pulled the harnessed recruit into the azure sky. When the arm reached its peak, it released the chute with the recruit attached, and both dropped to the earth.

Chappell, a star football player at Case Western, volunteered for the army in 1941, ten months before Pearl Harbor. Born and raised by a blue-collar family in Cleveland, Ohio—Chappell's father was a mail-man—his ethnic origin was Germanic. He told his recruiter why he signed up: "There is going to be a war. I want to be in it."

Chappell's sardonic humor, punctuated by his signature half grin, was evident on his military application. With youthful bravado, he listed his profession as "actor." Initially placed in an artillery unit, he soon moved to the military police. Because of his hard-nosed, ornery disposition, the job fit Chappell like a glove, but for one problem: Chappell frequently became the man in need of policing. Chappell put it best: "I got into a couple of scraps."

Under investigation for several incidents, the young MP gained exceptional notoriety as a brawling bad boy. His infamy caught the eye of General Robert Beightler, then commander of the 37th Division. The division was training in Camp Shelby, Mississippi.

"General Beightler bawled the hell out of me, but later made me his personal bodyguard," Chappell later recounted. The young private continued to impress the general, who recommended him for officer candidate school.

"There were a couple more scraps," Chappell recounted. "I ended up reporting to OCS with my shirt ripped to shreds."

As at Case Western, Chappell applied himself diligently to the training. Upon receiving his commission, a major commented: "You finished here like a gentleman, even though you weren't dressed like one the day you came in."

The newly minted second lieutenant was transferred to a replacement depot, where they slated him for deployment to Europe. Chappell wasn't keen on the idea.

"I was supposed to be put in a cavalry unit and they were gonna ship me somewhere else," Chappell remembered. "For a young guy, I was pretty obnoxious. I wanted more training, so I personally confronted a full bird colonel and told him I would go anywhere, but I would not go to a replacement depot to just be a replacement troop. The colonel sternly looked at me and said, 'Looks like you're looking for trouble. There's only one place for you.'

"'What's that?' I responded.

"'Paratroops.'"

In 1942, Chappell became one of America's fledgling paratroopers. The airborne were then, and still are, a special breed of warrior. The men volunteered from all walks of life, some from the "wrong side of the tracks." Airborne units subjected raw recruits to an exceptionally rigorous regimen of forced marches, calisthenics, and running, conditioning the men for the unique rigors of landing and fighting behind enemy lines. Airborne training was notoriously exhausting, both mentally and physically. The airborne had a high washout rate.

"After I got in," said Chappell, "I found out what the hell the colonel was talking about. It was tough."

Chappell got in on the ground floor of America's airborne efforts. The 82nd Infantry Division had just split in half, creating the 101st and the 82nd Airborne Divisions.

Airborne troopers were elite soldiers set apart by their smart-looking khaki M-42 jumpsuits, bloused into jump boots. After completing four jumps, they earned their precious silver jump wings. This decoration was highly coveted by regular infantrymen in World War II and still is today. Airborne troops strutted around the regular infantry like game-cocks, referring to them dismissively as "legs."

The early airborne troops were a paradoxical mix of youthful wildness and Spartan discipline. Troopers were encouraged to believe they could lick any five men, thanks to their superior training. As a paratrooper Chappell established impossible standards for himself, far above the norm, propelling him to do extraordinary things.

With his deep green eyes, slicked-back blond hair and Herculean physique, Lieutenant Chappell fit his nickname of Flash Gordon like a glove and easily obtained all the revelry he wanted. Chappell summed up the experience in one sentence: "There was plenty of wine, women, and song."

The paratroopers put the myth of their revelry to the test in nearby Phenix City, Alabama, a small town on the other side of the Chattahoochee River known for its rundown bars. One infamous incident involved a townie stabbing a paratrooper in the back during a drunken brawl at the Lone Star Tavern, killing him instantly. The barkeep allegedly allowed the assailant to escape through the back door. Upon hearing of the incident, the jump school paratroopers rose from the barracks and tore the Lone Star Tavern to the ground with their bare hands.

✳   ✳   ✳

Chappell's commanders, however, noticed him primarily for his outstanding military prowess and assigned him the role of gatekeeper for airborne recruits. His job: to wash out men.

"I got up the next morning and went to the towers. I stood around like a big dumb hick trying to figure out what I was doing. The sergeants stared at me. I stared back. I wanted to ask them what the hell I was going to be doing or I was going to act like I already knew. I went into the office, sat down. Several sergeants came in."

"So, you're the new lieutenant?"

"Yeah," Chappell responded.

Chappell's presence alone made it understood—Chappell was taking over. It was time to get to work. Beginning by improvising, Chappell developed the course that would turn a group of raw recruits into a well-oiled, professional outfit. In typical fashion, Chappell made it up as he went along.

Chappell also taught hand-to-hand combat in sandpits near the jump towers. Most of his knowledge that he used in training recruits came from personal experience.

"I taught myself," Chappell explained. "There are only a few basic moves you need to know: chops, kicks, and a couple of throws." Chappell mastered these motor movements, becoming an expert in disabling armed opponents. He taught young recruits how to kill enemy sentries silently and how to defeat ground troops with their hands. Despite his mastery of hand-to-hand fighting, Chappell was still a pragmatist, saying, "The easiest way to kill a man is to shoot him." Nevertheless, the hand-to-hand training he perfected would one day save his life.

In the middle of 1943, Chappell's life changed forever when he met Colonel Garland Williams. The colonel, as Chappell recalled, was chief of the Narcotics Bureau in New York City before the war. He was a friend of Bill Donovan, and Donovan sent him to pick out paratroopers for service in the OSS. Apparently, Chappell's congenial touch caught Williams's attention. Chappell opined, "I gave him a real hard time. Williams then took me aside and said, 'They are going to put you in charge of training.'"

With his typical sardonic smirk, Chappell responded, "Been there, done that."

Nevertheless, the young lieutenant was ordered to report to Washington, D.C. After flying in on a C-47, Chappell flagged a cab, which he took to the same nondescript building that Stephen Hall had earlier reported to. Wearing his neatly pressed khaki jumpsuit, silver wings glistening in the light, he swaggered up to the guard desk. "The guy sitting there didn't look very impressive."

"I'm here to see Colonel Williams."

The next thing Chappell knew, four guys came out of nowhere and began to grill him.

"Who are you?" barked one of the men.

Chappell threw back an insult, he remembered, thinking to himself, *They're full of shit.*

The young lieutenant's blustery attitude got him through the door and beyond—he fit right into OSS culture. They had recruited him because he understood the necessity of taking risks.

Chappell continued to work his way through the corridors of the old brewery, requesting to see Colonel Williams.

Williams's aide responded that he needed an appointment.

"I'm sure I do," Chappell responded, "but where is his office?"

Once Chappell finally tracked down Colonel Williams, the colonel greeted Chappell and asked him a few questions about the quality of the paratroopers. After the conversation, an aide escorted Chappell down a long hallway into the office of "Wild Bill" Donovan.

Chappell remembered his first meeting with Donovan:

"He looked like Kris Kringle in a uniform. He rarely raised his voice. He had presence. He only raised his voice when he got excited."

Donovan got down to business and the two men discussed the necessity of inserting commandos in an operational group. The OGs needed highly trained soldiers, men who could drop into enemy territory and fight. They would work as a team and perform on their own initiative.

After shaking Chappell's hand, Donovan told him: "Howard, we are putting you in charge of the German Operational Group." The OSS had selected Chappell to train and command the American shadow soldiers who would fight within the borders of Nazi Germany itself.

3

Odyssey

THE PROW OF THE BRITISH LUXURY liner cut through the emerald waves of the Atlantic Ocean, flanked by several destroyer escorts. Her prewar colors of white, red, and black were slathered under a dull coat of naval gray with the forlorn hope of blurring the ship from searching eyes on German U-boats. In the bowels of the ship one could discern remnants of an opulent past; vestiges of mahogany and brass still adorned the bulkheads. The British Navy had converted the ship into a troop transport, her finery crated and warehoused for better times. Now she was hauling human cargo, troops destined for North Africa and Europe, including over a dozen operatives from the OSS Special Operations branch, among them Hall and Lukitsch.

Ship life, mirroring the monotonous repetition of the ocean waves, quickly led to incessant boredom. The men strolled between the port and starboard sides of the promenade, smoking and talking to no end. However, the tedium was punctuated with rigid naval procedure. Upon their embarkation, the captain had briefed the troop passengers with austere British formality. At least once a day, a lamp would illuminate and an alarm would sound general quarters.

On the long trip over, the men had nothing better to do but joke with one another. The tomfoolery was endless. Numerous bets were made as to who would make another seasick first. The men mixed spoiled food into each other's meals and groused on unsavory topics to make the stomach churn. There was nothing to do but watch one another's hair grow. Hall's hair grew faster than the others. When he would peek out from the rows of six-bed racks, his friend Joe often exclaimed: "No! The

Head! Get it back in there!" With all this horseplay, the men had no choice but to bond. Lukitsch and Hall, who had earlier developed a close camaraderie, became the best of friends as they developed a deep respect and admiration for one another.

The uneventful trip spanned several weeks. Having traversed over a thousand miles of the Atlantic Ocean, the convoy finally found its way to the shores of North Africa. The ship docked in Algiers. The men's first stop turned out to be a replacement depot, or "repo depot." In the midst of olive drab pyramidal tents, Hall, Joe, and two other operatives were put on temporary duty as platoon leaders of an African American company. Their responsibilities included mail screening and censoring, as well as conducting "calisthenics, close order drill, and hikes." Regarding the black soldiers, Lukitsch said, "These are good men, and lots of fun." At the time, the US Army racially segregated most black units and assigned them white commanding officers. Hall, Lukitsch, and the two others experienced America's early race relations first-hand. Nevertheless, they treated the men fairly, challenging them with physical training the same way they would white soldiers. As a result, the men admired them. The experience stayed with Lukitsch for the rest of his life.

During field hikes with the African American troops, Hall and Lukitsch were strangers in a strange land. Maneuvering in and out of the tiny North African villages in the mountains outside Algiers, they got a firsthand glimpse of the nomadic Arab lifestyle. Lukitsch wrote to his wife: "Incidentally, they still dress as you remember them from your geography, with rope around robes, legs and sandals—most of them barefoot. Every once in a while you'll see a tiny burrow with baskets on each side and a cloaked Arab riding in between." He wrote about the idiosyncrasies of local culture, noting that the children, who often serve as a bridge between cultures, constantly needled the men for cigarettes and candy.

After their brief stint with the African-American unit, Hall and Lukitsch received orders to travel to the OSS base in the mountains of Chrea, near Algiers. Located in a mountainous pine grove, the operatives base was less than fifteen miles from the city limits of Algiers. Nearby, the British SOE had its own base in a luxurious seaside resort. The area included grounds for parachuting and other covert training facilities. Winding down a dirt road on the side of the piney mountains, Hall and Lukitsch arrived at their new assignment. They were given the duties of instructors. Hall handled demolitions training. While they bided their time, they provided demolition training to OSS Special Operations recruits on their way to occupied Europe.

4

Desperados

THREE LARGE OLIVE DRAB six-by-six GMC trucks pulled through the main gate of the exclusive Congressional Country Club near Bethesda, Maryland. Incongruous guardhouses flanked the ornate entrance. An obstacle course obstructed the once-manicured fairways. Soldiers staged mock patrols through the woods. Washington's intelligentsia and members of Congress were noticeably absent.

The trucks wound down the paved road, arriving in front of a squat white building that once housed club employees. In the fall of 1943, the lush greens of the Congressional Country Club had become the stomping grounds of America's first special operations teams.

Recently promoted, Captain Chappell stood on the side of the road, hands on his hips, elbows tilted forward in a gesture of assertion. His square-jawed profile revealed a cocksure confidence. Three dozen olive drab-clad men hopped out of the trucks and fell into formation in front of the young captain. The military crispness of their movements rendered their diverse backgrounds undistinguishable.

The line of men stood at parade rest, feet six inches apart and hands folded behind their backs.

A more eclectic group of desperados could not be found: former Luftwaffe pilots, Jewish escapees from German death camps, renegade Poles, and world-class athletes. They shared two things in common: They all spoke German, and they all wanted vengeance for the suffering of their families at the hands of the Third Reich. Sixty years later, one recruit reflected, "The whole bunch were the craziest people I have ever met in my entire life." Chappell briefly introduced himself and announced their mission: to go behind enemy lines and strike at the heart of Nazi Germany.

Chappell's German Operational Group (OG) was finally ready. For the past several weeks, Chappell had been training the Italian, Greek, Yugoslav, and French teams on the basics of parachuting. Now, he was to be in charge of his own men.

The precursor of the Green Beret teams that would follow years later, the OG units were segmented into teams based on the countries in which they would operate. The basic unit of organization consisted of four officers and thirty enlisted men, divided into two sections of seventeen men. Each section required a variety of men with different functional skills: radio operator, medic, demolitionist, weapons specialist, and team leader. But all OG operatives had two things in common: "aggressiveness of spirit and willingness to close with the enemy."

Over the next several weeks, Chappell's job was to forge his men into a team, separating the wheat from the chaff. "If you had soldiers," he said, "you know good soldiers from bad soldiers. . . . All of my men were sharp; if they weren't, they were gone." One of the officers working with Chappell summed him up this way: "Howard had very high standards. If you didn't measure up, you were gone in thirty seconds."

Chappell had complete control over his unit's training. "I just made up whatever I wanted." Chappell was in a unique position. Because his kind of unit was new and unique, he was allowed a free rein. Unlike an officer in a conventional infantry unit, he was not under the thumb of an overbearing commander. He formulated his own dynamic training curriculum. Chappell's ability to improvise was his most exceptional asset as a soldier. Like a master ironworker, Chappell forged his men into a fighting unit, pounding them with a grueling regimen. They endured physical hardships such as humping long distances in mock patrols. The men learned hand-to-hand combat skills, everything from parrying a bayonet to killing an enemy sentry silently with a blade or a garrote. Chappell also emphasized demolitions instruction to prepare his men for sabotage. The recruits delighted in cratering several of the sleekest fairways in the country club's golf course.

The dining room in the main country club mansion was converted into a movie theater. Here the men learned German unit designations and insignia, and how to properly gather and assimilate tactical intelligence.

The training for an OG operative was informal and rank was dropped. The mission always came first.

During training, one of the recruits caught Chappell's attention. At five foot ten and two hundred pounds, with black hair and a swarthy complexion, the Spaniard Salvador Fabrega was a character among characters. A cook by trade, Fabrega was multilingual. When he was once challenged regarding his language abilities, he responded, "I schpesk seven different languages—Engleesh de best."

Before the Spanish Civil War in the 1930s, Fabrega owned a seagoing restaurant, a boat that featured a kitchen. He wined and dined his patrons on the open seas. During the civil war, Fabrega fought for Franco. With the arrival of World War II, he left Spain to fight in the French Foreign Legion. Later he deserted, which carried the punishment of death by firing squad. On the run for several months, the daring man changed his identity. Using his many connections and his exceptional fast-talking guile, he stowed away on a ship to the United States.

Arriving in New York City, Fabrega talked his way into a maître d' position at New York's famous Copacabana nightclub. During the immigration process, immigration officials moonlighting for the OSS recruited Fabrega into the nascent clandestine service. Here he now stood in front of Chappell with the other OGs.

"I liked him from the start," Chappell later said. "He started out about two hundred pounds. When I was done with him, he was a lean 170.

"Fabrega was loaded with nervous tics. If you didn't like one, he'd give you another. His most famous one, when he knew he was caught making a minor infraction, was a pitiful dog look. He would go, 'Ooops, who's to say? Me not know?' and look all pathetic . . . and speak in Croatian or some other language that no one understood."

Chappell reflected on their bond. "I trusted all the men in my unit, but with Fabrega I trusted my life."

Despite Fabrega's antics, he developed a close loyalty to Chappell, often referring to him as "Boss."

The happy-go-lucky, clever Fabrega possessed another important skill:

Fabrega was a master scrounger, and could "acquire" anything at the drop of a hat. His motto was "Tell me what you need, and I will 'organize' it for you." One of the recruits at the CCC made a dare while on leave: "Can you get us some girls?" Fabrega responded, "How many do you want?" "Six," we replied. "I'll be back," he said. Whaddaya know, he came back with six girls.

Fabrega and the rest of Chappell's men learned how to drive German motorcycles, trucks, and even small tanks at Fort Belvoir, Virginia. Much to the captain's dismay, the desperados were not all exceptional drivers.

"I drove across a field [in a tank] and promptly drove straight into a trench. The net effect was that the tank appeared to be driven by a drunk," one of the recruits lamented.

After their brief stint with vehicle training, the German OG hit the rails and traveled to Chappell's old haunt Fort Benning, where they were integrated into the airborne training program. To maintain their cover as normal soldiers, the OSS issued them regular army fatigues. Once barracked, one of Chappell's old jump sergeants summoned the men to the parade ground and told them:

While in camp, you always run, never walk. Even to the mess hall. Those who cannot handle the physical requirements will wash out and have to return to the infantry. Them that make it are going to be the toughest sons-of-bitches in this man's army. And them that don't make it, we don't want them no-how.

The training proved arduous. Each man pumped out hundreds of push-ups, performed countless windmills with arms outstretched— where the shoulders burn horrifically—and endured many forced marches with eighty-pound rucksacks. The airborne's training and toughening (T&T) program soon merged into jump training. Parachute training was still in its early stages. The first step, jumping out of moving trucks, taught the body to absorb the shock using a parachute roll. The next challenge in the training took place at Chappell's jump towers. The thirty-four-foot tower was the first test, to see whether a man feared heights. Most of the men passed this initial screening. Next they faced Chappell's 250-foot blackened steel tower.

Chappell decided to impress his men with a feat of derring-do on one of the massive towers. Chappell removed the harness from the nylon risers of an already opened parachute and wound the risers around each wrist. Once at the top, he looked down at his men, ready to perform a death leap. Their necks craned to see him at such a dizzying height and they shielded their eyes from the sun. Chappell leaped from the tower. All the way down, the captain held the parachute risers attached to the white parachute silk with his bare hands. He landed and executed a perfect parachute roll.

One of the men commented that "Flash Gordon [did this] just to prove his disdain for safety and good sense." Such derring-do and fearlessness epitomized Chappell's character.

The final stage of parachute training consisted of four qualifying jumps from an airplane at five hundred feet above the earth. The drill instructor divided the OG into twelve-man "sticks" and they boarded separate C-47 cargo planes. The engines made a steady drone as they approached the target drop zone. Over the drop zone, the men stood up, and each checked the chute of the man in front of him.

Next, the jump sergeant barked, "Stand in the door," then, "Hook up."

The men grabbed the static lines attached to the backpacks on their T-5 parachutes, inserted the static lines' eye hooks into the jump wires, and moved to the open door of the C-47. Icy air hit the face of the first men in the stick.

Most of the OGs summoned the courage to jump out of the planes. After twenty feet of freefall, the static line pulled out their parachutes, which blossomed into white silk umbrellas. But the jump was not without risk. Equipment failure was an ominous threat, and incorrect parachute rigging meant death. Also, the shock of the harness on the chutes when they deployed caused "strawberry burns" from the tight buckles and snaps on the harness. And when they landed, the men had to roll properly in order to distribute the force of the impact. Landing correctly proved especially difficult, and men broke legs and ankles. Approximately twenty percent of the German OGs washed out during jump training, and one almost lost his life. One of the OG men recalled the incident:

> We called him Fuck-Up. He was very good as a radio operator, but he wasn't in good shape and he was an alcoholic. We could always find him at the nearest bar. And that's exactly where he was before our fourth qualifying jump. We yanked him out of the bar and he wasn't in good shape. We threw him out of the airplane and he woke up on the ground wondering where he was. His last recollection was that he was at the bar.

That evening, livid with rage, Fuck-Up filed into the barracks with the rest of the men. After the men fell asleep, the maddened radio operator stole an M1 Garand from the rack, loaded an eight-round clip into the magazine, and stalked Chappell. The man pointed the gun directly at Chappell's face, threatening to kill him. Chappell fearlessly walked up to the man.

"Soldier, let me have it."

Chappell gazed into the man's eyes. Moments passed with no words exchanged. The radioman trembled, his finger poised on the trigger. In a fluid sweeping motion, Chappell snatched the rifle away and gruffly snarled, "I'm not going to report you because we need you. Shut up and go to sleep."

The next day, the men formed up at the parade ground and ceremoniously donned their new M-42 khaki jumpsuits. The commanding general presented them with their silver jump wings, a coveted honor for any soldier.

✳ ✳ ✳

With their silver jump wings on the breasts of their M-42s, the OG men returned to Washington, D.C. The new paratroopers went out on the town, carousing with chests puffed out, wearing their smart class A uniforms and jumpsuits.

Secrecy for America's first special forces unit became an issue, and Chappell had to do something about it.

> With all these men walking around in paratrooper boots and uniforms, cab-drivers would pull up, toot their horn, and say, "Congressional Country Club?" I ran down into Donovan's office and raised holy hell. "I don't want my guys being trained here." And I got them yanked.

The security-conscious Chappell persuaded Donovan to move America's secret warriors to California's Catalina Island. Located twenty miles off the Southern California shoreline, Catalina was an ideal location for amphibious warfare training.

Known for its green hills and red-roofed vacation homes, Catalina was a resort town. However, Chappell's men were headed for the other side of the island, a compound of dilapidated wooden buildings that served as a summer camp before the war. Life was soon to get a whole lot more Spartan for the German OG.

The men embarked upon survival training. Dumped in the remote, unpopulated section of the island, they split into six-man teams, and Chappell instructed them to live off the land for five days. Armed with sharp knives and .45s, the men were expected to forage for berries and edible foliage. Some of Chappell's men, however, discovered a better opportunity. Industrialist Philip K. Wrigley, the owner of the entire island and the son of the founder of the famed chewing gum company, kept a herd of dairy cows near the woods. The men shot one of the cows, and one man who was an experienced butcher carved the animal for dinner. Healthy and practically unscathed, these full-bellied German OGs rolled back into camp. Chappell interpreted the men's resourcefulness as a positive trait and did not chastise them excessively. Instead, he filled out an IOU for Mr. Wrigley's dead cow.

Before the OGs completed their training, Chappell received a message: "Donovan wants to see you." Without hesitation, Chappell complied. He boarded a ferry back to the mainland and took the next plane to Washington, D.C.

In D.C., Chappell made a beeline for the Q, where he reported to the American spymaster. His gray hair parted and his brilliant blue eyes sparkling, Bill Donovan was affable. With a smile, he addressed the captain. "Howard, I have just the thing for you."

Chappell quickly retorted, "Before you go any further, I'm really happy where I am."

"But, this is great," Donovan said with glee.

With respect and a hint of guarded optimism, he responded, "All right, let's hear it." Chappell was thinking to himself, *This is going to be some harebrained idea.*

Sixty years later, Chappell couldn't recall the exact nature of the mission Donovan proposed, except that it was somewhere deep behind enemy lines. Donovan dreamed up all kinds of missions on a daily basis—some of them daring, some harebrained. "His imagination was unlimited. Ideas were his plaything. Excitement made him snort like a racehorse."

When Donovan proposed Chappell take on this mission, Howard's answer was calculated: "General, I've got over forty men back at Catalina waiting for me. These forty men are imbued with the idea that we are going to execute a sabotage mission against the Third Reich. If I take a job now, I am going to have to leave all these men sitting out there."

Donovan shot back, "Oh, I know. You can take two or three of them with you."

"I know, sir. That wouldn't do it, though."

Donovan crumbled. "I can see your point. Thanks for coming in."

Chappell's loyalties lay with his men. They had endured numerous trials and tribulations for his sake, and he was not about to give up on them. He had a vision, an obsession—getting his entire team inside to strike at the heart of the Reich.

5

The Plan

STEPHEN HALL'S FATE RESTED on selling an idea. In the early morning hours of Thursday, June 22, 1944, his opportunity for making his plan a reality arrived. The OSS plucked him out of the demolitions school in Algiers and gave him orders to fly to Caserta, Italy, on "temporary duty." The date coincided with the third anniversary of Hitler's invasion of Russia, and the Allied invasion of Normandy was only in its third week. Hall hoped the interminable months of training and the dull grind of Algiers had come to an end. Nearly a year had passed since Hall penned his pivotal letter to the OSS "[that he] could block the Ampezzo Highway and [the Brenner] railroad beyond."

In Italy he met with a room full of officers from Company D of the 2677th OSS Regiment and laid out his plan. The 2677th was the unit that would facilitate Hall's mission.

The meeting took place in a rustic villa in Caserta. Cigarette smoke wafted up to the rafters as Lieutenant Hall took his place in front of a wall-sized topographical map of Italy. The young lieutenant needed to convince the ranking brass of the 2677th that his plan made sense. "The project had to be drafted as carefully as a case before the Supreme Court," recalled Hall.

Seizing his moment on stage, Hall dramatically laid out his plan to first sever the main communication and supply routes leading up to the Brenner Pass and then blow up the main route through the pass. With the zeal of a preacher, he worked the room, enthusiastically selling his plan to decision makers in the 2677th. One of the most important of them was the man who would become Hall's case officer, Second Lieutenant

Michael Jiminez. The swarthy Latino, who had more combat experience than anyone else in the room, controlled logistics for Company D's SO missions in northern Italy. A fellow OSS agent described him with one word: "tough."

Lieutenant Jiminez and Company D's Captain Vince Lossowski, described by an OSS agent as "a man of complete confidence," had both fought in Spain for the Abraham Lincoln Brigade, a group of Americans who battled against fascist dictator Francisco Franco. While they were not necessarily card-carrying communists, many Lincoln Brigade vets were "philo-communists," as one OSS man described them, and yet they were also "some of OSS's most dedicated" operatives. Their specialty: working with communist partisan movements in northern Italy while running OSS agents. Because of their prior associations with communism and their perceived collaboration with communist partisans, Jiminez and Lossowski would later find themselves in front of a congressional committee.

Like so many military plans, Hall's proposal looked good on paper, even irresistible. At that point in the war, the Army Air Corps' bombing raids had failed to stop the flow of men and matériel through the Brenner Pass to the German armies in Italy. Trying a fresh approach, dropping one man or a small team behind the lines, seemed to make sense to the top brass. Such a small covert operation could be executed with minimal resources. And, of course, there was the OSS mission mantra: "If you don't risk, you don't win." Ominously, however, Hall was the only man in the room who had been on the ground in the mountains of northern Italy.

Hall quickly won the support of the new commander of Company D, a Virginia tobacco farmer who, like many others in the company, was new to special operations. The commanding officer of the 2677th, Colonel John Riepe, proved to be a tougher sell. Riepe "approved the plan in principle," with one caveat: "The air cover [aerial photographic reconnaissance] would be the determining factor." The OSS would use aerial photography to prove or disprove the existence of secondary supply routes leading from the Brenner. Jiminez also approved the plan, with some reservations.

Safety was a grave concern. Missions behind enemy lines became exceedingly dangerous after Hitler issued a secret directive effectively nullifying the Geneva Conventions for the treatment of spies. In retaliation for British operatives who had executed a wire-bound German soldier taken prisoner during a commando raid on the German-occupied Channel Islands, Hitler instructed German forces to execute summarily any operatives captured behind the lines. Hitler stated: "In future, all terror and sabotage troops of the British and their accomplices who do not act like soldiers but rather bandits, will be treated as such by the German troops and will be ruthlessly eliminated in battle, wherever they appear." This applied to uniformed and non-uniformed personnel, armed and unarmed. Although German commanders on the ground interpreted the order differently, Hall and the other operatives realized that being captured would likely result in a death sentence.

Hall was willing, even eager, to face the risk of death. In a memo, Hall noted with jubilation that "The conclusion of this conference seemed unmistakable, if the air cover revealed a clear route, the operation was approved."

After making it through the approval wickets of the 2677th, Hall was ready for prime time. For three and a half hours he briefed the plan in great detail to Army G-3 and Allied Army Italy (AAI) officers. The meeting went well. According to Hall's summary, "All military aspects of the proposed operation were discussed, and no [serious] objection whatsoever was found to the plan. . . . All the officers showed considerable curiosity about my many details of the plan and background information and exhibited great enthusiasm for the scheme." Colonel Riepe signed off on the plan, put his pen down, and turned to Hall with a look of reserved satisfaction, saying, "You have blanket approval of this." A general in the meeting also expressed his approval, stating bluntly, "Go ahead and do it." Roderick Stephen Goodspeed Hall was at the threshold of the adventure of his life.

Jiminez gave Hall free rein to choose most of his team. First pick: his best friend, Lieutenant Joe Lukitsch, a trained demolitionist. For the vital position of radio operator, Hall selected Joseph "Stan" Zbieg, from

Bridgeport, Connecticut, a specialist second class in the navy. The life-line of any OSS mission was its radio and its operator. A radio operator reports mission essential intelligence back to base, arranges supply drops, and, if need be, sends word for extraction. This mission would also need an interpreter, and Hall chose an operative he knew from Al-giers, a man named Victor Malispino. The New Jersey native and Italian speaker was ideal because of his family ties to northern Italy. For maxi-mum sabotage capability, each member of Hall's team had received cross-training in demolitions.

The OSS organized Hall's mission in uncharacteristic fashion, mak-ing it part of a larger operation. The OSS selected Major Lloyd Smith to command the umbrella mission, known as Eagle, of which Hall's mis-sion was to be a part.

A varsity wrestler from Penn State University, "Smitty" was the OSS's latest rising star. Six months earlier, a C-47 carrying US Army nurses had crash-landed in German-occupied Albania. Nearly all the women and the pilots survived. Armed with only a .357 Magnum, Smith infil-trated Albania to rescue them. Threading his way through difficult ter-rain infested with German soldiers and unfriendly communist partisans, Smith brought out the nurses and crew, earning the Distinguished Ser-vice Cross.

Smith's "prime responsibility [was] the organization of the parti-sans, liaison between the partisan groups and the OSS, and command of activity in the region." Smith's guiding hand was presumably ex-pected to rein in the exuberant, often overly optimistic Hall, a verita-ble loose cannon.

Hall's prime responsibility was "the attack upon the communications route." OSS assigned Hall's specific mission the code name Mercury. In a breach of code-name etiquette, the radio for the mission was also un-wisely dubbed Mercury.

Before he could launch his mission, Hall needed to learn the basics of parachuting, so OSS headquarters sent Hall and Lukitsch back to Al-giers for a crash course in jumping out of airplanes. After qualifying, he returned to Italy and joined the other members of the team, who had already qualified as paratroopers. Now training for the mission went into high gear as Hall got the team hardened up.

The team would need mountaineering equipment, so Hall took on the role of quartermaster. "Maps, sleeping bags, foreign money, climbing gear, radio ciphers, medicine, and just about a thousand damn things— all weighed and triple checked." Hall requisitioned the mountaineering gear from the legendary First Special Service Force (known as the "Devil's Brigade"). Months earlier, this famous mountain unit had been instrumental in breaking through Kesselring's Winter Line shielding Rome. Hall was given access to the unit's warehouse and obtained climbing ropes, mountain pitons, snap links, cold-weather uniforms, skis, and even two mountain ice axes.

With gear in hand, the team trained for eight days on white-capped southern Italian mountain peaks. In the mountains outside Caserta, they practiced their hiking skills. On remote cliffs outside Naples, the team worked on rock climbing. Lukitsch wrote to his girlfriend Eleanor about the rigorous exercises: "My muscles have never ached more in my life."

The team also sharpened their demolition skills, cratering several of the mountains' cliffs and creating landslides. Landslides were essential for blocking mountain roads. Finally, they sharpened their command of the Italian language. Victor Malispino gave each man a crash course in conversational Italian.

The following week, the team acquired the additional supplies and equipment it would need on the mission. Again, they acted as their own supply officers, because Company D was changing its location and there was no one to make arrangements. Mission essentials included ammunition, small arms, and demolition equipment such as blasting caps, prima cord, and fuse lighters. All the equipment had to be loaded into cylindrical parachute drop containers. Buried in a box marked "balloons" were forty-eight condoms. The men of Eagle and Mercury missions now seemed prepared for all possible developments behind the lines.

By July 31, the men were ready and Hall took a moment to type up a letter to Captain William Suhling, commander of Company D:

Dear Captain Suhling,

Our operation against that certain supply route is all ready to shove off, and, in fact, we may be gone by the time you read this. I am sure you will never regret the interest and "push" you gave it. The scheme has expanded quite a bit since its first conception, owing to the favorable partisan conditions in the area, and we have high hopes of accomplishing things on a large scale. The principal aims now are: tactical and supply liaison with a very large and well organized partisan military group in the area; Complete blocking of the critical supply routes, both R.R. and highway; destruction of locomotives, trucks, and fuel stocks; establishment of a courier route into Austria; gathering, through a net to be set up, as much military intelligence as possible, with special attention to the following items—troop and supply movement and/or disposition, location of German Command Headquarters, German plans for using gas (this has appeared in our reports of our agents very recently), results of air bombing. I can imagine we may also have the opportunity to gather info on the political situation and on persons suitable to take over local government in the event of troop occupation or German capitulation. Needless to say, we won't crowd the air waves with this kind of poop, but, if we do get it, it will be available at the right time. . . .

We're going in with several thousand pounds of equipment for the partisan group, and expect to re-order by radio quite a bit more. Food is not included as we shall live off the land.

Well, I guess that's all there is to tell about it. It has certainly been a great pleasure knowing you, sir, and I hope we see each other again before long.

Best Wishes,
Steve

As a final step in the preparations, the men stowed their personal luggage and belongings. The last man to check in his belongings was Lieutenant Hall, who brought a single brown suitcase.

6

Boondoggle

SHORTLY AFTER THE SPRING of 1944, after Stephen Hall departed for North Africa, Howard Chappell's German OG group finally received its call to action. The team boarded trains to New York City and embarked on a Liberty troopship with orders for an unknown destination. The ship was packed with regular infantrymen and forty of America's first special forces. The men all took part in a guessing game regarding their final destination. Only Chappell knew they were steaming to North Africa.

Aboard the top deck, they leaned over the rail and observed the grandeur of the Hudson River. The New York skyline disappeared in the mist of the hazy morning. On their starboard side, the Statue of Liberty held her torch high in the chalky white sky.

The Liberty ship maintained formation in a convoy to avoid the torpedoes of the enemy wolf packs. The journey was uneventful. Most of the men played cards, shot craps, and were bored out of their minds. One wise OG attempted to concoct an alcoholic elixir made from aftershave and Coca-Cola. Needless to say, several of the men ended up doubled over and writhing in sick bay.

The trip led to deeper bonds among Chappell and several men on his team. One member whom the captain took into his confidence was Sergeant Eric M. Buchhardt. At five foot eleven and 175 pounds, Buchhardt was a dynamic and creative member of the team. He invented a sighting system for 60mm mortars, later submitted to the army for consideration as a service-wide protocol. Besides demonstrating creativity, Buchhardt could patch and dispatch effectively. "He was a medic,"

Chappell explained. "He could put a bandage on you and all that kind of stuff, but [he was also] a first-rate demo man."

After weeks at sea, a foreign port finally came into sight through a thick fog. Excitement rippled through the OGs as they began to approach land. A tugboat came out to conduct the ship to its mooring near the wharf, and the men prepared to disembark. Chappell mustered his men, but oddly one of them was missing. As they could no longer linger on deck, they walked down the rusty gangplank. The briny odor of seawater permeated the air as seagulls screamed in the distance. The din of Arab port life was punctuated by an oddly familiar voice. A swarthy man in civilian attire was on the dock pestering the new arrivals.

"Mister, mister, you have cigarette?"

Several of the men shuffled by the stranger in disdain. Buchhardt kindly complied, offering the bum a Lucky Strike. Dumbfounded, Buchhardt turned to Chappell.

"Jesus Christ, that son of a bitch looks like Fabrega."

Chappell responded, "Yeah, the reason that son of a bitch looks like Fabrega is because he *is* Fabrega."

It was a classic Fabrega moment. The man could elude any sort of trouble and hustle an advantage out of any situation. Eager to make landfall before his comrades, Fabrega conned the pilot of the tugboat to let him on before they had even entered the port. He managed to arrive an hour early and "acquire" civilian clothes. As Fabrega impressed Chappell with his unique skills, the OGs arrived in North Africa ready to strike at the Reich.

Once ashore, the operators found themselves in Oran, an Algerian port of two hundred thousand. Three-quarters of the population were of European descent. Founded by Moorish traders in 903 BC, the Barbary Coast town had been sacked countless times by a wide assortment of European and Middle Eastern navies, armies, and pirates and rebuilt over and over. The ambience of swashbuckling still lingered when Chappell and his men landed.

Oran had been captured by the Allies in 1942 and became an improvised depot for men and supplies on their way to the Italian front. The city fit Chappell and his motley crew like a glove. Unfortunately, they were in the *wrong* city, where no one knew who they were or why they were there.

The OGs filed ashore with the rest of the troops. Chappell's first stop was the commanding officer of the replacement depot, or repo depot, to which the OG had been assigned. A replacement depot was essentially a holding tank for men who were to be shipped off to existing units to replace combat casualties. Chappell entered the white stone building serving as headquarters for the repo depot. He requested a meeting with the commanding officer. Chappell was ushered into the general's office, located prominently in a cluster of stone buildings set aside as repo depot HQ.

With signature bravado, he extended a calloused hand. "Sir, my name is Captain Howard Chappell of the OSS."

The general looked at him, sneering. "Who the hell are you?"

"OSS. Office of Strategic Services."

"We don't know anything about OSS," responded the general. "You are to report as replacements for other units."

At this time of the war, very few people had any idea what the OSS was, because the OSS was still a secret organization, existing only on a need-to-know basis. OSS's headquarters was equally disorganized and had not formed an office in Oran by the time Chappell arrived, nor had they sent instructions to anyone in the city. One of America's highly trained operations units was marooned in a bureaucratic nightmare. No one knew who they were, and it was beginning to look like this crack unit would soon be used as replacement cannon fodder in chewed-up units. In fact, the commanding general did decide to send Chappell's OG to England to be used as replacements for airborne units.

Chappell refused the general's orders, while he made repeated requests to other high-ranking officers. But his requests fell on deaf ears. With no radio, telephone, or other means to communicate with OSS headquarters, Chappell took matters into his own hands.

"After almost getting court-martialed in Oran, I learned that the OSS had a secret base in Algiers," he recalled.

Algiers is the main port city in Algeria. However, it is several hundred miles from Oran. Chappell devised a plan to get there.

"Fabrega, I need a truck."

"Boss, what are we gonna do with a truck?"

"Sooner or later, we're gonna need a truck."

Meanwhile, Chappell told four of his stealthiest OGs to "liberate" supplies from the army. "I had my guys stealing pillowcases, towels, and anything we could get our hands on. We were robbing the repo depot blind."

Chappell hid the truck and placed all the stolen booty inside the cabin. The liberation operation went on for weeks, while the men went about their training, trying to kill their boredom. Their one outlet was a weekly rum ration. Chappell remembers one day in particular: "At the time, I didn't drink a lot and I would put my whiskey ration in my footlocker, which was padlocked." When he returned from riding his motorcycle, the lock was still on but the whiskey was gone. He summoned Fabrega into his tent.

"You got a problem, Mister Fabrega?"

"What's da matter?" responded the Spaniard.

"Somebody's a-stealing my whiskey."

"Oh?" He flashed his best puppy dog face.

"You go get the first sergeant, and I'm going to tell him that you have the other key for the footlocker."

Fabrega responded sheepishly, "Okay." He turned, hesitated, took another step, and then turned back around. "Meebee eef you check een half of an hour, eet weel be back."

With a sardonic smirk, Chappell responded, "Ya think?"

Chappell returned to find his liquor had "magically" reappeared. "Fabrega didn't take it, but he knew who did."

The pilfering of regular army supplies continued, and the bed of the truck was soon filled. Chappell's plan was to sell the goods to the local Arabs in exchange for francs. They would use the cash to purchase tickets for the local train running from Oran to Algiers.

Chappell ordered Fabrega and Buchhardt to go to the local souk and consummate the deal. Sitting on his motorcycle, which he had also liberated, Chappell watched as Fabrega made a swiping motion with his hands, signaling the deal had been cut. All the loot was converted into francs, which Chappell promptly used to purchase more than three dozen one-way train tickets to Algiers.

Before departing, Buchhardt scrawled "Somebody lost me" on a piece of paper and left the sign on the windshield of the six-ton truck they had been using as a storage shed.

As the men made the winding journey on the rails, they looked out at the rocky, dry Algerian landscape dotted with adobe huts. They were finally moving forward toward a mission. Making his way through the train cars, Chappell noticed the men's pilfering skills were still intact.

"Why did you take that?" Chappell eyed an army duffel bag.

"We didn't take it."

With half a smile, Chappell responded, "Whaddaya mean, ya didn't take it? It was not on the train and now it is in here."

One of the men sheepishly answered, "Well, it was 'liberated.'"

Chappell firmly placed tongue in cheek. "Shall I ask who liberated it?"

"We don't know."

After riding the rails for half a day, the men jumped off in Algiers, perhaps the greatest of the old pirate harbors on the Barbary Coast.

"In Algiers, I was unable to make arrangements for a German mission," Chappell recalled. "We were offered a British mission to jump into the Black Forest to organize resistance and to destroy ball bearing factories. The British never got the mission organized, nor did they get approval from the OSS in Washington."

But the same communication problems that plagued Chappell in Oran continued to beset him in Algeria. In the OSS, the right hand did not necessarily know what the left was doing. Frustrated, Chappell, on his own initiative, caught a flight from Algiers to Caserta, Italy, where the OSS had a base. Chappell recalls pleading with an OSS officer there: "Sooner or later, somebody is gonna wake up. You are going to realize the whole group of OSS operators are just sitting in Africa. When they do realize it, the shit is gonna hit the fan."

Chappell later remembered the difficulty he had getting his team assigned to an operation behind the lines in Germany:

> The OSS was so fucked up. No one there knew anything about my
> group for Germany and suggested that I go to Brindisi [where the OSS
> had another base]. I returned to Algiers, but there still were no orders
> from Washington. So, I returned to Caserta, leaving the rest of my
> group in Algiers. After a week in Caserta, I felt as though my men and
> I were orphans. The hardest part was keeping my men and officers
> from learning how screwed up everything was until I could get things
> straightened out.

Eventually, Chappell found the right person, who assured him, "I'll take care of it." He was good to his word—within days, the men jumped on a plane headed for Italy.

7

The Jump

ON THE NIGHT OF AUGUST 2, 1944, Major Smith's Eagle team gathered under the gaping 104-foot wingspan of a Halifax heavy bomber. The moon cast an eerie glare on the scene, partially obscured by fluffy cumulus clouds. Hall looked at the other members of his team. Each wore a camouflage "striptease suit." The suits were a special operations favorite because they concealed either civilian clothes or a military uniform and included an internal backpack, a pistol holder, and a scabbard for an agent's dirk. The suits also served a more basic purpose: they would keep everybody warm during the long two-hour-plus flight through the Italian substratosphere.

Major Lloyd Smith led his Eagle team, dressed like camouflaged astronauts, through the rear hatch of the bomber and picked his way along the cigar-shaped fuselage. The cramped compartment was crammed to the gills with parachute supply containers full of equipment essential to their mission behind the lines. After the team found their seats, the pilot pulled back on the plane's throttle. Blue smoke oozed out of the four Bristol Hercules XVI radial engines. At 1,615 horsepower, the engines soon propelled the plane at a nice clip of 250 miles per hour.

The Halifax leveled off at ten thousand feet. Hall recalled, "We sweated rivers—and froze later. . . . The ride was painful, we were cramped in amongst the containers of supplies, the roar of the engines was overwhelming—also naturally, the prospect of a parachute jump into enemy territory at night, or any other time, is not too comforting."

The bomber traveled more than six hundred miles up the boot of Italy. During the journey, Hall climbed up to the cockpit and found out

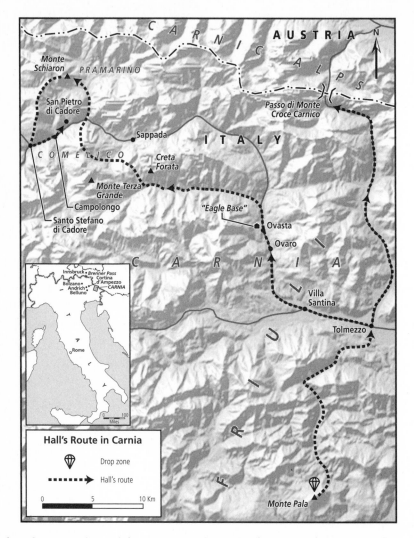

the plane was bound for Monte Pala in the foothills of the Alps of Carnia in northern Italy. Known for its panoramic vistas, the mountainous region is located on the northeast corner of Italy along the Austrian border. Hall did not realize the drop zone was so far away from the Brenner. The news stunned the blue-blooded young officer: "It was bad news for me, as it was eighty-five miles from the Cortina area." Initially, Hall thought the drop zone would be closer to Cortina and the southern approaches of the Brenner Pass. Hall would need to travel a great distance on foot to even come close to his objectives. He knew that in order to accomplish the mission, he would have to traverse some of the most heavily guarded and rugged terrain in western Europe.

A crew member removed the wooden hatch covering a hole through which agents parachuted, known as the "Joe hole." Through the hole, Hall saw the glow of white tracer rounds floating up near the plane, and explosions muffled by the incessant roar of the Halifax's engines. He strained his eyes, trying to make out signal fires lit by partisans below to mark their destination. A few fires burned in the distance, but the pattern was incorrect. The plane appeared to be in the wrong location.

The pilot's voice crackled over the intercom as he spotted the *assumed* correct fires on the ground. The red jump light flickered on and the green light pulsed. The men were at the ready. Major Smith, followed by interpreter Victor Malispino and radio operator Stan Zbieg, disappeared through the blackness of the hole. Next, Joe Lukitsch and Hall swung their legs over, looking down.

"With a full moon, the tumbled hills far below looked eerie; the fires looked small and distant," Hall recalled.

Once again, the pilot flipped on the jump signal. Hall jumped first through the hole, followed by his best friend, Joe Lukitsch. The static line, attached to the back panel of the British X-type parachute, pulled the white silk from the pack tray, "opening with a crack."

In a horrifying moment, Hall realized his shroud lines had become tangled, and he began to fall through the air in a death spiral. He suddenly faced the fight of his life, desperately trying to untangle the shroud lines. If the lines continued to twist, the chute would collapse. Remembering his brief training, he frantically jerked the parachute risers (attached to the shroud lines) up and down. After he had fallen three hundred or more feet, the twist finally came undone and the silk canopy blossomed like a giant white mushroom.

As Hall struggled with his risers, Joe Lukitsch "sailed past, like a shot out of a cannon," recalled Hall. Eventually, his chute also opened, below him, where he was drifting. Glancing down at the surface of the mountain below, Hall realized he was looking straight down at "two wicked spikes of limestone." The rest of the mountainside was rock and forest. Guiding the risers, he was able to navigate between the two limestone pillars, which could have hung him up yards above the ground. Landing with a thud, he did a couple of back somersaults, flipping into a gulley covered with saplings.

In complete silence, Hall assessed his surroundings, some of the most lush, bucolic scenery on the face of the earth. The Carnic Alps loomed in the distance, white limestone rock faces covered in patches of verdant woodland. Lukitsch and the rest of Smith's Eagle team were nowhere to be found.

Hall pulled out his razor-sharp stiletto and cut his way out of the harness. Next, he pulled out his parkerized Union Switch and Signal .45 and waited, motionless, for twenty minutes. At two a.m. he slowly began moving to a hill. The other team members suddenly appeared, and Mercury and Eagle were united.

The mission was not intended to be a blind drop, although that is what it became. The partisans and an OSS secret agent, code-named Fred, failed to meet the team at the drop zone.

The Eagle and Mercury teams hid in a deep swale, with the men taking turns standing watch. Smith took the first watch at 4:30 a.m. About half an hour later, Hall heard people moving near the camp. Smitty decided to move the team somewhere safer. With the first rays of dawn, Eagle's interpreter, Victor Malispino, spied people apparently trying to signal the team with a red flag. Smitty and Hall moved closer for a better look.

To see who was out there, the men needed to come out of hiding. But they did not know whether the signalers were friendlies or German sympathizers. As the pink fingers of dawn crawled across the sky, the operatives spotted a farmhouse near the edge of the valley. Major Smith and Captain Hall decided to gamble on the occupants of the house. They approached, praying they would be met by friendlies. At this critical moment, in one fell swoop, they could fall into German hands. Most of the locals were also aware that, in typical ruthless fashion, the Nazis sometimes tested the loyalties of Italian civilians by parachuting Germans disguised as Allied agents. Any family that helped the agents would be sent off to a concentration camp or summarily executed.

Hall knocked on the door. The owner, a civilian, at first thought Hall was a German, but then realized he was an American. Luckily, the civilians occupying the house were connected to the local partisans. Smith had chosen the right place.

Hall and Smith established trust quickly, and within ten minutes about twenty men and women appeared, all wearing the type of red scarf worn only by a local partisan faction known as the Garibaldi. "They set up a collection point beneath a large oak and all hands started to hunt [for our] containers and pile them up by a tree," Hall recounted. Without the contents of the cylindrical parachute containers—plastic explosives, arms, rations, radios, and the obligatory cigarettes—the team would be powerless.

By noon that day, the teams had linked up with the partisans and were on their way back into the mountains. Their supplies were toted by mules to a nearby cave.

As the mission began to take shape, Hall began recording his thoughts daily on cigarette paper. It was the beginning of a small diary which he would keep every day of his mission. It was also a dangerous violation of a basic rule of spycraft. Hall jotted down how the team reacted in the first day's operation: "We felt that we had been granted a miracle. The whole operation was in full sight of Nazi operation towers in the land below and the lack of reception and [the] hideous rock pile we landed on should have made us all casualties and prisoners. Aside from cuts and bruises, we were all lucky." According to the young operative, the Nazis would not be on the team's trail for another week.

Although they had avoided the Nazis, the team had landed on the fault line of Italy's slow-burning civil war. In occupied northern Italy, the six principal antifascist political parties—namely, the Partito d'Azione, the Communists (including the Garibaldi Brigades), the Socialists, the

Christian Democrats, the Liberals, and the Republicans—had formed a loosely bound resistance movement known as the Comitato di Liberazione Nazionale per l'Alta Italia (CLNAI). But the groups often fought each other as well as the Germans. They represented a complex mix of competing political movements all vying for power.

The OSS supplied the groups with money and arms, trained them, and helped them to fight the Germans. In this area of Italy, the CLNAI held the support of the bulk of the civilian population. Luckily, the sparsely populated Mt. Pala was in a remote and wild area with few roads, making it difficult for the Germans to access the area.

The drop zone was far enough south of the Austrian border that local sympathy lay with the Allies. And the German troops here were stretched to the limit; not every town could be occupied. Only the town of Tolmezzo was garrisoned by Germans. Nevertheless, only four hours earlier, the drop zone had been occupied by a German platoon.

In his various operations, Hall would run with both the communist Garibaldi and the nationalist Osoppo partisan groups controlling the Carnia area. Like in Mao Zedong's famous analogy, the American and British missions were the fish swimming in the friendly sea of civilians sympathetic to their cause. When he would later move his operations farther north, near Brenner, Hall learned that pro-Allied sympathy could never be assumed. Thirty years earlier, that portion of northern Italy—known as the Tyrol—had been part of Austria, and a large portion of the population was loyal to the Reich.

A few days after the drop, Lukitsch and Hall decided they would separate from the Eagle team and move north in order to carry out the first steps of Hall's mission. They soon met a British SOE agent, named Major Manfred Beckett, and a local detachment of the Osoppo. The detatchment was an amalgamation consisting of various other fighters: members of the liberal Partito d'Azione, Christian Democrats, and monarchist officers who had disbanded after the king fled Rome on September 8, 1943. At its height, the Osoppo numbered approximately two thousand men. They claimed to be politically unbiased, but according to Major Smith, they seemed "pro-democratic and anticommunist." The brigade fought in companies armed with Breda light machine guns, Italian rifles, and Sten submachine guns. They also possessed several 81mm mortars, courtesy of the British.

As occupied Italy teetered on the brink of a messy civil war among its partisan groups, American operatives were often caught between factions harboring disparate political and ideological agendas. Over the next few days, Hall and the Eagle team got to know the Osoppo.

Later, the team met the leaders of the Osoppo's rival group, the Garibaldi. Dubbed the "Gees," the Garibaldi were the communist-led resistance units. Organized throughout northern Italy, from Piedmont to Friuli, they were highly aggressive and strongly antifascist, and they did a large part of the fighting against the Nazis. They were named for Garibaldi, the hero of the Italian nation, in order to downplay their links to the Communist Party and to keep their ranks open to communists and non-communists alike.

Ominously for the West, the Gees had a clear political agenda for postwar Italy. "All their leaders, including battalion and company platoon commanders, were rabid communists," wrote Smith.

The area where Hall and the Eagle team had landed was dominated by communist partisans. Ironically, the team included several OSS operations officers who had communist sympathies themselves—Jiminez, Lossowski, and OSS agent Irving Goff, who handled Eagle as well as more than a dozen other missions. Many of the agents Goff sent behind the lines were communists, and the intelligence they provided was known as the "Goff chain." The communists saw the end of the war as a chance to seize control. In a strange twist of fate, Hall, a blue-blooded conservative, was soon working with communist partisans as well as being handled by men back at base who were communists.

Over the next several days, Eagle met several downed airmen and an escaped British POW who had been captured in Tobruk.

As Stephen Hall's team moved northwest toward Cortina, they turned down an offer of assistance from the Gees. "[The partisans] offered to give me a fifteen-man guard for reconnaissance, but said we'd probably be caught—I declined, to save men's lives," Hall wrote.

One night, Hall and the team treated themselves to the feather beds of the best hotel in town. Because the partisans occupied Carnia in such strength, Hall and the Eagle team implemented a daring plan. They would destroy all the major bridges and roads leading into Carnia. Since the region could not be occupied in strength by the Germans, the area became effectively a "zone libre" (free zone). The team played a key role in effecting this change by blowing the bridges and lines of communications into Carnia. Instead of spreading their troops too thin, the Germans were just biding their time as they built up reinforcements in Tolmezzo, the largest city in the region.

The next day, Hall began one of his most important contributions to the partisan movement in that area of northern Italy. Hall recorded in his diary, "Had class in demolitions . . . lasted three hours. Set in blue charge of plastic as demonstration. Had one of [the men] take notes." As they trained the partisans, he and the other Allied missions were bringing them hope. Men such as Hall were raising troop morale, illustrating to the partisans that they were not alone in their struggle and that their cause was righteous.

One evening in the second week of August, the team dined and drank wine at the house of a doctor sympathetic to the partisan cause. That night, they had a meeting to plan the blowing up of their first objective: a reinforced concrete bridge, located near the Austrian border, that Allied bombers had failed to destroy. Later that night Hall and Lukitsch slept in the attic of a local house.

In the early morning of August 9, the day the mission was to begin, Hall and Lukitsch planned to climb a local mountain known as Creta Forata for a general recon of the terrain. However, billowy white cumulus clouds moved in and obscured the mountaintop. They canceled their climb, never getting an opportunity to survey the area. Instead, the men did something that day that reminded them of home: they went fishing. Because of the war, food remained scarce in northern Italy. So, "[we] went fishing, to try to get fresh meat, but there are no fish in Carnia," Hall lamented in his diary.

The team waited until 10:30 p.m., when they finally boarded a truck driven by the partisans and traveled several miles closer to the Austrian border, a few kilometers north of Tolmezzo. After concealing the truck, Lukitsch and Hall led the small party creeping toward the bridge, which was so deep behind enemy lines it was practically unguarded.

Once there, Hall identified the load-bearing columns on the reinforced bridge. Hall recorded in his diary: "Joe and I placed charges. One-hundred and fifty pounds of dynamite. Twenty-five pounds plastic. [Ignited by] black time pencil."

At 1:30 a.m., Hall checked his watch and blew the charges right on schedule—but not all of them. Only the two outside charges detonated, blowing out some of the pillars, known as "stringers," of the reinforced concrete bridge. The inside charges fizzled out. The bridge, however, was badly damaged and could no longer support heavy loads. Hall would have to make plans for the Garibaldi partisans to finish the job the next night.

Unfortunately, the explosion stirred a hornet's nest nearby: a German garrison. Now the team was on the run. Caught in the middle were the civilians of the nearby village.

Hall's destruction of the bridge near Tolmezzo led to German reprisals: entire villages were burned to the ground, houses raided, and civilians hanged and shot. The attack on the bridge precipitated a German raid on the nearby town of Villa Santina, in which a number of civilians were killed. Although Garibaldi partisans engaged the Germans and drove them back to their fixed positions at Tolmezzo, the team's actions would cause terrible reprisals on local civilians by the occupying German forces. As with all insurgencies, however, a small number of men had successfully tied up a much larger number of troops from the occupying army.

During the first two weeks of August, Hall spent time getting his bearings. Summertime in Carnia was gorgeous. Sunlight poured through the peaks onto the vast valleys below, illuminating the small towns and villages. With the built-in protection provided by the free zone and blown-up bridges, the Eagle team moved about the area with comparative ease.

Though he was more than eighty miles from the Brenner Pass, Hall was still attempting to implement the initial stages of his plan by targeting unguarded bridges that were important communication and supply routes. In the second week of August, Gees trained by Hall targeted the bridge initially damaged on August 9. This time, the bridge suffered such serious damage that road travel became impossible.

Hall then arranged a reconnaissance mission to scout out another target—a bridge over the Drava River, which turned out to be heavily guarded by German troops. Hall was beginning to realize he faced tremendous challenges. The plan he had worked so hard to draft was beginning to evaporate in the face of the reality of so many German troops in the area.

Nevertheless, their success with the first bridge raised their spirits. Hall and the Gees returned to the village of Ovaro, where Eagle established a base camp. After the mission, they were "wonderfully received" with cheese, wine, and grappa.

On August 12, 1944, Stephen Hall turned twenty-nine years old.

"Being my birthday, I drank to my health with milk at 12:01 a.m.!"

Having served the appropriate "time in grade," Hall sensed a pending promotion. In typical OSS fashion, he took the initiative and promoted himself, placing the shiny silver captain's bars on the collar of his jump jacket. With their signature initiative and bravado, many OSS operatives behind the lines followed this informal practice of self-promotion. Many operatives felt the self-promotion gave them a leadership edge in the eyes of the partisans.

The next morning, the team split up into three sections. Smith and Malispino took charge of radio operations at base camp, while Lukitsch worked eastern Carnia. Hall would be accompanied by the partisans hiking westward out of Carnia, to an area called Cadore in the Dolomite Mountains, where a single brigade of Garibaldi partisans operated—the Calvi Brigade.

Captain Hall spent the following day plotting his next move before starting for Cadore, taking refuge in a partisan safe house in Comelico. While eating breakfast, he encountered an unexpected surprise. Like divine intervention, a local girl entered the house, informing him that a German patrol was near.

"I scrambled upstairs just in time," recalled Hall.

Hall hid in the attic of the house, writing a report to Smith. After the patrol passed, he emerged unscathed, wearing a trench coat. "Walked through the town, passing several people, although the night was misty," Hall remembered. Hall then bicycled with the partisans to his next mission. The next day the sun beat down on them as they pushed up the mountain. The steep mountain roads forced the men to dismount and walk their bicycles. Rain came down intermittently and the sky became "black as a hat."

Approaching the target bridge at night, they cut the phone lines leading to the nearby Nazi garrison and posted guards around their position. Hall inspected the target. "Crawling on slimy wood underneath the cataract as usual, the target was misrepresented being much stronger and more solid," he recounted. After digging holes next to the pylons, he placed fifteen pounds of plastic between the timbers. Hall then planted fifty pounds under the keystones of the bridge. The detonation echoed through the nearby mountains. One of the keystone charges fell into the river, but the bridge collapsed at 3:20 a.m. Hall noted in his diary, "Very tired and sore . . . ducking woodchoppers (Germans) napped in alpine hay loft for two hours."

Over the next few days, Hall's small band made their way toward Comelico and Cadore, to the Dolomites. Abandoning their bicycles, the partisans worked together to transport Hall farther northwest. They picked him up in a sidecar motorcycle and drove him through the winding, verdant mountain roads. The driver fought in the Calvi Brigade, a leftist brigade named after a Comelico hero in northern Italy's war of independence against Austria in 1848.

Reclining in the comfort of the motorcycle sidecar, Hall took in the beautiful Italian countryside. After several hours, they arrived in Pramarino, in Cadore, a remote mountainous region with few roads and virtually no Germans. The partisans hid Hall away in a mountainside hut.

Relaxing after his long journey, Hall reveled over his latest victory, munching on wild strawberries and sipping fresh milk. Hall dined with the partisans, who lit the fireplace in an empty house and made polenta, a cornmeal mush traditional throughout northern Italy. Hall had already eaten the dish so frequently he dubbed it the "yellow peril." In an attempt to vary the cuisine, the young operative gathered coral mushrooms and fried them, washing them down with a pint of fresh milk.

As the men relaxed with full stomachs, the owner of the house, an Italian of ancient German descent, showed up at the door. Hall scurried to the loft and listened to the partisans speaking to the man. "I could have reached over the edge of the open attic and touched them. The boys gave this man 200 lira and said if he reappeared or told anyone he would be shot because they were Garibaldi. Twenty minutes after he left, I was out of the house with all of my gear," Hall revealed. It was another close call. That night Hall slept in the woods, getting soaked when it rained in the early morning hours. Hall ominously penned in his diary, "heard shots near house during night."

Over the course of his dealings with the partisans, certain conflicts came to light. Many of the partisans were battle-hardened soldiers, having endured years of combat. They could boast of numerous campaigns, from the deserts of North Africa to the wintry plains of Russia. Some of the Italians resented the presence of an inexperienced young American officer, especially one as cocksure as Hall. Nonetheless, most of them were happy to see Americans fighting side-by-side with them.

Near the end of August, Hall decided to sharpen his mountaineering skills, climbing Mount Schiaron, one of the highest mountains in the Crode dei Longerin chain, part of the Carnic Alps. He would need these skills near Brenner. Fir trees dotted the landscape, and jagged gray pillars of limestone pierced more than nine thousand feet into the blue Italian sky. Hall and a partisan guide pushed their way up the winding paths past local civilians working the alpine glades. Once on top, Hall wrote, "although cloudy, could see all major roads, valleys, and as far south as Piave." He noted that the meadows near Pramarino offered an ideal drop zone.

- 52 -

Life for the OSS operatives in northern Italy was an endless game of cat and mouse with the Germans, and the stress of constant fear weighed on Hall. To make matters worse, food was scarce for the team. Hall called in for a supply drop and waited several days for the goods. At one point his Mercury team was down to two small loaves of bread and a hunk of cheese, but fortunately, Gees arrived with polenta.

Back at the OSS outpost in Ovaro, a horrified Major Smith watched as German reinforcements poured into Tolmezzo. Hordes of White Russians and Cossacks, recruited to support the German army and now refugees from the Eastern Front, were pushing into the region. The German allies brought their families and all their worldly possessions, including fifty camels.

Smith radioed Jiminez on August 15:

Tolmezzo is being strengthened daily. Germans number two thousand. Troops billeted in garrisons and public houses. We expect drive against partisans this area and effort to open and keep roads open we blocked. Tolmezzo populace all fascists. Can it be bombed?

Meanwhile, as Hall still waited for the supply drop, lighting signal fires along the drop zone, important intelligence fell almost magically into his lap. The political commissar of the Cadore Brigade handed him a written report of troop dispositions in the area. Most importantly, they gave him two maps detailing the fortifications and troop presence along the Brenner Pass. The information was essential to Hall's larger plan.

That evening the men celebrated dinner with squirrel fried in butter. A marksman who eventually became one of Hall's chief lieutenants provided the squirrel. Known as "Tell," he was a forester by trade, and his nom de guerre came from the legendary archer who symbolized Swiss independence, William Tell. As a punishment for insolence, the original Tell was ordered by an Austrian official to shoot an apple off his son's head. Tell won fame by splitting the apple in two. But soon after that, he split the Baron's heart in two, igniting the independence war of Switzerland from Austria.

Since 1943, the contemporary Tell had worked with the partisans, rising through the ranks of the Calvi Brigade, eventually taking command of a company. Hall described the charismatic Tell as a "firebrand."

Later that night, Hall wrote in his diary, "Stayed up till 12. *No drop. Best night we've had.*" The men spent another day on the mountain. Food was once again running low, so Tell picked mountain mushrooms.

As the dark, starry quilt of evening descended on the Alps, the cigarette paper Hall used for his diary was running out. He looked into the black sky and saw the giant nebula of Andromeda, and the star constellations of the Perseus group. Once again, he lit fires for a drop. Once again, nothing came.

The supply issues frayed the Gees' confidence in Hall. The promise of a drop, but no delivery, aroused suspicion. As Smith recalled, "They were accusing me of not supplying them with arms because they were communist. They knew I wasn't communist, but I took the approach that if they were fighting Germans that is all that mattered." He followed the old adage "the enemy of my enemy is my friend."

The restless Hall could not remain idle while awaiting the drop. To inhibit German troop movement, Hall coordinated a small partisan operation, planting explosives above a mountain road near Lake Dobbiaco. The charges detonated effectively, causing a landslide. He reported the attack to Smith, who radioed back to base. Smith wrote:

> Hall states, rock fall from Croda dei Baranci: plugged road and railroad defile between cliffs and Lago Dobbiaco. Todt [German and Italian construction workers] working day and night on four kilometer detour. SS troops being concentrated in passes Routes 51 and 52. And on foot path passes to protect passage of foot troops. Hydroelectric stations for Venice at Lozzo and Lago S. Croce. Can cause ten day black out if drop is received. Our mission will fail unless requested supplies are delivered immediately.

By August 28 the supply situation had become desperate. Smith radioed Jiminez: "From Smith, to whom it may concern: What the hell is the cause for the delay in my drop? . . . If delay is caused by usual incompetence, will personally break some goddamn necks upon return. Let's get on the ball for a change."

Smith reported back to base on Hall's behalf: "Partisans ready to block all minor roads thru the Alps there with rock falls and mines upon receipt Pramarino drop."

Over the next several days, Hall experienced something all soldiers go through—sheer boredom. With his cigarette paper depleted, Hall carved a pipe to satisfy his urge for nicotine. He was in communication with Smith on a regular basis. The supply drop was beginning to look like an impossible fantasy.

With time to spare, he spied on a nearby Nazi work party: "Waited in bushes until 5:30, seen by one man and three children who walked right over me." As Hall gathered information on the Germans, the SS gathered information on the OSS. In nearby Padola, the Germans ransacked a local partisan's house, confiscating shotgun shells and taking several men for questioning in Bolzano.

On September 1, the thirtieth day in Hall's diary, the world had now been at war for five years. Hall awoke to the sun shining through thin white cumulus clouds. After lunch, he took a nap in the loft of his mountain house. As he slept, two men crept into the loft with cocked pistols while he was sleeping. One of the men barked, "Are you Captain Hall?"

"Possibly," Hall responded. "Who are you?"

Hall's .45 was at his feet. "I thought they were fascist spies at first," he wrote later. "After a couple of minutes it developed that they were my bodyguards. . . . Some bodyguards!" The two would later prove to be overly protective. Hall groused, "They hang on me like glue."

At about two in the afternoon, a motorcycle arrived with a message from Major Smith suggesting a conference. After arriving at the Eagle base headquarters, Hall sent out the mission-essential intelligence he had gathered, including a map of the Brenner defenses, to the OSS base.

After receiving the message and the map, Captain Irving Goff from OSS headquarters immediately responded to the message, confirming the high value of Hall's information: "Brenner defense plan of maximum importance."

The map would shape Hall's plans for the Brenner, pushing him deeper into northern Italy to his final destination. Before embarking on another journey, he reposed and, that evening, penned: "General celebration. Reviewed all radio messages—future plans and means of achieving. Had some ice cream! On radio news, got a little tight on some stinky rum, a great release for tired nerves."

The ice cream must have come from the locals—because of bad weather, the Pramarino supply drop had never arrived.

8

"No"

FORCED TO USE EVERY POSSIBLE means at his disposal, Howard Chappell hustled, stole, connived, and weaseled his way through the grid-locked military bureaucracy. In spite of the threat of a court-martial, the team finally made it into Italy. He felt like they "had finally found a home." Geographically, at least, he was one step closer to his ultimate goal: thrusting his team of OGs behind enemy lines and into the heart of the Reich. Chappell's men were now administratively attached to Company A of the 2671st Special Reconnaissance Battalion, Separate (Prov.) OSS.

It was September 1944. The company was known as the Italian OGs. An ancient medieval hill town less than two hundred miles north of Rome, Siena became home to Company A's new base of operations, chosen purposely because it was belly-to-belly with German lines. Siena marked the tip of the northern advance of the American Fifth Army. After the June liberation of Rome, the Allies had slowly crept up the spine of the Italian boot. The Allies had divided their armies: the American Fifth Army slogged up the western coast; the British Eighth up the eastern coast. Their advance was hampered by a lack of enough Allied troops. The Allies had siphoned off troops from Italy for the invasion of southern France in mid-August, and Britain had also sent troops to Greece to suppress the civil war led by communist rebels (which, ironically, the OSS and the SOE had helped foster).

While the Allies were withdrawing troops, Hitler replenished his own, sending eight new divisions to Italy. The route used by German reinforcement forces: the Brenner Pass. While Kesselring's army group fought for time, German construction crews worked behind the lines building a vast defensive barrier in the rugged Italian mountains known as the Gothic Line.

By autumn, heavy rains had turned Italy into a watery quagmire. Mud slowed the Allied advance as it hit the German defensive line. A combination of weather, terrain, and stubborn German defenses turned the Italian theater into a stalemate. Churchill wrote: "The Italian theater could no longer produce decisive results." Meanwhile, in western Europe, the Allies had broken out of Normandy and were advancing on the borders of the Reich. As the Italian winter approached, the Allied soldiers were losing morale. One officer summed it up best: "I wished that I were dead, if I had to stay in Italy another winter."

Despite the slow pace up the Italian spine, "The situation, oddly enough, best served the overall Allied strategy for the Italian theater— that of [occupying] the maximum number of German divisions." The Germans would have to send many troops stationed in northern Italy farther south to help bolster their defensive line. At the same time, the insurgency in the north would occupy whatever German troops were still there.

Behind the lines in northern Italy, the OSS and their British counterpart, the SOE, were helping organize and supply the Italian insurgency. Tens of thousands of partisans harassed the Germans behind the lines. The OSS successfully organized the Italian resistance into an effective "fourth arm," complementing the Allied land, air, and sea forces driving into northern Italy. The OSS supplied the insurgency with money and guns, and even food, when they could make a drop. These small bands of partisans, aided by groups like the Eagle and Mercury teams, tied up thousands of Axis troops who otherwise would have reinforced German armies farther south and on the eastern and western fronts.

✳   ✳   ✳

After getting his men situated in barracks on the outskirts of Siena, Chappell strolled toward a rustic stone villa adorned with a blood-red tile roof and mossy stone bulwarks. The picturesque building was the headquarters for OSS missions behind the lines.

Chappell made his way past an armed guard into the villa. He worked his way through the operations room, a maze of filing cabinets and thick mahogany bureaus. The dot-dot-dot, dash-dash-dash of ciphered Morse code echoed in the background.

Behind a wooden table, with a large map of Italy above his desk, sat a tall figure in a khaki field jacket. Captain Albert Materazzi had the look of a man of action. The thin OSS officer was a very busy man. He was personally running more than half a dozen missions behind the lines, issuing orders, monitoring intelligence, and sending supply drops as needed. The villa was the nerve center, and Materazzi was fondly referred to as "the Brain."

The twenty-nine-year-old operations officer was born in Hershey, Pennsylvania, of Italian descent. After graduating from Fordham University with a degree in chemistry, Materazzi completed a fellowship at the University of Rome and then earned the equivalent of a doctorate in chemistry. An expert on cartography and print lithography, he worked for the army map service and taught in laboratories at Fort Belvoir, Virginia. The OSS recruited him for his keen mind and his command of the Italian language.

Chappell walked up to his desk, introducing himself as the leader of the German OGs.

"I don't remember exactly what Howard said to me," Materazzi later remarked. "However, I do remember that he wanted to bring his entire team on a mission. I knew . . . [it] would have never have worked. . . . I made short shrift of Howard and dismissed him."

Much to his chagrin, Chappell walked out of the villa with no results. Ever the ornery and stubborn character, he would return the following day and practically every other day.

9

Bridges and Molotovs

RAIN SPATTERED STEPHEN HALL'S face as he climbed the southeast shoulder of Mount Terza Grande. After a few days' rest at the Eagle base camp in Ovaro, Hall was back in the field, reconnoitering the mountains of Cadore. The day of September 3, 1944, became stormy and cold in the Italian mountains, and the clouds were low. As he climbed toward the summit, a herd of sheep "nearly ate my clothes off," Hall recalled. The top of the peak contained a thin layer of light, powdery snow. From this vantage point, the border of Yugoslavia stretched out over fifty miles away. Perched virtually on top of the world, Hall wrote a final sentence before turning in:

> Clear evening sky. . . . Cumulus, cold as the deuce but could see breath, high wind all night. To bed at 8:30 p.m.

Later that afternoon, moving with the ease and precision of a master mountaineer, he made his way down the peak. The weather improved dramatically. "A clear brilliant blue sky, looks perfect for drop. Clearest day we've had yet." Once at the bottom, Hall received news that his demolition instructions had paid off. The Gees had blasted a railroad bridge and a cliff face to block a German supply route.

The partisans continued to harass German supply lines, ambushing a convoy and capturing three trucks. They killed four Germans, wounded five, and took several prisoners, including the commander of the Sappada garrison. The partisans asked Hall what to do with the prisoners. He recorded his answer in his diary: "I said not to kill them; plan to send wounded sergeant back to Sappada to demand surrender—Joe to do this with thirty Gees." Hall wanted Joe Lukitsch to arrange the German garrison's surrender. Hall's advice revealed his basic humanity, even in an inhumane world. Especially behind enemy lines, both sides frequently did not take prisoners. Earlier in the operation, for instance, two Nazi prisoners had been captured by the Garibaldi partisans. They were interrogated by Lloyd Smith, who cryptically reported in an Eagle radio message: ". . . they were shot that evening."

At Sappada, Hall planned to blow out the mountain road and bridge, blocking the route for German reinforcements. The young OSS officer left immediately to pick up "boom dust," also called Aunt Jemima.

While Hall's demolition team was moving up the road toward the bridge, a hysterical Italian woman ran out of a house, crying, "The Germans are here!" Hall quickly turned the newly captured trucks around and off the mountain road and moved his partisans to the small village of San Pietro di Cadore. Fearing for his life, Hall took up a position in the alley with a grenade: "Heard a scurry of running feet: Looked around: no partisans! Women and kids still in street, so I took off, figuring Gees had plan. . . . I did not see any of them again for two hours." During the chaos, the partisans had abandoned him.

Fitting into the local environment proved one of the most difficult aspects of operating behind the lines. Earning the trust of the Italian partisans and understanding their capabilities was also challenging. In San Pietro di Cadore, Hall had overestimated the loyalty and reliability of those around him. It was proving difficult for a blue-blooded American from Connecticut to work reliably with these partisans.

The partisans were not cowards. Many of them were seasoned combat veterans, having served in Russia, Greece, Africa, and the Balkans. Some even fought in the Spanish Civil War. Others endured hard lives as immigrants in European mines and in the factories of France and the Low Countries. However, Hall had a likeable side that was intoxicating to those around him. He was an adventurous man with a boyish charm. At times a naive dreamer, Hall could be fun and affable. Although the men recognized natural leadership and military authority, Hall lacked these traits. But they also knew he could be a source for two important commodities that any insurgent needed—money and guns. Yet, Hall had not been able to deliver these in any significant capacity. Nevertheless, he offered hope and reinforced the righteousness of their cause against the Germans.

After waiting twenty minutes in the alley with grenade in hand, Hall returned to the town village square. Out of nowhere, eleven SS suddenly arrived on foot. Hall scurried to a hiding spot and devised a plan. New to partisan warfare, he chose a novel way to fight: "I asked all civilians for wine bottles . . . made up grenades by packing bottles with plastic and short time fuses," remembered Hall. Fortunately, Hall never had to use the bombs. The Nazis conducted a brief patrol of the town and moved on.

Hall walked to the nearby village of San Stefano di Cadore. Except for a wounded partisan and a guard, the village was empty. Seemingly in the nick of time, he walked to the upper part of the village. He wrote: "Looked over just as Nazis drove up with forty men and surrounded building [containing the wounded and took them out]." Knowing he had to keep moving, Hall walked six miles into the hills and that night slept in a barn.

The next morning, the OSS officer linked up with the Garibaldi partisans and proceeded to interrogate some Nazi prisoners captured the day before. The Germans caught up in the net numbered more than a dozen, including SS Polizei Lieutenant Willie Auerbach. The partisans kept the POWs in a cow pen. "After interrogating Nazi prisoners, a second lieutenant, sergeant major, and eight workers," Hall recounted, "[I] got their parole! Sent whole gang north."

It is difficult to determine whether Hall had the authority from the partisans to free prisoners. However, the fact that he did so once again shows Hall's compassion. Additionally, it is likely the partisans feared German reprisal if they executed the prisoners. It is also possible they were freed because food was so scarce.

※　※　※

Meanwhile, more than thirty miles south of Hall's position, Eagle base camp was in a terrible fix. The Germans had gathered Cossack units outside Tolmezzo in late July, but they never entered Carnia before the second half of September. Major Smith angrily reported to OSS:

> 10,000 white Russians (Cossacks) and 1,000 SS troops camped between Tolmezzo and Amaro. Fighting is now at Villa Santina. This is it. They are making effort to open and keep open escape routes. No ack ack other than heavy machine guns. For Christ's sake come over and dive bomb while still concentrated. Let dive bombers escort all possible arms and ammo. Drop to 3 white sheets forming V. Point of V faced into wind. Drop on DZ Ovasta. This area is HOT. We are almost out of ammo. Send grenades, rifles, machine guns, mortars, Piats [antitank weapons], rifle grenades, medical supplies. Answer immediately.

Eagle base camp found itself in the path of a massive invasion. A terse response followed:

> Air force will not take action on targets, unless position exactly located. Suggest you give precise coordinates, plus description in relation to other terrain features. Where are SS and Russian troops bivouacked? . . . This is present situation re drops. Owing to priority in other European theatres to obtain number of planes, need to fulfill even small fraction of request.

While Eagle sweated out the pending Cossack advance, Hall used the time to regroup and assess the situation. Once again, Hall returned to base, as he had before, in a partisan motorcycle. When he arrived, he noted the mood at camp: "Disheartening. Bad news all around. No messages, no drops. Nothing all around."

At the Eagle base camp, the sky was a solid overcast. Hall became bored, especially with all tobacco gone. As he collated all the intelligence, he realized that the mission was, in fact, beginning to bear fruit. He sent an update to OSS headquarters via radio:

> Routes 50, 51, and 52 completely cut by Eagle and Garibaldi at Perarolo Defile on September 3, half ton of dynamite collapsed railroad tunnel, cratered road, resulting landslide from cliff buried both. Repairs will take at least three weeks.

With the intelligence on the wire, the men at Eagle camp kicked back for a game of poker.

Stephen Hall woke up to a clear day. He got ice cream on his way to the nearby town. While returning to base, he received news from an excited Garibaldi, stating that a BBC signal had arrived. The message: supply drop imminent. During the next week, Hall finally received the long-awaited drop. With fresh supplies, he planned to blow additional bridges.

＊　＊　＊

Tensions arose between the conservative Hall and the leftist Gees. Hall recorded in his diary, "quarreled with Nemo [Giuseppe Guglielmo] on red views." Nemo was a battalion commander in the Calvi Brigade. The argument was, in many ways, symbolic of the mounting internal pressure between the team and the Garibaldi partisans. But differences were eventually set aside, and afterward the two men competed in a friendly game of target practice. The bullet holes they made in the red-brown larch planks of a mountain hut in Pramarino are there to this day.

One day in the middle of September, after snatching an hour's worth of sleep on a stove in the rest camp, Hall, along with Major Smith, went on a raid with the rest of the partisans. Smith remembered the day:

> Climbed to the plateau, leaving Hall and a few partisans to construct a sixty to eighty yard abatis [an improvised blockade of felled trees], which Hall booby-trapped. Tell and the rest of us continued

about two miles further north. . . . And I kept a discreet twenty-five to fifty yards from the group. The [German] garrison was in a relatively open field on the right side of the road, about 150 yards [in front of us].

The group took positions along a fence and fired a volley, after which Tell called on the garrison to surrender. "The Germans answered with a sustained burst of heavy machine gun fire," Hall wrote. Tell, whose authority was growing steadily, ordered an immediate withdrawal. The men obliged.

Meanwhile, Hall mined another bridge, planting charges underneath its pylons to cover their retreat. While Hall worked underneath the bridge, "two German soldiers passed by. . . . I was very quiet, but continued work." After Hall laid the explosives, Tell, Smith, and his interpreter joined Hall's party. Looking down at his watch, Hall noted it was 7:00 a.m. He lit the fuse. It fizzled out to no effect. Hall sent a partisan to light a second fuse. "Perfect detonation," Hall wrote.

After returning to base camp with the rest of the team, Hall conducted a reconnaissance mission and used the opportunity to teach a partisan, code-named Florida, how to drive a motorbike. Hall humorously noted, "Hell of a time, as Florida had never ridden one. Spilled twice." They also evacuated a wounded partisan on the rear seat of the cycle. Meanwhile, German troops and thousands of Cossacks were making plans to descend on the area, like a coiled spring ready to unravel. They had had enough of Hall's dynamite.

Near the end of September, Hall received several messages that would dramatically direct the future course of his mission. The most important was a message that came from OSS headquarters through Smith's radio: "Get intelligence teams to Brenner." OSS headquarters also wanted to know whether partisan groups were operating in the Brenner area. As luck would have it, that very same evening, a British sergeant and six escaped POWs showed up—"very tired." After Hall arranged for their food and beds, a British soldier gave him an important piece of information. He told Hall about partisans in west Cadore, closer to the approaches of the Brenner. With this new information, Hall "decided to speed over immediately, [and] get in drops there," Hall penned in his diary. The information that partisans were operating close to Brenner, and the pressure of not fitting in with the communist Garibaldi partisans, compelled Hall to move farther northwest toward the Brenner. Instead of blowing up unprotected bridges and railroad defiles in the Carnia area, he was now, finally, going after the Brenner targets and maybe even the Brenner Pass.

In his diary Hall recorded with glee his response to the information: "Decision: yes." That night he also noted he would need a radio operator. He would note the same thought many times later.

10

Bored in Siena

HOWARD WHEELER CHAPPELL WAS experiencing something every soldier feels in war: a hefty dose of monotonous, mind-numbing boredom—
precisely the kind of thing that makes men do foolhardy things. To distract
his team, each day he led them in physical training. To maintain his men's
sagging spirits, they also enjoyed games of football on the local soccer field.

Fortunately, Mr. Fabrega kept everyone entertained. His colorful personality, knowledge of numerous languages, and quick wit made him the
most liked.

When one of the OGs complained about always eating the same
food, Fabrega hatched a plan.

"Not to vorry, I vill get you de chicken," quipped the swarthy
Spaniard.

The Spaniard hijacked a jeep and drove to a nearby farm village. Eyeing a gaggle of hapless fowl crossing the street, he sped down the main
throughway, flattening chickens in his wake. One farmer emerged from
his house, screaming at Fabrega as he dashed out of the vehicle and
scooped up the feathered carcasses. He returned with his spoils, greeted
with cheers by the hungry men. That night they prepared a feast.

Every day, undaunted and incapable of sitting idle, Chappell
pestered, poked, and prodded the Brain for a new mission. Sixty years
later, Materazzi remembered he was "a real pain in the ass."

11

The "Evil Genius"

WITH HIS PIERCING STEEL-GRAY EYES, August Schiffer stared at the men and one woman in his command. With the arrival of autumn, the change in seasons brought the forty-two-year-old to Northern Italy as the new Gestapo chief of the region. His cool sun-bronzed face and deep forehead crease furrowed as he glared at his audience. "This headquarters did not accomplish anything to defeat the enemy and that must be changed!"

Schiffer delivered his fiery speech inside the gloomy walls of the Corpo d'Armata, located in downtown Bolzano. The building, a former Italian military headquarters, is built of brick and stone. Epitomizing utilitarian government architecture, it casts an eerie pall over the town to this day. The building fit the man known fearfully as the "Evil Genius" like a glove. He, like his Führer, had come a long way from his former profession as a house painter. Unbeknownst to him at the time, his command of the Bolzano and Belluno area of operations fatefully linked him to Stephen Hall.

Schiffer's rise to power began in December 1925 when he became a member of the Nazi party. The party rewarded his loyalty in 1933 with the coveted Gold Party Badge, reserved for only its most ardent and fanatical members. He proudly displayed the medal on the lapel of his uniform.

His introduction to police work began in 1933 when he joined the Kriminalpolizei, the Criminal Police branch of the Nazi Party. At the time, the secret state police, or Gestapo, had yet to be formed. For several years before the war, Schiffer rose through the ranks of the criminal police. As the years rolled by, the rise of the Gestapo gave Schiffer the opportunity for a career in their ranks. The Gestapo promoted Schiffer to the lofty rank of major. Performing a brief stint as commander of security police outside of Zhytomyr, the location of Hitler's headquarters in the Ukraine, Schiffer honed his skills in intelligence work. He began recruiting and organizing informants. Months later, the Gestapo tasked him with the training of intelligence agents.

In August 1943, Schiffer's rise was impeded by a lung ailment. He traveled to Berlin to convalesce. Upon recovery, he returned to duty in October 1943, and the SS named him Chief of Section IV (Gestapo), where he commanded secret police units in Trieste, Italy. The weather in Trieste became too much for his lungs, so he changed duty stations to Bolzano.

Schiffer became Deputy Director of Section IV of the Secret Police, which was headquartered in Bolzano, and included command of the Gestapo and the criminal police forces. As a counterinsurgency expert, he possessed broad authority superseding that of most military units in the area, causing many in his organization to fear him. "In several instances where Schiffer's instructions were not executed properly, he threatened his men under the point of a gun to carry out his orders immediately. . . . Without hesitation, [he] would have liquidated us," recalled one of Schiffer's men.

In October 1944, the beady-eyed, broad-shouldered Schiffer traveled to Bolzano with his entourage. Perhaps the most striking of the group accompanying him, an individual who "followed [him] willingly to Bolzano as [his] secretary," was the beautiful, seductive, and opportunistic Christine Roy. Also known as Christa, the young woman was born in Berlin in 1921. An ardent Nazi and Schiffer's mistress, Roy took full advantage of the power and opportunities afforded by her position. According to one contemporary, she was "generally known as the queen." He further stated: "Lower employees were afraid of Christa Roy and carefully avoided any possible trouble with her, because they knew that one single word said by her to her superior and lover, August Schiffer, would have been enough for them to get transferred or suffer some other punishment."

Under Christa's spell, Schiffer went to great lengths to make her happy. He reportedly arrested an Italian woman from Bolzano for the sole purpose of acquiring her lavish fur coat, which Christa coveted. One member of the criminal police explained, "She attached herself to Schiffer just for speculation purposes so that she could enjoy the trappings that came to her through her boss." It was also said of her that she was "a female without feelings." During interrogations, she didn't seem to mind the "most disgusting tortures." Gestapo personnel under Schiffer's command feared her greatly.

Christa Roy was part of only one half of Schiffer's double life. Schiffer was a family man, married with two children ages nine and two. He loved them deeply, but saw them rarely due to the war.

Schiffer's "muscle" was Albert Storz, a thirty-two-year-old native of Salzberg, heavy boned with a stocky build. Bushy eyebrows obscured his blue-gray eyes. His thick head of brown hair was combed straight back without a part, just like his boss's. He was vulgar and loud and articulated his movements with his strong, heavy hands. During his outbursts, his gold incisor tooth gleamed. Storz's duties were chiefly in connection with Gestapo prisoners, and he handled most of Schiffer's prisoners. He was an extremely brutal and sadistic person who carried out, often personally, beatings and torture. Besides being Schiffer's muscle, he was also his chauffeur.

Schiffer's right-hand man was Heinz Andergassen, who was called the very "incarnation of sadism and brutality" by a fellow officer. He was roughly the same size as Storz and just as violent. Andergassen was also a heavy drinker.

Schiffer's position gave him plenary power. Despite holding the mere rank of major, Schiffer commanded most of the Gestapo outposts in the area. His command area included the large cities of Cortina, Belluno, and Bolzano.

The SS commander in the same area, Major Otto Schröder, indirectly fell under Schiffer's authority and was known to be similarly ruthless. Schröder commanded a Waffen-SS battalion named, appropriately, Einheit Major Schröder. Barrel-chested with strapping muscles and six foot three, Schröder was responsible for instituting a "reign of terror" with his SS battalion. According to postwar US Army Counter Intelligence Corps (CIC) reports, his operations entailed numerous atrocities:

> Informants are able to swear to the fact of at least 360 men being hung [b]y meathooks beneath the chin. At times, groups varying from four to sixteen were hung in the public square or in the woods near town, with orders to leave the bodies there two days. At least one-hundred persons were kept in prison at all times to furnish subjects for reprisals. The headquarters was known to have contained torture rooms, whipping rooms, and electrical shocking rooms.

One particular incident of reprisal occurred after a partisan booby-trapped a German target range. The partisans had attached a photo of Hitler and an explosive to one of the targets, along with a sign that said in German: "Aim Right." Furious, the Germans ripped the sign off the target, detonating the bomb and killing three of Schröder's men. In retaliation, Schröder initially ordered the execution of fifty partisans held in a Belluno prison. Schröder then whittled down his initial order to nine prisoners. The nine were hastily hanged, including a common prisoner who unluckily bore the same name as one of the partisans. Nevertheless, after Schröder heard they hanged the wrong man, he personally went back into the prison and shot the correct partisan.

✷ ✷ ✷

The clean mountain air of Bolzano helped clear Schiffer's lungs. With his authority in place, the general methods and attitudes of the secret police unit in Bolzano began to change. Schiffer had complete and utter loyalty to the Nazi cause. He was determined to follow every possible lead to root out the insurgency, which meant destroying the insurgents and the Allied agents who supported them, whom Schiffer called "terrorists." He understood through his long years of training that exploiting human intelligence sources was the key to battling an insurgency. The Nazi officer ruthlessly employed torture and what he dubbed "intensive cross-examination" techniques to extract information from captured individuals. He considered himself a patriot, but to Schiffer, the ends justified the means.

During the course of interrogations, Schiffer broke men with torture. Schiffer recounted that "under the term of 'intensified cross-examinations,' members of the Secret State Police understood application of methods of torture with the purpose of extorting information. . . . They were ordered for the first time by a directive of [Heinrich Himmler]."

Directives reveal that Schiffer worked within Gestapo regulations:

> The fight against resistance movement was steadily increasing in intensity. Individual commanders or commanding officers during intensified cross-examinations applied—according to local conditions—such measures which guaranteed the desired results. But intensified cross-examinations were always applied only to chief officials of partisan groups and only 'in such cases when it was impossible to obtain a confession. . . . It was necessary to use these methods in order to compel the stubborn terrorist chiefs to make any statement at all.' Naturally, I ordered such intensified cross-examinations myself with the result that I was able to prevent . . . attempts at sabotage or similar terrorist acts.

In his defense, Schiffer stated, "I expected that their confession would clarify the problem and uncover further clues."

In sadistic fashion, Schiffer employed a variety of brutal practices. First, the "swing":

> Wrists of the person under questioning were cuffed, either by a rope or by handcuffs and then the arms were pulled over the knees in such a manner that it was possible to insert a bar between the elbows and knees. The body, which, more or less, balled itself together, would then be suspended with the ends of the bars wresting on rungs of a double-ladder. In many cases, this procedure alone sufficed to make the delinquent confess. If this was not sufficient, however, the person under

questioning was beaten on his sitting part with leather whips . . . also
beat on the feet. . . . I also let women be cross-examined in the Swing.

Schiffer dubbed another torture technique "suspending": "In this
case, wrists of a delinquent were cuffed behind his back and he was suspended by his wrists between the two sides."

Schiffer also sadistically used electric shocks: "I brought from Trieste
a small induction apparatus with which it was possible to generate electricity by rotating a crank. . . . Usually, the poles of the induction machine were applied to the cheeks of those who were hanging in the
swing or were suspended from the ladder."

Schiffer had the power and techniques of torture. He was ready to
defeat the enemy.

12

The Mountaineer

HALL DID NOT WAIT for a radio operator. By the end of September, he set out on the expedition toward the Brenner. Alone, he traveled through the treacherous mountain terrain armed with a submachine gun, a .45, and a heavy backpack. Snow capped the peaks above two thousand feet. Hall had become a man like Hemingway's Robert Jordan, living for the moment and on an epic mission. For the cause, he threw aside the trappings of privilege and pushed himself to the limits of human endurance. He pushed through lush, piney forests; hiked up hills; and scaled the mountains with a rope and pickax:

> I made up my pack and started out, contouring the peaks, just the line where the bare rock jumps from the steep scrub slopes. It took three days to make the fifty-five miles. It involved 32,000 feet of climbing. . . .
>
> I've seen more gorgeous scenery than three men will in a lifetime—sunrises and sunsets among the peaks, moonlight glimmering on glaciers, storms swirling around tremendous pillars of rock, cataracts, forest glades, ancient villages.
>
> But full enjoyment is not truly there when you are on eternal guard against guns appearing behind every rock and shadow. The 'threat' never leaves you, asleep or awake; and I have not yet laid down to sleep without a pistol in my right hand.

Since his arrival in northern Italy on August 6, Stephen Hall had hiked, biked, cycled, and climbed hundreds of miles, earning him, in his own words, "a pair of legs of cast iron."

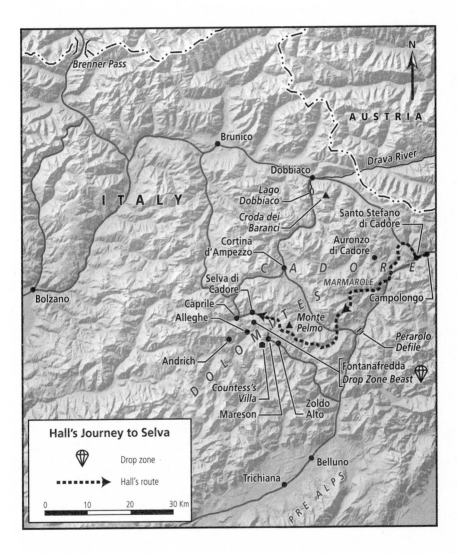

Hall's Journey to Selva

- N
- AUSTRIA
- Brenner Pass
- Drava River
- Brunico
- Dobbiaco
- Lago Dobbiaco
- Croda dei Baranci
- Santo Stefano di Cadore
- Cortina d'Ampezzo
- Auronzo di Cadore
- CADORE
- Selva di Cadore
- MARMAROLE
- Caprile
- Campolongo
- Alleghe
- Monte Pelmo
- Bolzano
- DOLOMITES
- Perarolo Defile
- Andrich
- Fontanafredda Drop Zone Beast
- Countess's Villa
- Mareson
- Zoldo Alto
- PRE ALPS
- Belluno
- Trichiana
- ITALY

Drop zone

Hall's route

0   10   20   30 Km

At one point Hall made his way through Nazi barricades, passing a hydroelectric dam at Auronzo di Cadore. As Hall circled the mountain trails, snow began to descend. The fluffy flakes fell from the gray canvas sky, blanketing the rocky mountain trails. The expedition became even more dangerous. Hall faced the threats of frostbite, hypothermia, and disorientation among the peaks.

One night, he slept under the noses of a Nazi garrison, in an abandoned World War I-era fort, and wrote a forlorn entry in his diary: "no food." The next day, after a "tiny breakfast," he continued a day of "very hard climbing." As he hiked and climbed, he reconnoitered the various mountain ranges through his binoculars, searching for Nazi troops. By a stroke of luck, he ran into a company of partisans who gave him a guide and much-needed supplies.

At the end of September, Hall crossed another mountain range, "climbing 2,000 meters up the flank of Mt. Pelmo." While traversing the crags, he memorialized the scene: "On foot, new snow just under cliffs with avalanches coming down." Hall avoided the avalanches that could have buried him, but the snow was ominously taking its toll on his body. As it came down, he scrawled: "Right foot frozen."

After three days of climbing, hiking, freezing, and starving, Hall found the partisans he was seeking. Officially created in the autumn of 1944, the Val Cordevole Brigade had become an autonomous and anti-communist fighting force. They looked upon themselves as an alternative to the many leftist partisan brigades operating in the area, such as the Garibaldi. The men operated south of Cortina in the mountain villages and valleys of Zoldo Alto, Falcade, Caprile, and Selva di Cadore. They invited people from all walks of life to join the insurgent group, although a communist leader of another group of fighters perceived them in purely Marxist terms, describing them as the "local representatives of the interests of the agrarian bourgeoisie." The Val Cordevole Brigade numbered roughly 150 men divided into four battalions. Many powerful individuals could be found on its roster, including their political "heart and soul," Arnaldo Colleselli. Colleselli later became a member of parliament for the Christian Democracy party, an organization that would rise to power in postwar Italy.

Former Italian mountain troops, known as Alpini, formed the core of the brigade. Commanded by their charismatic leader, Ettore Davare, they fought for Mussolini in the Balkans and in Russia. Born in 1915, Ettore had been a sergeant major in Mussolini's Alpini and had survived the Italian retreat at Nikolayewska, on the outskirts of Stalingrad. In 1943, after the collapse of Mussolini's government, Ettore headed for the mountains and, like many other young men, joined the partisan movement. He built his own brigade. One partisan described him as standoffish and determined, particular and reserved, "even if smiling in front."

Once with the brigade, Hall began to bond with the partisans and make his plans. In the distance, he could hear the roar of Allied planes bombing the Brenner. Over several days, he was able to gather intelligence on the Brenner as well as Cortina, where he would base his operations.

After discussing his intel with Ettore and the other partisans, he sent his findings back to Major Smith via courier. In his diary he wrote: "Message to base on Brenner biz." He also forwarded a plea for a supply and explosives drop. Back at base, Major Smith relayed a desperate message to headquarters: "Hall can blow the Brenner if his supply drops are sent. . . . Utmost haste necessary. . . . This is the last message from us until drop comes."

Hall spent the next day in his sleeping bag nursing a bad cold. He was going beyond what his body could handle, and suffering psychologically as well. Evidence suggests he was in the early stages of a deep and dangerous depression. In spite of positive developments on the Brenner, Hall's physical exhaustion and influenza caused him tremendous suffering.

On the sixty-third day of Hall's diary, his entry recorded an amazing scene. Looking into the sky, he saw Allied Liberators flying all morning. The partisans made a large Italian flag on the ground to signal the planes. After finding Allied propaganda newspapers in some of the drops, "there was a great thrill all around."

✻   ✻   ✻

Over one hundred miles to the south in Carnia, like a compressed metal coil, the German army sprang into action. Axis troops from the SS, Wehrmacht, and Italian fascist units marauded across the Italian countryside in a *rastrellamento,* the Italian word for "raking up." Like a plague, hordes of Cossacks spread across Carnia, attempting to root out and destroy partisan forces. Directed by the brilliant Field Marshal Albert Kesselring, the action was intended to destroy the enemy operating behind their lines and keep the German supply routes free, thus eliminating the knife held at their backs. Kesselring knew that his line of defense farther south could hold until the spring of 1945 at best. The Germans needed to remove the partisans and clear the supply lines so they could construct a new line of fortifications.

Thirty miles to the south of Hall's position, German SS troops, fascists, and over three thousand Cossacks poured out of the garrison town of Tolmezzo. At Eagle camp, Major Smith faced his worst nightmare. After the air corp failed to act on countless requests to bomb the garrison, the Germans finally struck hard, sweeping into the entire Carnia region of Italy. For the Cossacks, it was bittersweet. After having been uprooted from the steppes of Russia and brutalized by Stalin, the Cossacks now fought for the Reich and for a new home. In exchange for liquidating the partisans, the Germans promised the Carnia to the horde.

The rastrellamento put Smith, Joe Lukitsch, and the rest of the Eagle mission on the run. The Germans already knew that several Allied missions were operating in the area. In an unsuccessful mass night drop, OSS headquarters foolishly dropped colored parachutes onto the white snow of the Italian landscape. Immediately alerted of enemy activity, the Germans launched a violent sweep. Eight hundred SS troops and two thousand Italian fascists blitzed Carnia. German agents and collaborators guided the Axis forces to partisan supply caches.

According to Major Smith:

The Republic Alpine patrol consisting of thirty men coming east from Frassaneit routed three hundred partisans from the adjacent mountains. My mission was with a company of the Osoppo that literally ran up the side of the mountain when this patrol fired on us.

In other areas, partisan brigades fought the Germans until the SS brought up heavy mortars and field guns. The Germans and Italian fascists stationed detachments in all the small towns and imposed a scorched-earth policy to deny the partisans shelter. The Eagle team remained in the mountains for more than a week with hardly any food or shelter. Many of the partisan detachments dissolved, with guerrillas deserting, changing into plain clothes and melting into the civilian population.

Lloyd Smith summed up the scene: "The partisans of Friuli had been completely routed."

※　※　※

Hall and Smith also reported to OSS headquarters the growing conflicts between the partisan groups. The communists were attempting to consolidate their power in the north in preparation for the postwar period. The first of several explosive messages from them would have a profound impact in later months:

> Nicholson, Rudolf and I are working to prevent a break in relationship with Osoppo and Garibaldini. Division Political Commissari are rabid Commies threatened to arrest Major Rudolph. The following statement has been made by same leader: "The time will come when we will also drive the British and Americans from Italy. . . . Russians are still in Ampezzo valley village."

Another message received at headquarters on November 18 came from either Hall or Smith. Albert Materazzi theorizes it was Hall because it came over another mission's radio, and Smith later categorically denied sending it:

> The present situation prevents official military activity due to too much political pressure by a few communists in control of . . . partisans.

Dangerous anti-British, anti-Italian and anti-American propaganda by ten men neutralizes any Allied effort to take the offensive against the demoralized enemy. . . . This appears to be deliberate sabotage of Allied plans and is even against the official Italian Communist Party and its directives. . . .

There will be little military action this winter if these suggestions are not carried out immediately and political activity prevents a peaceful settlement in this zone after Armistice.

All OSS Italian agents this region must be under my command. Union of Osoppo and Garibaldi prevented by communism spread by our agents. Unless these agents are placed under my command and are told of such at once and I am consulted about the entry of all OSS personnel this region, my mission is coming out.

This was perhaps the most important radio message Hall ever sent. According to the Brain, when the message was received back in OSS headquarters, "the shit hit the fan," and investigations were launched. Several months later, like those of a tiny stone tossed in a pond, its concentric rings would ripple all the way to Washington. One historian said:

The communists were becoming increasingly cocksure, difficult to manage, and conspiratorial as their power in the north grew. As Mercury warned, the OSS's communist agents were spreading propaganda which was preventing union with the center and right of the committee of national liberation. . . . Plainly, the communists intended to try to seize power in the north of Italy and were resorting to every means to obtain American arms supplies and gold to enable them to do so.

Hall was the first to foresee that this political issue had the potential to sink the entire OSS. In question were the political views of not only the OSS agents, but of some of the operations officers handling Hall's mission. The issue would become a political football in months to come. In hearings in front of Congress that resembled witch hunts, Jiminez and Lossowski would be unfairly put under a political microscope that would taint the entire organization. Later, this congressional testimony would be used to block the creation of a postwar OSS, or CIA. Congress and political pressure would assert the OSS was infiltrated by communists and was one of the reasons the agency was to be disbanded by executive order after the war on October 1, 1945.

❆　❆　❆

Smith ordered Hall's close friend, Lieutenant Lukitsch, to return to an OSS base in Italy by plane. Smith cryptically added: "Lukitsch is coming on Lysander to fully explain the situation to you." The political consequences of the radio messages regarding communist OSS operatives would have profound impacts in the coming month, when General Donovan appeared before Congress. The fate of America's first centralized intelligence agency would hang in the balance.

Ironically, Eagle, accompanied by three downed airmen, escaped Carnia through the help of the communist Garibaldi Brigade. With partisan guides, they walked hundreds of miles behind enemy lines, avoiding countless German patrols, to Yugoslavia and the safety of Tito's communist partisans. Eagle eventually returned to OSS headquarters in Italy in the spring of 1945.

❆　❆　❆

Several companies of German Gebirgstruppen—mountain troops— clambered through the icy peaks as the exhausted and frostbitten OSS officer Stephen Hall ran for his life. The German Alpine mountain troops were some of the Reich's best, highly trained and renowned for their esprit de corps. Known for the edelweiss insignia on the side of their field caps, they had fought in nearly every Nazi theater of the war.

For several days, Hall and his Val Cordevole companions fled, at one point fighting a gun battle with German mountain troops in the village of Alleghe. Hall, accompanied by Ettore Davare, the brigade commander, then headed for the hills with the Val Cordevole. The brigade's "officers and noncoms . . . knew every trail and crag of all the Dolomites."

Using their knowledge, they effectively evaded the crack German mountain troops.

Hall's group climbed the mountains for several days and were once again attacked by German troops with heavy machine guns. The insurgents hid at the edge of a forest as the Germans fired blindly. "We watched the tracers smack on the rock all around us . . . they never saw us and finally went away," remembered Hall. The partisans melted away. Fortunately, so did the rastrellamento, at least for a while.

The pause allowed Ettore and Hall to regroup the brigade and erect a field headquarters. Over the course of these operations, Hall became a close confidant of Ettore. With Hall once again fighting fevers and bedded down in his sleeping bag, Ettore gave him a red leather-bound book to read. The book, a novel called *The Scarlet Pimpernel*, is set during the French Revolution. The main characters, a group of English nobles appalled by the bloodshed of the Reign of Terror, disguise themselves as Frenchmen, infiltrate Paris, and save French nobles from the guillotine. Ettore had received the book as a gift from a friend, a mysterious woman of alleged noble lineage, called the countess. We may never know if Hall realized the portentous significance of this book. It was an omen of the sequence of events and relationships that would come to define his journey. As usual, Hall penned a significant diary entry: "*The Scarlet Pimpernel* from C."

13

The Countess

IN THE DEEP OF THE NIGHT, Hall and Ettore crept through the woods on the edge of the village of Mareson. By the light of the moon, they saw a house hidden in a patch of forest on the side of a mountain. The charming and picturesque home was adorned with bulky pine window frames and a heavy oak door, a balcony on both levels. As they hid in the woods near the villa, Ettore craned his neck to get a closer look. Tucked in his pack, Hall had his leather-bound copy of *The Scarlet Pimpernel*. He planned to return the adventure novel to its owner.

Ettore looked for the signal: a pine branch on the rightmost windowsill meant they could enter. A white handkerchief meant they could not. Scanning the façade, he spotted the branch, and the two moved forward, slouching to keep their silhouettes low in the silver light of the moon. As if they were in a fairy tale, "Once Upon a Time" was inscribed above the threshold of the front door. As they stepped in, they saw a woman seductively lying on a divan, surrounded by hand-painted murals. (The murals exist to this day, preserved for their beautiful artistry.)

Born of Swiss nobility in 1907, Isabel de Obligado was tall and svelte, with a wasplike figure. Some said she divorced or separated from an Argentinean noble, giving her the title of Countess. She was a woman of power and influence. Elegant and well dressed, she carried herself with distinguished presence and beauty. She appeared younger than thirty-eight, concealing her age with flowing, copper-dyed hair, one of many elements that masked a double life. In the summer of 1943, the local villagers said, she arrived out of nowhere (most said from Rome), with the trappings and finery of wealth. Her sporty Lancia coupe was the only privately owned automobile in the area.

After tea and talk with Hall and Ettore, she revealed "bits and pieces about the local Nazi government" in which she served. Hall recalled she possessed a "tangled background." After the armistice of September 8, 1943, when Italy dropped out of the war, German forces occupied most of Italy and the Reich annexed for itself the northern provinces of Belluno, Bolzano, Trento, Udine, Gorizia, and Trieste. The regional counsellor, Dr. Hubert Lauer, appointed her to the post of Delegato Podestarile, essentially giving her the powers of mayor of the municipality of Zoldo Alto, which included the tiny hamlet of Mareson. The seductive countess's connection with Lauer could be deemed in today's vernacular as "friends with benefits." In her own words, she described Lauer as "a very great admirer of mine."

Lauer was known for riding around south Tyrol "in a Farnum automobile, with a bodyguard of thirty Nazi toughs," recalled Hall. However, like the countess, Lauer was not as he seemed. Though he embraced the trappings of a true German official, at heart Lauer was an Austrian patriot. A US Army report after the war described the Austrian in this manner:

> Dr. Lauer used his position, his influence, and his authority to benefit the population, without being partial to partisan groups. In administrative functions, he was both anti-fascist and anti-Nazi, and steered away from political connections. In his control of the gendarmerie, Dr. Lauer was able to suppress a large part of the terrorism which had taken place.

Such were the environs in which Stephen Hall operated. Not everyone was who they made claims to be; ally and enemy often intertwined. The countess was probably a double agent, but she was then as mysterious a figure as she remains to this day.

In subsequent days, Hall became acquainted with her upstairs rooms, a combination of sugar and spice. One room was filled with confections—flour and sugar to satisfy her sweet tooth. Her home-cooked cakes were enjoyed with tea. Another bedroom was filled with weapons and ammunition for the partisans, and a third room housed a radio. Despite her official position in the Nazi regime, she appeared to side with the partisans. One operative noted another of her many assets: "She could shoot a machine gun and set off bombs, could do everything."

Isabel de Obligado was actually an Allied agent working for France. In 1944, the French were already looking ahead to the end of the war. Both France and Britain recognized the necessity of a strong Austria in the face of the expansion of communist Russia's influence, especially through its nearby and soon-to-be satellite state, Yugoslavia. France was interested in creating a buffer zone in the Tyrol, part of the new Austria, to minimize the threat of another knife in the back such as they had experienced when Italy invaded France in 1940. The countess served France's broader interests, furnishing them with intelligence; in fact, a French spy chain operated out of Bolzano.

Though her motivations remain unclear, her actions speak volumes. One episode in September 1944 highlights her influence and courage. When a partisan kidnapped a German noncommissioned officer, the countess offered herself as collateral and guarantor of a prisoner exchange. The partisans returned the officer to the Germans, who did not torch the village.

As a result of her influence, the villagers described her as a goddess. Hall's return of *The Scarlet Pimpernel* marked the beginning of their affair, as the countess fondly recalled:

> We were bound together . . . because we were the only two cultivated beings and the only *"gens du monde"* in this partisan ensemble [who were] *"gens du peuple,"* (common people)—or people all paid with a price in gold for doing what they did—and it was very natural that Steve as a consequence appreciated me enormously—and I, him—and we made our confidences to each other.

The two developed the strongest bond known, falling in love.

14

Green Light

DURING THE SECOND WEEK of November 1944, Howard Wheeler Chappell made his usual rounds at the nerve center to pester the "Brain" to get his team behind enemy lines. After countless denials and dismissals, Chappell finally received the answer he wanted to hear.

Since October, OSS headquarters had tried numerous times to send Stephen Hall a radio operator, but fate had always seemed to intervene. Planes had been grounded by bad weather and operators had been peeled off for other missions. The OSS had been forced to communicate with Hall the old-fashioned way, via courier.

In the middle of October, Hall fell under the command of the Company A operations officer, Captain Materazzi. At the same time, another team, called Aztec, operating under Captain Materazzi's operational control, had informed him that an additional operational group was needed to work in the area above Belluno. There were a lot of partisans and not enough Allied operatives to supply and train them. Materazzi spliced two objectives together: organizing an OG team for the area and getting a radio operator for Hall.

Materazzi gave Chappell the mission of taking a three-man OG party to Cortina and linking up with Stephen Hall. Now the responsibility for delivering an Italian radio operator to Hall fell on Howard Chappell's shoulders.

For Chappell, the mission was a major step toward realizing his longstanding goal, to take his entire German Operational Group on a mission to pierce the heart of the Reich. The three-man advance team was only the beginning. He could use Hall's knowledge of the area and, more specifically, the Brenner, to achieve his ultimate objective. As one of Chappell's men stated: "Howard wanted to go through [the Brenner] to get to Germany."

The timing could not have been better for Chappell. By the middle of November, his OGs were getting restless. Five Jewish members of the team had mutinied, demanding placement in the OSS's secret intelligence branch. They wanted their own missions to strike back at the Reich. Over a year and a half had passed since the team had been formed. Chappell craved action.

Since no safe drop zone near Hall had been established, Chappell planned to drop near the existing OG team, Aztec, that Materazzi had on the ground. Captain Joseph Benucci led Team Aztec. Hailing from New Jersey, the handsome, five foot eight, chestnut-haired Italian was fondly known as "Capo" by the partisans. Deftly handling the behind-the-lines drama of multiple partisan groups, the Brain felt Benucci provided some first-class intelligence, but was otherwise a "bullshitter." Nevertheless, through Benucci's Aztec team, Hall had now come under the Brain's sphere of influence.

The Aztec mission had dropped into the Belluno area on October 13, 1944. Gathering intelligence and liaising with the local partisans, Joe Benucci was able to somehow establish contact with Hall and set up a lengthy courier route. Messages had to pass from Benucci's base camp outside of Belluno through more than thirty miles of rugged terrain and roads infested with roving German patrols. The OSS considered getting a radio to Hall as the highest of priorities, and now Howard Chappell was going to attempt to bring it to him.

Chappell assembled and prepared all the gear needed for the behind-the-lines mission, code-named Tacoma. Machine guns, ammunition, grenades, and winter clothing came out of Company A's supply sheds.

Chappell wanted to bring his entire team, but the Brain limited him to a three-man team. His right hand, Salvador Fabrega, was of course his first choice. He also needed a radio operator, but none was available from his team. The OSS provided a seasoned behind-the-lines operator whom Chappell had never met, Corporal Oliver M. Silsby. The lanky operator was a veteran of two prior missions behind the lines in Yugoslavia. Intelligent, blond-haired, and blue-eyed, the Detroit native had a suave demeanor and a calm smoothness. Silsby was also an expert operator, specializing in Morse code and cipher pads. At the time, Morse code messages were coded in cipher from one-time pads. Pads were printed only once, one copy given to the base while the other was given to the radio operator. The cipher was considered unbreakable.

On November 25, 1944, Materazzi sent a message via Aztec to Hall that would link him to Chappell: "Chappell team coming next . . . drop will include [radio] operator for Hall." Unfortunately, Hall would never hear the news.

15

Mission Impossible

HALL LOOKED DOWN AT a transcribed radio message from headquarters. The Brain had sent the radio message a week earlier, but it took days for the courier to carry it over the mountains from Belluno to his hideout.

> Inform Hall. Narrow gauge railroad near Cortina d'Ampezzo greatly used. Cut if possible. Attempting to solve winter supply problems. Project working whereby fifteen bombers under fighter cover would make mass daylight drops in secure partisan areas. Fifty tons using three-hundred chutes . . .

Hall's supply problem had become precarious. Many of the groups he worked with, including the Val Cordevole Brigade, were hobbled by the lack of new supplies and men. Furthermore, Hall dealt with constant communications issues, making contact with headquarters difficult. The winter elements of the rugged Dolomites also took their toll on the captain's body. His famous cast-iron legs started to falter under the constant pressure of evading the Germans chasing their brigade.

Hall made preparations for the next phase of his Brenner assignment: to disable the Cortina railroad. He worked with an electrical engineer familiar with the railroad, a man who knew the blueprint of the tracks in detail. As one component of their supply lines, the Germans were using a narrow-gauge rail to ferry troops and supplies from the main Brenner line through Cortina and points farther south. The Cortina line was electric. Various substations supplied the electricity to the railroad tracks. Four huge mercury condensers regulated the electric current on the railroad. High-tech for their time, these condensers were housed in one small unguarded and unoccupied building, making them an Achilles' heel for the entire railroad.

One particular electric substation was located at a critical choke point. The substation housed two of the large mercury condensers. Destroying it could cripple the railroad; the German industrial base was in tatters from Allied bombing raids, and replacing such high-tech components would take months. Hall planned to carry forty pounds of plastic explosive to destroy them. The main challenge before Hall was getting to the substation. The only way to reach the site would be to traverse unfriendly territory in the open while German patrols roved through the countryside.

Hall also planned another secondary target, this one far more audacious and the masterstroke in his Brenner plan: He would coordinate the destruction of one of the primary railroad tunnels in the Brenner Pass. Hall had envisioned the scheme a month earlier, while working with a group linked to the Val Cordevole Brigade, a group he had met through Professor Colleselli. The group was called the Bolzano Resistance Movement. Comprised of fewer than twenty men, they operated deep in German territory in Bolzano and were headed by an industrialist executive named Dr. Manlio Longon. Hall furnished the explosives, code-named "marmalade," to be transported on a truck to Bolzano, where members of the Bolzano Resistance Movement would plant the explosives and charges in the tunnel.

Other aspects of his plan involved using the Val Cordevole to sever the Brenner railroad once it emerged from the pass. Furthermore, he would use the brigade to perform reconnaissance and identify "pinpoints"—or vulnerable places—along the railways and pass the locations to the air corps. Bomber raids on Hall's pinpoints would ideally cause landslides, further blocking the route.

Before the objectives could be met, plans for both major targets fell through at nearly the same time. Hall's plan for the substation at Cortina was the first to be compromised, when Hall's main confederate, Tell, was captured in mid-November.

✳   ✳   ✳

In the fall of 1944, the inadequate resupply of the OSS-sponsored partisan groups in northern Italy was exacerbated by the Warsaw uprising. The Allies diverted most available long-range aircraft in the Mediterranean theater to Poland in order to supply the uprising. OSS and SOE "bent all efforts" to deliver as many supplies as possible, but winter weather was also grounding the airplanes and preventing supply drops. The Allied advance up the Italian boot had become snarled, and the war in Italy would see another winter. Under these circumstances, the theater commander, Field Marshal Alexander, issued a direct order to all partisan bands to lie low.

These factors combined to create a perfect storm of circumstances gathering against the operatives and partisans. With Allied bombers grounded by poor weather, the Germans could afford to pull units off the line to conduct anti-partisan mop-up operations. The partisans ended up unfed, ill clothed, ill equipped, and under German attack.

"The effect of the theatre commanders' directive to 'lie low' on partisan morale was naturally depressing," noted an OSS historian.

This situation forced many partisan groups to disband for the winter, including brigades controlled by Eagle and Mercury. Eagle fell directly in the crosshairs of a renewed German rastrellamento, challenging the supply problems for all the partisan groups.

✳   ✳   ✳

Meanwhile, Stephen Hall was alone. Rain fell on the Italian Dolomites as he wrote his next diary entry:

Sent long letter to Joe B. [Benucci, leader of the Aztec mission] and radio gram on DZ [drop zone]. But Batista ['Battista,' Giovanni Andrich, electric engineer who supplied Hall with plans for substation,] brought five old Colliers [magazines] around at 3 p.m. 1939 etc. Also Elks magazine. All quiet . . . Listen to radio news in the evening. Bitch of a cold with bronchitis—Unheated room. To bed with honey and milk hot. Over the course of the next few days it rained and continued to read magazines all day.

It was getting colder in the Alps. In the freezing recesses of the attic where he hid, Hall wrote a more upbeat diary entry: "Holiday today special food—pasta! Simon [a partisan] brought grappa in the evening."

The next day it began to snow and drizzle. Nevertheless, Hall's bronchitis improved. He read every word in his five *Collier* magazines, including the ads, and penned a fateful entry: "All marmalade should have been shipped by this time."

16

Weaving the Web

Roughly forty miles west of Andrich, in a dreary industrial office at the Corpo d'Armata, Major August Schiffer, wearing the smart field gray uniform of the Gestapo, worked intently at his desk. The double silver runic symbols of the SS adorned the collars of his immaculate uniform. His hat, emblazoned with the SS death's head skull, lay flat on his desk. Through a combination of luck and perseverance, Schiffer was on the edge of a breakthrough. The major had put his years of police training and counterinsurgency skills to good use.

Schiffer was a master at connecting the dots—finding small pieces of evidence and reconstructing the facts. His first big break in the case came with the apprehension of an informant caught driving a truck loaded with Hall's "marmalade." In a strange twist, the driver, perhaps named Foppa, turned out to be an informant for the Germans. The information gleaned from this single thread allowed Schiffer to roll up the entire Bolzano Resistance Movement, the cell affiliated with the Val Cordevole Brigade.

Through Foppa, Schiffer was able to connect the dots to one of the most important members of the Val Cordevole: Professor Colleselli. When Colleselli was brought in for interrogation, the ever-present Christa Roy, serving as Schiffer's stenographer, dutifully chronicled his statements—given under torture—so that they could be examined and analyzed during and after each session. She is said to have "[taken] an active part in the arrests and enjoyed the prisoners' mistreatment." Later, Christina Roy remembered bringing in Colleselli:

Professor Coleselli [sic] was arrested in a school building in Belluno. Major Thyrolf and Schiffer drove me to Belluno. . . . Coleselli was [then] taken to Bolzano. Before being taken to Bolzano he was subjected to an interrogation in Belluno. Coleselli was not mistreated. Coleselli confessed immediately and indicated that he was a sympathizer of the Christian-Democratic Party and that he was in contact with the commandant of the Brigade Val Cordevole, principally with the Capo who had the cover name of Ettore. Coleselli confessed further that he had received the order to get demolitions by the chief of Committee of Liberation in Bolzano, the director of the Magnesium works, Dr. Manlio Longon.

Schiffer detained Colleselli and then turned his attention to bringing down the next major figure associated with Hall's plan, Dr. Manlio Longon. The dots he was connecting now were crucial because Schiffer quickly learned of the Val Cordevole Brigade and its leader, Ettore, and it would not be long before he heard rumors of an American captain. Armed with information gleaned through the interrogation of Colleselli, Schiffer arrested over a dozen people within a short period of time, detaining them in the Corpo d'Armata. Unfortunately, most of the resistance members arrested were part of Hall's plan to blow up the railroad tunnel in the Brenner Pass. One by one, Schiffer's Nazi thugs brought them to the "machine room," a dank, industrial, stone-walled room lined with rusty pipes and valves. It became Schiffer's asylum for brutal torture and interrogation. Schiffer cunningly described how he snared Dr. Longon:

I carried out the arrests in the following manner: I let Dr. Longon be invited to the office of the Referent for Industry of the highest commissioner for the Operational Zone Alpenvorland . . . where I arrested him. In the course of the investigation, it came to light that part of the members of the Bolzano resistance movement were in contact with an American captain who issued the various instructions for preparation and carrying out of the blow up projects and similar acts of sabotage. The name of this American captain was not known at the time. It could only be asserted that this American captain was in contact with the Val Cordevole Brigade and with another brigade which was communist. Dr. Manlio Longon was chief of the Action Party and, undoubtedly, a chief personality in the Bolzano Resistance Movement.

Dr. Longon himself was a key figure, as Schiffer recalled: "It was Dr. Longon's assignment to pick out the men who would carry out the intended and planned operation of blowing up the [tunnel]."

Schiffer personally "intensively interrogated" (tortured) Longon for hours, gleaning information on a key agent in the ring who previously eluded him, known as Mario. Through his cunning, Schiffer found a way to get Mario. At about the same time, Schiffer also snared a smaller fish, an agent code-named Friggo. Friggo fingered Mario as a "chief enemy agent." Around Christmas 1944 Schiffer offered Friggo a deal. If he found Mario for them, he would be set free. Schiffer "allowed him to escape" from his cell in the Corpo d'Armata and he "declared himself ready to locate the chief agent Mario and deliver him into my hands."

Friggo was successful in carrying out his end of the bargain. Once Mario was apprehended, Schiffer invited Longon into his office with Mario present. "Longon recognized Mario immediately and was obviously surprised to see him under arrest." Schiffer's suspicions were validated. Longon's connection to the driver of the truck carrying explosives threw dirt on what would be his shallow grave. With this final revelation, Hall's entire plan to destroy the railroad tunnel in the Brenner evaporated.

Schiffer's machinations did not end there. He was now intent on finding the mysterious American captain and the commander Ettore. First, he drained Longon of all actionable intelligence and then determined to "execute the death sentence upon Dr. Longon." Insidiously, Schiffer decided to carry out Longon's execution in such a way as to be untraceable. "I made a suggestion . . . that either the arteries of Dr. Longon be cut open in his cell with a piece of glass and that he be left bleeding to death, or that he be strangled . . . the killing of Dr. Longon was supposed to remain a secret, at any rate; that is why I gave the order that Longon's corpse, after his hanging, be brought back to the cell where a suicide by hanging was to be staged." Longon was hanged by a small rope and placed in his cell in the prescribed manner, a conniving bit of theater to stage a suicide.

All the while, time was running out for the blue-blooded American captain. Schiffer's dragnet around Stephen Hall tightened.

17

La Montanara

HALL AND HIS GROUP slowly climbed up the base of the mountain. After working its way to the crest, the small group set up a partisan brigade headquarters in a cow barn in a hidden valley.

By the end of November 1944, what was left of the Val Cordevole Brigade had slipped farther into the mountains of Fontanafredda, Italian for "cold fountain." The area is a beautiful landscape, with terrain nearly a mile high, snow-capped peaks, and towering larch trees.

Along with the rest of his partisan brigade, Hall was on the run, as the Val Cordevole gradually melted into small bands of men.

Hall chose a small group of the best soldiers:

I finally picked up a bunch of ex-noncoms from the alpine troops. They don't come any better. We are all on skis and go swishing over the snow fields and passes like the Finns.

Lack of supplies continued to plague the small band as they looked hopefully at every plane in the sky. On the night of November 25, the men were awakened from their sleep by the drone of a plane's engines.

"I had my suspicions [about the plane]," Hall wrote, "and told the men not to light the signal fires. It was a tough decision to make."

Still suspicious, Hall gave the order to pack up, and he and the partisans moved another five miles to snow fields on Mount Pelmo. The area they occupied was known locally as the little flower meadow, although Hall described it differently:

It was just another icicle shop to us, very cold with five feet of snow. An hour after we had moved, three groups of Nazis appeared over the rim at the basin at Fontanafredda. They were investigating the plane business. Seeing a dead camp, they came no nearer to investigate.

Undaunted, on December 12, Hall received word, via courier, of an imminent supply drop from fighter-bombers. He ordered his men to wait at the drop zone for days while avoiding German patrols. The men were in rough shape: "They suffered from influenza, dysentery, frost bite, and bloody feet," Hall wrote. Eleven days passed after OSS headquarters had informed Hall of an imminent supply drop. Finally, at 4:00 p.m. on December 23, after having received no supplies, Hall made the decision to send his men home. He promised to get a radio, saying, "Maybe in a month we can start work again," lamented Hall.

"They did not want to quit, but I knew that in their weakened condition, that it was too dangerous for the situation."

Drearily, the men prepared to leave Hall and return to their homes. Before departing, they sang La Montanara, "The Mountain Girl," to honor Hall and his efforts to help them. It was one of the most legendary of the Alpine songs:

> *Up there in the mountains*
> *Among woods and valleys of gold*
> *Among the ruggèd cliffs there echoes*
> *A canticle of love.*
>
> *La Montanara, ohè!*
> *You can hear sing,*
> *We sing the Montanara*
> *And who does not know it?*
>
> *Up there in the mountains among banks of silver*
> *A hut covered with flowers,*

It was the sweet little dwelling-place
Of Soreghina, the daughter of the Sun.

As the men trailed off into the dusk, the song brought tears to Hall's eyes. It was a pivotal moment; the entire mission seemed lost. Hall was alone.

And then, a miracle. "An hour later, as I was gloomily contemplating the fire alone, a courier stumbled in the door. There had been a day drop by five fighter planes the day before," Hall recalled. The drop site was close by.

The supply drop allowed Hall to regroup the partisan brigade. The men started rounding up supply canisters and parachutes, which they buried before the Germans were able to react. It was the shot in the arm the men needed.

"We got mortars, funny papers, machine guns, soap, carbines, cigarettes, explosives, and a pile of assorted stuff . . . It was a great Christmas for everybody."

With the added momentum the supply drop provided, Hall felt that his mission was back on track. With his men supplied, he left the partisans for the familiar arms of the countess.

18

A Lover's Christmas

RODERICK STEPHEN GOODSPEED HALL had been behind the lines for five months. He had dodged countless patrols, blown up bridges, and helped organize and coordinate partisan brigades. Furthermore, his efforts had to revolve around the politics and mixed loyalties of the partisans in the region. His legs of cast iron were numb and his feet frostbitten, encased in an inch of grease. He was running a fever and was physically exhausted. His only refuge was to be found in the arms of the countess. He would spend this Christmas with her, as she recalled:

> [Steve] passed Christmas with me in my house, which was the center of the partisan movement. Christmas Eve I kept him, because I saw that he had a fever and that his feet were very badly wounded on the heels. I took a great deal of care of him, and we made a little Christmas tree together. He was on the [couch] with my furs around him, because he was shaking with fever—and he must have had a premonition of misfortune . . . because he told me that he would not return to America, and that I was his only true friend in whom he had absolute confidence (he did not like the Italians and did not get on well with the partisans).
>
> The life was hard for him, and the food did not agree with him. So I saw him getting thinner and more and more depressed—and with all that he had his feet frozen on the right side—and all my attentions did not suffice, because he ought to have remained repose for a time, and *that* he could not, or did not wish, to do . . .
>
> I believe that no one can tell you as well as I the truth about the life of Steve—moral and physical—in these mountains . . . following

a mysterious law—and in this making to love him all those who knew him—most of all myself, who know him better than the others.

The countess adored Steve Hall, and she deeply understood him. She understood he was on a mission—and, perhaps, a personal journey. Hall felt alone, being one of the only OSS officers near the Brenner in northern Italy.

Hall wrote:

So with the local Hitlerites digging the jive at a dance hall a mile and a half down the road, I spent a delightful Christmas Eve with an old friend, the Countess. Cookies, tea, apples—and at midnight candles on the tree. We talked about our respective families so far away. By morning the fever was gone and I left to follow my men.

It is possible Hall also told her about his next mission. Perhaps he gave her details on how he was planning to destroy the mercury condenser in the Cortina transformer substation. Hall may have informed the countess it was a one-man job and told her that he would ski from Selva to Cortina, plant the charge, and ski back. With little cover, Hall would have to ski undetected through heavily garrisoned Cortina,* plant the charge, and somehow ski back to safety. It was a suicide mission and she would have known it. She may have tried to talk him out of it.

The countess went on to describe Hall's demeanor:

[Steve possessed] a great depression, moral and physical and spiritual, from which he suffered. He seemed to have great sorrow in the depth of his heart . . . which deprived him of the joy of living for long moments. He sometimes made allusions to me, but I always avoided

---

*Cortina was a huge sanatorium for German sick and wounded soldiers. The area also contained over one hundred members of the Japanese intelligence service who were based there.

that he say too much to me—for fear that he would regret it afterwards—they are so delicate, the feelings—and so easily wounded that I preferred not to touch upon it. Now I regret it so much, so much.

No one will ever know for sure Hall's true state of mind prior to the mission. What we do know is that he was desperate. In severe pain, alone, and trapped in the icy mountains, he stood on the brink of his own demise—or glory. Still, the mission needed to continue despite the fact that capture was highly likely. His position was deep behind enemy lines in an area swarming with SS troops. But perhaps in his own mind, death or capture was an easier solution to the suffering he endured.

With little warning, Hall left Christmas morning. He felt alone, more alone than he had ever felt in his entire life. Hall did not know it, but Captain Chappell was on his way to meet him.

19

Tacoma

HOWARD CHAPPELL LOOKED around at his men, the dull drone of four Rolls-Royce Merlin engines beating in the background. The plane slowly lost altitude and leveled off over the tiny Italian village of Valmorel in the Italian Pre-Alps.

It was the day after Christmas, and he led a three-man team, code-named Tacoma, three hundred miles deep behind the lines. Nearly a month of false starts and scrubbed missions delayed Tacoma from getting to Hall. Now Chappell was finally on his way. Looking through the Joe hole into the blackness, the craggy outlines of the Dolomites and fir trees flashed before his eyes hundreds of feet below.

A T signal fire set by the partisans pierced the inky blackness of the night sky. The Polish crew flying the Halifax flipped the switch, and the green jump light pulsed. Cylindrical metal parachute containers packed with submachine guns, ammunition, uniforms, and shoes for the partisans dropped from the plane before Tacoma.

Chappell approached the hole. While not a C-47, the Halifax gave him the same feeling.

"Stand in the door, hook up," he muttered to himself, the same phrases he barked countless times to his men in training jumps.

He stared down the Joe hole as he hooked up his static line attached to the blowout panel in the back of his X-type British parachute. Flashing his signature smirk to Fabrega and Silsby, he dropped through the hole into the blackness. Chappell free-fell for about fifteen feet until the static line pulled out the panel and pulled the white canopy from the parachute harness's pack tray. The cold mountain air hit Chappell's face as he looked up and grabbed the risers on his chute. Below, the signal fires edged closer as he floated gently down toward them. The partisan drop zone, code-named Azure, was nestled in a bucolic mountain meadow covered with snow and flanked by high Alpine fir trees.* Fabrega and Silsby were not far behind "Flash Gordon." The team dropped close to one another and, upon landing, were greeted by a motley crew of partisans dressed in civilian clothes and tattered uniforms.

The drop zone and the tiny mountain town of Valmorel were located about ten miles from Belluno, and over 150 miles from Bolzano. Chappell's mission was to first link up with Hall and then to approach the Brenner, bringing in the rest of the German OGs. Cortina and Captain Hall were about forty miles to the north. The seemingly short distance cut across some of the most rugged mountainous terrain in Italy. The route flowed through bridges and tunnels guarded by hundreds of German and fascist troops.

The partisans gathered up the ten tons of metal parachute containers. Small arms, ammunition, uniforms, shoes for the partisans, and most of Tacoma's equipment were found. Along with partisans, old men, women, and even children helped gather the containers. One young partisan in the gaggle of bodies remembered Chappell's godlike presence and, sixty years later, after hearing mention of his name, stated flatly: "Rambo."

Unfortunately, the men's personal musette bags with toothbrushes, cigarettes, and other knickknacks were missing. And most unfortunately, the radio generator or power pack for charging the radio batteries was not found. This equipment powered the radio for communication with their base. It was critical to Tacoma's success. A lack of power for the radio would haunt Tacoma for the rest of the mission.

The beauty of the Azure drop zone was its remote location. It took Germans hours to navigate the mountain trails to get there. Unless they pre-positioned troops in the area, the partisans would be long gone before the Germans could reach the meadow.

---

*The Azure drop zone is now a park, which includes an Alpine-style pub frequented often by old partisans.

After rounding up the supplies, the partisans took Chappell and his men to Captain Benucci's Aztec team mountain hideout.

Fabrega remembers: "One of the partisans then led us to a rendezvous point where Captain Benucci awaited us. This was about a four-hour hike from our DZ. The zone was quite quiet, and at about two a.m., Captain Benucci led us to the house where he had been living and where we were to stay."

Chappell greeted First Sergeant Nick Cangelosi, Aztec's weapons and ordinance specialist. Twenty-four years old, five foot six, black-haired, and raised by immigrant parents from Sicily, Cangelosi joined the OSS from the 504th Parachute Infantry Regiment and mastered the techniques of survival behind enemy lines. Cangelosi typically led most of Aztec's raids and was the mission's de facto leader with the partisans.

"It was right after Christmas and Chappell reminded me of Santa Claus, he hit all of us with the biggest smile you have ever seen," recalled Cangelosi. Chappell radiated confidence, working the room and greeting Aztec's quiet, hardworking radio operator, Sebastian Gianfriddo. Described as extremely loyal, competent, and a "good listener," the black-haired, hazel-eyed "Sebby" was Aztec's radio link to OSS headquarters.

Inside the one-room mountain safe house, Chappell, Fabrega, and Silsby exchanged greetings with three partisans. They gave the trio such inglorious noms de guerre as Blondie, Blackie, and Brownie—the unimaginative code names came from the colors of their hair. Standing out from the three was Brownie, or Aldo Palman, a handsome five foot ten, with chestnut-brown hair—he was a force to be reckoned with. Hailing from Belluno, Brownie was a warrior.

Chappell later said of Brownie, "[He] had so much courage and he seemed fearless."

Prior to meeting Chappell, he and another partisan had walked into Belluno, where they spotted two German machine guns in a local armory. They disarmed the guards, threw the machine guns into a German truck, and made multiple trips back to the armory to grab more equipment. Brownie's daring would earn him Chappell's respect.

After Tacoma met the partisans, Fabrega put his culinary skills to work. Cangelosi remembered how he would gesture with his hands when he needed whatever food Aztec had laying around to prepare the meal. "He was exciting to watch, as his eyes sparkled and his hands were waving up and down," recalled Cangelosi.

"Bello! Bello!" With a flurry of a couple pots and pans, Fabrega threw together the meal.

"He was a great cook, he always seems to make something out of nothing," recalled Cangelosi.

"We slept here that day and waited for our equipment which was brought to us. We remained here for three days because Captain Benucci learned there was a rastrellamento," remembered the animated Spaniard.

Typically in a rastrellamento, the Germans would pull thousands of troops off the main battle line and sweep an area for partisans. For Aztec and Tacoma, it was a hard fact of life and an almost weekly occurrence. Staying alive in the war-torn Pre-Alps was a tremendous effort for anyone operating behind enemy lines. Surviving the elements compounded the stress: snow, below-zero temperatures, and the resultant frostbite remained a constant torment. Tacoma, Aztec, and the partisans learned to change safe houses every night and stay on the move. Sixty-five years later, Cangelosi described the experience as a constant "rat race where we were hunted every day."

Fabrega recalled being hunted like live game:

We all moved into a house midway between San Antonio and Trichiana. This was about five kilometers from Captain Benucci's house and every night one or the other of us would walk over carefully, to avoid detection, in an attempt to get our equipment. We finally succeeded in getting some of it to our place. While here we checked our equipment and made plans for our trip to Cortina di Ampezzo [and Hall].

20

Messages in Bottles

STEPHEN HALL PICKED UP his skis leaning on the venerable larch tree in front of the countess's villa. Fastening the brown leather straps, he pulled his aching and burning feet into place, each one "literally as hard as boards." He paused to reflect on the journey that lay ahead. He dreaded the trip. The long journey to Andrich snaked along the Marmolada range, and the sun did not shine for long stretches. He was unaware Chappell was on the way.

Hall swished up and down the slopes along wooded mountain trails, making his way to his "den in Andrich," Hall's safe haven. The trek to Costa Annetta's mountain home took hours. The courageous Italian woman offered her home and sustenance, but her courage came at a high price. Had the Nazis caught her, they would likely have burned her house to the ground and hanged her from a meat hook in the town square.

Instead of resting, Hall focused on his next order of business and completed a plan of action for the Val Cordevole Brigade's next mission. It is likely he planned the strike on the Brenner rail line as it emerged from the pass.

Bored and once again suffering from the flu, Hall holed up in the tiny unheated attic room in the kind woman's mountain house. With "nothing to do but listen to [his] mustache grow," Hall occupied his mind reading *Ivanhoe* and, later, old copies of *Colliers* magazine. Inevitably, his weary thoughts turned to home, and he started a letter to his family. The letter, addressed to his father, summarized many of his activities since November:

January 1

Dear Ray,

If I ever get out of this mess, I will be the softest touch in this country for soul-saving organizations for 50 years. I am in what you might call a strategic gopher-hole which gives off all the signs of being a baby volcano before long. Anyhow, I've got some back pay coming to me and when I do get through, we'll try "that fishing trip." So start your annual leave. . . .

Anyhow, out of all of the various battalions, brigades, squadrons, and armies which I've organized (and seen die), I've finally picked a bunch of ex-noncoms from the Alpine troops.

But hell knows if we'll ever get this mission through. Looks like a baby volcano for sure: to wit, Kesselring will move back to the Alps here soon and you can't do much when you are plunk in the middle of their damned battle line—that is, not for more than about 20 minutes, and my function, among other things, is to live, if possible. If there were two of us, it might be different. Oh well, as I say now, I'll cross that mountain chain when I get to it! Maybe I can get out, if the Teutonic population gets too numerous.

If not, I'll be saying goodbye and thanks for giving me life. I've made mistakes and haven't got very far as standards usually go, but no one can say I haven't done a lot of things with life, or enjoyed it.

So long, Ray,
Steve.

The first clear, blue-sky days lifted Stephen's spirits as he dug through a layer of snow, hitting the earth next to the wall of Annetta's house. Gently, he placed the letter inside a gray-green wine bottle and reburied it next to the wall.

The letter conveys the nervous bravado of a man caught between severe external and internal strife. His hyperbolic descriptions of his exploits reveal both the bravery and fear of a true risk-taker. His bravado is understandable, considering he recognized and perhaps welcomed the bleak prospects of his own fate.

Furthermore, severe frostbite is often accompanied by significant amounts of pain and nerve damage. Hypersensitive nerves can make those afflicted feel the sensation of pins and needles. The chronic pain likely affected Hall's spirit.

The facts on the ground colored Hall's myopic view of the war. In Italy, the winter had set in, and Allied movement along the front once again ground to a halt. The Germans continued slowly withdrawing up the spine of Italy toward the Brenner Pass, which they would certainly use to escape from Italy into Austria. Allied intelligence also falsely reported the Germans planned to fortify the Alps above the Brenner, creating the so-called Alpine Redoubt—Hitler's planned location for a final holdout. His perspective likely worsened when he learned of the Battle of the Bulge. During the opening days of the battle, hundreds of thousands of German troops hit a thinly defended line in Belgium's Ardennes Forest, creating a massive bulge in the Allied lines. Many wondered if the war had once again turned in favor of the Axis.

✳ ✳ ✳

During the second week of January, Hall left the safety of his den and conducted a reconnaissance of the area from a nearby peak. From the towering crags spanning over a mile across the Italian landscape, Hall took in the scenic view. But the beautiful day came under the shadow of news from days earlier. Schiffer captured several members of the Val Cordevole and the Bolzano Resistance Movement (Bolzano CLN), and "the whole organization was blown." The Gestapo captured several of the men involved in his operation. Under torture, he learned, Tell talked.

Hall recorded Tell's dismay at what had happened after Tell's capture:

> The fascist secret police picked up one of my key men! Under threat of torture, Tell capitulated, leading Nazi patrols to the hiding places of eleven of my men. The day after that he returned with twenty Nazis to the house I was staying at. Of course I had cleared out. They beat up my hosts, an elderly couple, and stole all their food, but did not burn the house down in the usual custom. This man, Tell, was

then to write down all he knew—it took him five days. So now the Nazis have all the goods on me.

Hall sarcastically spun his reversal of fortune of what Tell's capitulation meant: "This plays in my favor, as I can now play in the open without airtight security. Besides revealing many of the contacts in my brigade, forty pounds of plastic explosive used to destroy a substation was now in German hands."

This statement reflected the brazen, almost irresponsible attitude Hall had for his own personal safety. Holed up in the upstairs room of a six-hundred-year-old house, the OSS operative jotted down this next diary entry:

Have upstairs room in complete secrecy. Woodworker below doesn't know I am here. Mother of owner had son die of hunger in Nazi POW camp. Cloudy.

Hall discovered all this in an odd twist of fate: the man who helped the Nazis capture part of Val Cordevole ended up informing Hall. Within Schiffer's chain of command resided a mole—more precisely, an Italian double agent with ties to the resistance who also worked for the Gestapo.

An Italian police officer, code-named Sette, was described by one Italian partisan as loyal "in every possible way," with great courage. Sette even enabled one captured partisan, nom de guerre of Giacomo, to escape by providing him with molds for the keys, a description of the movement of guards, and a map of the prison. However, his dealings were ambiguous. As another partisan leader put it, "there was one police officer whose loyalties we never really knew." Sette served as driver for the local Gestapo branch in Belluno ultimately under Schiffer's control. Most likely, he met Hall through the countess.

Hall described his ability to make associations with such characters: "This all sounds rather like storybook stuff, but actually it's rather prosaic. They're all worried over their own skins and it's just a matter of picking on the ones who are most worried and most useful. I've become something of a myth to them, 'the American who's been here five months that no one can catch,' so that helps."

Over the course of the next few days, Hall relaxed with the partisans, reading nine issues of the 1933 *Literary Digest*. His respite ended with the arrival of a letter from Benucci containing a fateful order: "Base requests Cortina R.R. cut." As six inches of new snow piled up outside the house, Hall made preparations for the mission to Cortina. After spending one more day in the house, Hall made a final entry in his diary: "Haze, clear at night. Will leave tomorrow at 4 a.m. to attack Cortina line. It's a one-man job on mercury condenser in station yard."

Once the ink dried, Hall slid the diary into another wine bottle and buried it deep in the fresh snow.

21

Journey to Cortina

"MY FIRST JOB WAS to get to Cortina and Steve Hall, who knew the area around the Brenner. Once there, my goal was to bring in the rest of my team," Howard Chappell recalled nearly sixty-three years after the war was over.

Getting to Hall, however, became practically impossible. The deep snows made the thirty-five-mile journey by foot perilous. Tacoma would have to hike over winding, snow-covered goat paths and through craggy mountain trails, along the way avoiding the thousands of German troops swarming around the Brenner.

To solve the monumental problem of getting to Hall, Chappell did what he did best—improvised. He devised several plans that read like a movie script.

According to Nick Cangelosi, first sergeant of the Aztec mission, Chappell's first attempt to reach Hall involved a coffin. Silsby and Fabrega hid under a bale of yellow-brown hay in a cart driven by a local partisan commander, while Chappell lay in a coffin fitted with special air holes. Across his chest, he readied his submachine gun.

After Tacoma made its way through one roadblock manned by machine pistol-wielding Germans, Chappell deemed the operation too risky and opted for his fallback plan, traveling to Hall via truck.

Chappell needed a supply truck with German markings and a German driver and guard. They planned to drive to Hall while the team rode in the back of the truck with a guard detail composed of German soldiers who had deserted to the partisans.

Obtaining a supply truck would not be a problem. Partisans drove them for the Germans.

"We planned to start moving northward to join Captain Hall, heavy snow made walking impossible. We decided to get a truck. That meant we needed someone wearing a German uniform to talk to Nazi guards at the road blocks," recalled Silsby.

"I need two German soldiers I can trust," he told one of the partisan commanders.

"We have several men that might work," responded a partisan chief working with Aztec. Shortly after making the request, the partisan commander delivered two Austrian deserters who came well recommended to Chappell.

Both deserters were Luftwaffe ground troops. The first was short, wiry, blond-haired, and orally challenged, with widely spaced teeth. Chappell nicknamed him Bobbie. His dark-haired companion, who deserted from the same unit, got the inglorious nickname of Fred.

Chappell kept the men at arm's length, not knowing their backgrounds. He gave them new clothes and shoes and forced them to do "housework," keeping the team's mountain safe houses in order. In a few days, the men resented doing menial work and complained to Fabrega: "We were sent here to be guides, not to do housework, we aren't doing any more work."

Several days passed and, coincidentally, the deserters' former unit, the 20th Luftwaffe Division, moved into Trichiana, only a few miles from the team's mountain safe house. That night Fabrega—who spoke German—listened to the men's conversations, searched their belongings, and discovered a cache of food, ammunition, and cigarettes. Based on Fabrega's eavesdropping and the amount of food they had hoarded, Chappell concluded that their plan was to return to their old unit, claim they had escaped from the partisans, and beg for leniency. For them, it was a perilous plan, since most deserters recaptured often faced the firing squad.

Keeping these unreliable men with the team posed a huge risk. They knew Tacoma's hideout and could identify them. The whole plan could be blown skyhigh if the two Austrians escaped. The lives of the partisans and Team Tacoma were at stake, and Chappell lived by a simple credo: the mission always came first.

"We must get rid of Bobbie and Fred," Chappell coldly informed Benucci.

The next morning Chappell walked by Silsby, shaving in front of a mirror in the safe house.

"What's up, Cap'n?" Silsby asked.

"We're going to get rid of the Austrians," Chappell coolly responded.

Silsby looked at Chappell with one eye and kept shaving.

Chappell strode over to the stable where the two men slept and confronted the two Austrians. "I don't trust you. I'm sending you back," snapped Chappell.

Shocked, the two Austrians nodded while exchanging nervous glances. They followed Chappell, thinking they were returning to the partisans. Next, Chappell cryptically told both men to hand over their shoes.

"The shoes were worth 75 to 150 dollars," he recalled. "Besides the shoes, I wanted to get their clothes, since the partisans needed them."

While Fred was removing a shoe, Chappell pulled out his knife and cut Bobbie's throat. Fred broke into a run and made it out of the stable. Silsby, still shaving, watched through an open window as Chappell bolted after Fred, brought him down with a football-style tackle, and beat him to death with a piece of firewood.

By nature, war is harsh, brutal, and callous, and it can awaken the dark side of human nature. The execution of Bobbie and Fred unveiled the dark side of Howard Chappell, but it also marked the emergence of one of the OSS's greatest warriors.

That night, Fabrega and Brownie dragged their bodies into a cave, burying them in a shallow grave.

With Bobbie and Fred gone, Chappell resurrected the original plan—walking to Hall. Silsby remembered the ordeal:

During the three weeks we made arrangements for the trip to Hall, it snowed rather heavily, and it was now about five feet deep. We were supplied with guides by Captain Benucci, who was to lead us to another brigade [Val Cordevale]. From there arrangements were to be made for our transport across the valley to Cortina.

After walking for two nights over very rugged terrain, we got halfway to our destination and were met by the man who was going to take us to Hall. He told us it was senseless to go any further. The snow had blocked all the passes.

Frostbitten, cold, exhausted, but undaunted, Chappell came up with another plan.

I devised a plan to dress in civilian clothes and ride a food truck that was driven by a pro-partisan. We were to take the truck in the mountains and ride to Belluno where we would stop overnight, waiting for early morning when control of the route was relaxed. We were then to make our way (with the truck) to the house of the contessa [de Obligado] who was in touch with Hall, and she would get us the rest of the journey.

Over the next few days, Tacoma made the arduous trek back over the mountains to Valmorel, and bought civilian clothes in preparation for their journey by truck toward the Brenner and Hall. That night a heavy snowstorm descended on the area.

22

Against All Odds

AS THE LIGHT OF DAWN CREPT over the countryside, the blizzard showed no sign of letting up. The puffy white flakes coated Hall's shoulders as he buttoned the collar of his khaki M-42 paratrooper jumpsuit, slinging his carbine and backpack across his shoulders. Gently, he put his swollen feet in his skis, remarking to a downed Allied airman who had found his way into the Val Cordevale: "This is the opportunity I have been waiting for. With this heavy snow I will have cover to get into Cortina to blow up the railroad transformer station." Hall's backpack contained a forty-pound explosive charge he made from plastic and a time pencil.

Hall waited patiently for Ettore. But the blizzard delayed the partisan leader from reaching Hall. The OSS captain pushed on without him. Unbeknownst to Hall, Ettore carried a special letter from the countess:

Dear Steve,

I have learned that you are moving today, but that your feet are not completely healed (equal to the situation). Someone has said that it is the spirit which is the strength of the man; sometimes the feet are the important thing.

It is for that reason only that I advise you to come to take care of them at my house for a few days, finally to be finished with this inconvenience. I think that here you will have more safety than anywhere else, and you will be able to sleep as much as you wish.

I have also a lot of things to tell you—not too important—but not stupid either. You can tell me some tales which you can make up for

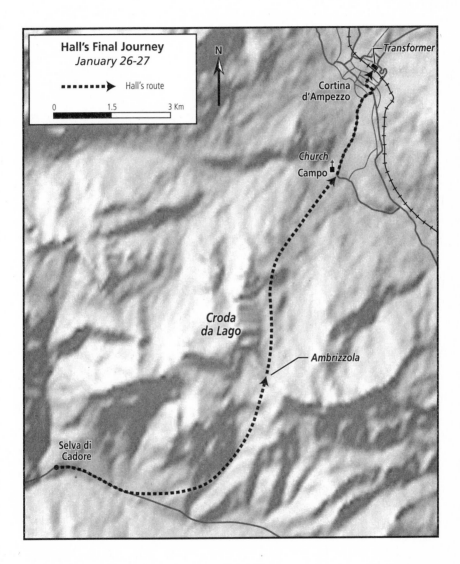

Hall's Final Journey
January 26-27

▪▪▪▪▪▪▪▶ Hall's route

0   1.5   3 Km

N

Transformer

Cortina
d'Ampezzo

Church
Campo

*Croda
da Lago*

Ambrizzola

Selva di
Cadore

me. In exchange I will make you the pommes de terre au gratin. Do you not think that you will have everything to gain in the exchange?

Here there is a pretty vent du diable (wind of the devil)—the good God invented this on purpose to make the window shutters clap; it may well be that He is also amusing himself with it. It must be heart-rending to look all day upon the land where so many wretched things happen.

Upon the hill everything is very well, and one finds life beautiful and interesting in spite of everything—and one sends you so many pretty curtsies and remembrances.

I. de O.

The two lovers shared stories and poems. Their stories to one another appear to have been one way of escaping the war. The relationship seemed colored by the romance of classics such as *The Scarlet Pimpernel*. A few days earlier, bidding farewell to his lover, Hall had left the countess's house. Isabel then had a premonition of Hall's death that she called a "presentiment of misfortune." The countess summoned Ettore and "told him to convince Steve not to go at this time, and to come [back] to her house in order to recover his health and feet," recalled the countess.

"I think that Steve would have obeyed me if he had ever received the letter but Fate willed that Ettore did not go that evening . . . and thus Steve departed alone," she recalled in a letter.

An hour after dawn on January 26, Hall pushed off from his safe house in the tiny Dolomite town of Andrich. The mountains cast an eerie shadow over the fir trees as Hall skied toward the rail station. Howling wind and frigid snow pelted his face as he made his way along the winding mountain trails. Hall's journey took him through seventeen miles of some of the most formidable terrain on earth. The miles are not a true measure of the journey, which only takes more than half an hour by car. On skis, the trip moves over mountains, down gullies, and into canyons. Hall's journey would take at least two days.

After a brief rest, he set out again on the morning of January 27. The blizzard worsened, with visibility reduced to an arm's length. Months behind the lines had taken a toll on Hall's body. He had lost weight and his legs of cast iron burned. Now his feet finally gave out and he began to freeze, likely developing hypothermia.

Spotting a small church, Hall took shelter in a small depression near a stack of cordwood. He took off his shoes in an attempt to soothe his aching, blackened feet. In the distance he could see the gray stone steeple of the Church of San Candido. Less than two miles from the transformer, he had stumbled into the small town of Campo, a suburb of Cortina.

Gentle flakes of snow fell around him as he lost consciousness.

Hall was deep in German territory. The Cortina area had been part of Austria before World War I, and most of the locals spoke German. To borrow from Mao's famous treatise on revolution, the guerrilla was the fish and the people the sea. The fish needed the support of the people to swim freely. Campo might as well have been Germany, with support from the pro-German population practically nonexistent. Hall was a fish out of water.

Had fate not intervened, Hall likely would have died in the snow. The pastor of the local church stumbled across him on his way to brush snow from beehives behind the church.

Hall lay outstretched on the ground, his carbine five feet away from his side. The priest approached him and began reviving a man he felt compassion toward. The captain offered no resistance, and mumbled feebly, "Sono stufo di quest vita" (I am fed up with this life).

The comment may seem out of character, yet considering his weakened condition the utterance was likely.

The priest carried Hall into a building near the church and gave him warm milk and food. Hall warmed his frozen body near the hearth.

The priest, who the locals considered antifascist, was of Austrian stock. Before the war he ministered to a parish in Austria. Though he was antifascist, Hall could not count on the priest to hide him, because the territory was notoriously filled with people sympathetic to Germany.

As Hall regained his bearings, a forest guard entered the house and demanded Hall's papers.

Hall produced an army identification card and probably told the guard he was a downed airman. It is possible Hall was disoriented and not aware how deep into German territory he had come. It is also possible he faced the hopelessness of his situation and thought he might find a civilian sympathetic to the Allies.

The forest guard feigned satisfaction with Hall's answer and left the room. But the guard suspected he had come across an Allied agent and called the German police in Cortina. About ten minutes later, two of the German police arrived and detained Hall. A day later, they returned to the forest guard and "commended [the forest guard] for his vigilance and, as a reward, allowed him to keep Hall's skis."

From this point on, the sequence of events surrounding Hall's arrest and detainment is difficult to piece together. The fascist police allegedly took him to Cortina, where they severely beat him. Despite continual abuse, he still maintained he was a pilot and kept his silence. In an act of honor, Lieutenant Willie Auerbach, who Hall had released from the Calvi partisans months earlier, was said to have been in Cortina but revealed nothing to his superiors about who Hall was. As a result, the SS instigated a search of the zone for more air corps personnel. Next, the police confronted Hall with the man who was formerly his main confederate, Tell.

According to Sette, Tell was first shown "the AGO card of Hall and he (Tell) identified him as the Hall of the OSS." Tell allegedly "identified Hall as head of the mission."

The documentation for Tell's betrayal comes from one source. It appears Sette, the mole in the Gestapo whom Hall had befriended, attempted to save the OSS agent. Sette claimed he requested Hall be transferred from Cortina to Belluno, "to liberate [him], but Hall was sent to Bolzano instead."

Another version of the story maintains that Hall was taken to Dr. Franz Lospichel's villa. The doctor held the rank of SS captain and served as commander of the Cortina d'Ampezzo outpost. Lospichel allegedly treated Hall with "the utmost kindness and consideration." They enjoyed a rather elaborate and festive dinner, where "the wine flowed rather freely," and an "animated and cheerful conversation" took place. The good SS doctor even prepared an extra bed in one of the villa's spare bedrooms. According to the groundskeeper of the villa, Hall remained there for two nights. On his final day at the villa, Hall allegedly shook hands with Lospichel and "told him that they would meet at Cortina for the skiing season at war's end."

The SS then moved Hall from Cortina to Bolzano by armed escort. He was driven to Bolzano by Lospichel's chauffeur, who Hall immediately recognized as a former employee of the Hotel Argentina, located in Cortina. They had crossed paths in 1937–38, when Hall stayed as a guest at the establishment. The captain asked about employees at the hotel whose acquaintance he had made prior to the war.

Unbeknownst to Hall, his journey was about to take a dramatic change of course.

23

Disappointment

IN HIS SMALL MOUNTAIN hideaway in Trichiana, Howard Chappell rubbed his hands together. The icy weather sharpened his thoughts as he reflected on his situation. Tacoma had walked miles over mountainous Italian terrain in a fruitless attempt to find Hall. Defeated, they trekked back to their base camp in Trichiana to link back up with the Aztec mission. Even the audacious plan to reach Hall by truck—driven by the partisans loyal to the countess—had failed. Five-foot snowdrifts blocked all the roads north to Hall, and the snow was still falling. Chappell faced a quandary on how to proceed. The answer came during a routine supply drop.

At the end of January, Joe Benucci and Aztec tried to recover parachute containers from an earlier supply drop. Aztec deployed around the drop zone when a German patrol blundered into the drop zone and started firing at Benucci and his men. Thinking they were ambushed, Benucci dove for cover in a thicket. Stepping deeper into the shrubbery, he found himself free-falling nearly forty feet. He blacked out and woke up moments later, looking right up at two partisans standing over him.

The partisans carried Benucci back to Aztec's and Tacoma's mountain hideout. They summoned a partisan doctor, who diagnosed the Sicilian captain with an internal hemorrhage. Moving any more could worsen his condition or even kill him. The doctor prescribed complete bed rest. But with the Germans constantly patrolling the countryside, staying in one place meant certain capture and possibly death.

Ironically, another local countess, Giuliana Foscolo, solved the crisis by inviting Benucci to stay at her sixteenth-century castle-sized villa, known as Casteldardo. Giuliana Foscolo was an ardent member of the Italian resistance. Elegant and fearless, she helped the Allied missions in the area and saved several downed airmen. Through her brother, she was also a confidante of Hall's lover, the Contessa de Obligado. Her stone mansion villa was located on the outskirts of Belluno. Today, its ruined tower offers a spectacular view of Mount Grappa.

Apparently, Benucci had met Giuliana Foscolo earlier and they had been romantically involved. "Joe Benucci loved women; he was always disappearing with them at times of crisis," recalled Nick Cangelosi. In Benucci's defense, he was responsible for furnishing the OSS with actionable intelligence, and to be successful, he had to gather information from the locals, women included.

Unfortunately, the hemorrhage injury was a reality, but Benucci turned his medical condition into a stroke of good fortune when Giuliana Foscolo offered him her assistance. For Tacoma, however, Benucci's untimely ailment would further delay Chappell's mission to link up with Hall. As senior officer, Chappell felt obligated to stay behind with the Aztec mission.

But the fairy tale scenario of being taken care of by a beautiful countess had a huge catch. The Casteldardo was also the 20th Luftwaffe Division's headquarters, staffed by twenty to thirty German officers and their security detachment at all times—Giuliana Foscolo was recommending that Benucci take shelter in the very belly of the beast. While the castle was the last place the Nazis would look for an OSS captain, Benucci by now had a ten-thousand-dollar price tag on his head. The plan did, however, have a small chance of success, as Casteldardo was a huge estate with dozens of rooms, and five rooms were walled off from the German staff headquarters. Giuliana Foscolo, a trained nurse, would care for the injured captain right under the Nazis' noses.

Twisting Benucci's rubber arm to okay the scheme proved easy. He later recalled the fantastic adventure:

The partisans carried me down the mountain. Waiting for us in a mule-drawn sled was the Countess. She held out her hand to me smiling—it was as if we were meeting on a pleasure drive. My first move was to change into her brother's civilian clothes, which she brought with her. I kept a grenade in one pocket and a loaded .45 in the other.

The sled pulled off. . . . It was dusk when we reached the villa; it was a huge bulk of white stone in the twilight—a beautiful mansion. The sled pulled up the long driveway and stopped right in front of the German sentries. . . . My heart started hammering. Although I'd been in plenty of rough spots, this was really something. For a moment I felt as though I could never walk past those two guards; then I felt the Countess's arm firmly under mine. Together we started toward them.

"Buona sera," remarked Giuliana Foscolo.

After climbing the stairs to the countess's bedroom, Benucci collapsed on the bed. Benucci stayed with her for twelve days, "eating five meals a day, drank dozens of eggnogs." Hiding under the noses of the very men who hunted him, Benucci alleges he heard the Germans rant: "The goddamned Americans."

During those twelve days, Benucci and the noblewoman allegedly carried on their romantic relationship. On one occasion, the German officers tried to enter her bedroom where Benucci was hiding. Giuliana haughtily fended them off by responding, "Men do not enter a lady's bedroom."

✳   ✳   ✳

Chappell decided he would remain with Aztec until the snows melted and the passes cleared, then proceed to meet Hall. Chappell was at a crossroads. When describing his mission more than sixty years later, he reflected: "You had to be there to understand it. We had to change course many times, but the goals remained the same." Gauging the circumstances, Chappell was once again improvising. Reaching Hall and the Brenner—and bringing in his OG team—would have to wait.

Chappell turned to the task that needed his immediate assistance: Benucci's partisans operating near Belluno. These groups needed supplies and arms, but most of all they needed training. Much like the Special Forces A Teams that would follow him in the years and conflicts after World War II, Chappell trained the partisans in sabotage and weapons handling.

While Benucci enjoyed all the creature comforts of Casteldardo, Chappell (and Aztec and Tacoma) remained on the run with the partisans. Two partisan bands, the Piave and the Seventh Alpini, supposedly operated under Benucci's command, but after his incapacitation, Chappell tried to take charge. Thanks to five planeloads of arms, ammunition, and supplies dropped on February 6, the captain had some leverage to influence their actions—or so he thought. And he began to plan two big jobs.

The first was to be a raid attacking a fascist garrison of three hundred men in the tiny town of Tarzon on February 7. Chappell planned an assault on the town barracks, using bazookas from the airdrop the night before. The team set out on an eleven-mile hike over rugged terrain to meet the Piave Brigade.

The Piave had several hundred men at any given time and operated out of the Conegliano area south of Belluno. German troops were keeping the Piave bottled up. Aztec painted a dim view of the Piave's military actions to OSS headquarters: "Due to the many fascists and German garrisons in the area, their military actions were limited."*

Unfortunately, the raid ended in disappointment. Silsby later recalled the incident. "When we arrived, the commander of the Piave Brigade, with

---

*Aztec helped build the Seventh Alpini from the ground up. Starting with a nucleus of fifty men, the unit was organized into small squads and battalions of men by Aztec's Benucci and his right hand, First Sergeant Nick Cangelosi. Their first order of business was to set up an intelligence net to ferret out spies and fascists within the partisan ranks and glean intelligence on local Nazi units. The brigade grew to over nine hundred by the end of the war. After its formation by Aztec, the group was constantly on the run from the SS. As Aztec reported: "The zone occupied by the 7th Alpini was constantly run over by the SS troops. With three and four feet of snow covering all mountains . . . extremely difficult to keep the men in the mountains and lack of food, lack of clothing, and SS troops made survival a constant battle. There were 360 men in this period caught and hung by SS troops in the 7th Alpini zone."

Nevertheless, led by Aztec's first sergeant and by Captain Benucci, the group set up several successful ambushes and even mined and blew up schoolhouses the Germans were using as barracks.

whom Chappell had made arrangements, gave some weird story about someone killing a fascist the day before and now all the fascists had moved from the barracks." It was a lie; the commander had simply lost his nerve.

Disappointed with the Piave's inactivity, Chappell's Tacoma team switched to the Seventh Alpini, a partisan group Aztec had spent months training and equipping. He also switched to another target—the railroad tunnel at Ponte nelle Alpi. Through the tunnel passed a supply route from the Brenner Pass and Austria.

With Benucci still incapacitated, Chappell linked up with the Seventh and plotted to destroy the tunnel. The operation began on the morning of February 8; under Chappell's direction, the partisans bored holes in the tunnel for the explosives. Next, he put the tunnel under observation and waited. Chappell planned to destroy the tunnel while a German supply or troop train passed through it.

With the rastrellamento looming, Chappell contacted the Seventh's commander, and called a council of war. Chappell recalled the drama: "[The leader] said if the Germans came in force, we would fight. I agreed. However, [the partisan commander said] if the Germans came in a small group, we would leave the area so as not to have any trouble. His decision did not meet with my approval, but I was forced to accept it."

Chappell prepared for a fight, ordering the Seventh to dig in six heavy machine guns. Chappell thought Tacoma, reinforced by three downed American airmen, and the Seventh Alpini held a superior position and could fend off any attack. Three to five feet of snow covered the ground, and the Germans could only reach the position by climbing a single narrow trail "without becoming helplessly bogged down in the snow. . . . I felt sure that we had the Germans in a trap they could not escape," Chappell recalled. He was about to learn another hard lesson in partisan tactics.

Silsby remembered how the attack unfolded: "They started coming about 0730 hours. I was counting them through the binoculars as they came up single file up the narrow mountain path. We had marvelous positions, and the partisans had just received a supply drop of arms and ammo two days before."

One Allied officer described the situation bluntly in his report:

> The Alpini were armed to the teeth with nearly every conceivable weapon except tanks and flamethrowers. The Settimo Alpini were attacked in Valmorel by approximately 100 Germans. . . . They were sitting up in the hills with heavy and light machine guns, mortars, bazookas, and all sorts of weapons. The Germans were winding up a valley towards them, looking rather tired and miserable, but had not seen them.

When the Germans were two hundred yards from Chappell's position, the Seventh did the unthinkable. "They took flight and fled without firing a shot, leaving their arms behind," recalled one officer familiar with the action.

"Before we knew it, we were the only ones left. And this Checco sent a man back to tell us we better come along! They had left one of the partisans who had been wounded in the leg behind," lamented Silsby.

Chappell was furious. He could not stand the thought of leaving a perfect position; moreover, his personal honor prevented him from leaving a man behind. Chappell lived and breathed the American airborne creed of leading by example. As the Seventh fled the area, Chappell ran through a fusillade of incoming rounds and charging Germans to rescue the wounded partisan, named Cherbro.

As he was unable to walk because of the leg wound, Chappell and Fabrega carried the man for several miles, up and down ravines. Reflecting on the moment sixty years later, Chappell quipped, "We committed the action known as 'getting the hell out.'"

The team and the partisans crunched through the snow and barreled up and down the steep, winding mountain trails. The SS were in hot pursuit, at times no more than four hundred yards behind them. The flight would prove an extreme challenge for a normal man. With exceptional strength and endurance, Chappell carried Cherbro in a fireman's carry most of the way to shelter.

Tacoma and the partisans eventually made it to the relative safety of San Antonio. With the Germans not far behind, Chappell set up a guard detail, placing men at observation points to watch for the SS. The OSS leader surveyed the lay of the land and mapped out an escape route, but was determined to fight if the Germans showed up. The team then transported the wounded partisan to a doctor in a hay-covered sleigh. Before he left, Chappell handed Cherbro a pistol for self-defense. It would come in handy later.

Starving, the men ate food Brownie had scrounged up, and a partisan commander came to Chappell with startling news: a German attack seemed imminent and he insisted the Seventh Alpini needed his help and weapons to fend them off. Looking for action, Chappell and his men rushed toward the alleged German attack:

> We started out to reinforce the partisans, quite happy to think that at last they were going to fight. When we arrived at the sector where the Germans were expected, I took precautionary measures and inquired into our own strength [and the] location of the enemy. . . . Just where the Germans were at was not quite clear, but there were supposed to be ten of them somewhere nearby. Both my men and myself became disgusted when we learned these facts and left. The ten Germans never did appear. I refused from that time on to have anything to do with this organization (the Seventh Alpini).

Disgusted and depressed, Chappell moved up to the mountains south of San Antonio and arranged for a meeting with the British Captain Paul N. Brietsche. Brietsche came from the UK Special Operations Executive (SOE) mission FRP.

Like the OSS, the SOE conducted guerrilla warfare and sabotage operations behind the lines in northern Italy, carrying out Churchill's charter to "set Europe ablaze." FRP worked with some of the partisan formations in the Belluno area, known as the Monte Grappa partisans, named after the mountain chain in the area.

FRP, later dubbed Bitterroot, had jumped into the Belluno area on September 1, 1944. Brietsche and Chappell got along well and swapped war stories. Brietsche had survived numerous brushes with death and a half dozen rastrellamentos.*

The two men met in the most conspicuous of places, an osteria (tavern) in San Antonio. The spirits dampened Chappell's depression over the state of the mission. As the jovial Brit recalled: "Chappell was infuriated, as he had not realized up until then this type of thing was possible, and had always great faith in the chaps he had, in spite of the fact that he had no experience with them. He just managed to get away himself, but stated that he was finished with partisan work and would rather like to spend the rest of the war in a small [hut] on the hillside with a radiogram and a hundred cases of whiskey. He was in this frame of mind when I met him in the osteria at St. Antonio."

A seasoned Allied operator who had worked behind the lines for months, Brietsche filled Chappell in on the complexity of the partisan political affiliations: Christian Democrat, socialist, communist, and the Action Party.

Most of the parties still exist in Italy to this day, but during the war, a low-grade civil war was being fought between the groups. After a few glasses of wine, Chappell took Brietsche into his confidence, saying he was "entirely finished with all of Benucci's partisans."**

---

*Brietsche related to Chappell his bizarre entry into the war in nothern Italy and told how he was dropped about a kilometer from the original drop zone only to be humorously greeted by SOE Major Wilkinson. Wilkinson was one of the first Allied officers in the area and was lying under a cow, milking it, when Brietsche landed. He turned to the young captain, saying: "Well, I warned base that this point was not a bloody dropping ground, anyway."

**Brietsche's assessment of Benucci was the polar opposite of his opinion of Chappell: "[Benucci] gave me lots of promises and for a few days I was satisfied he would carry them out. Benucci's behavior over the whole matter needs a separate report and has no bearing on the final outcome. It took me two weeks to realize the type of man I was dealing with, it was incredible to believe that an officer of his description would possibly be given a position of responsibility. . . . The full story of Benucci's actions then came out with ample evidence to support everything. It was then that I nearly created an 'international crisis' by sending in the true facts to base."

In his report written after the war, Brietsche stated: "Impression gained—excellent fellow. [P]artisan opinion—first class, but though he was rather young and inexperienced for the job, and too keen to go off by himself and do his own jobs. My idea this is a good thing as long as one includes a certain amount of partisans every time." Chappell was a man of action who was just now learning how to be a partisan leader.

The conversation went into the wee hours of the night and concluded with Brietsche suggesting Chappell should take over two partisan brigades: the Tollot and Mazzini Brigades. Fortified with grappa, the Italian elixir of choice, Chappell agreed. That moment marked a new beginning for Chappell as a partisan leader.

24

Caught in the Web

THE CAR CARRYING STEPHEN HALL pulled into the long flowing driveway of the Villa Polacco on the outskirts of Bolzano. Originally owned by a wealthy Italian family, the bucolic estate lost its luster when it was overrun by the Gestapo, who made it their headquarters. They escorted Hall into the villa's kitchen and served him supper. In English, Major Rudolf Thyrolf greeted his captive at the dinner table and made small talk.

Thyrolf, thirty-nine and born in Warsaw, served as commander of the German security police in Bolzano and was technically Schiffer's superior. His blond hair parted to one side accentuated a smooth-shaven, oval-shaped face, but his boyish features masked a deep ruthlessness.

As August Schiffer entered the room, Thyrolf dispensed with the pleasantries of a polite greeting and dinner. The mood shifted to a more sinister tone. In his crisp English accent, Thyrolf played "good cop," while Schiffer, with his guttural German accent, became the "bad cop." Seductively seated in a chair, Christa Roy recorded the interrogation. The two Gestapo officers pressed Hall for information.

"I'm an American soldier. You can't force me to make any specific declarations," Hall retorted.

"You're an enemy agent, not a soldier," responded Thyrolf.

"I am wearing the uniform of a US soldier and am not required to disclose anything more."

Captain Hall was captured wearing an American paratrooper uniform. Under the Geneva Conventions, he was not required to disclose anything other than his name, rank, and serial number. The technicalities of the

Geneva Conventions did not interest Schiffer. In his eyes, Hall was a terrorist.

Thyrolf continued playing good cop, as he explained to Hall that any information he divulged would not be revealed to American authorities. Hall once more refused.

After dinner, they took Hall to a room they said was reserved for "prisoners of honor."

The next morning, the party was over. They took Hall to the Corpo d'Armata, where he found himself at the very approaches of the Brenner—as a captive.

Guards first took Hall to Schiffer's office, where Major Thyrolf and Schiffer awaited. They took him to the machine room, Schiffer's execution cell and the site of so-called intensified cross-examinations.

During the torture, Schiffer began putting together his many threads of information and connecting the dots that would lead to Hall's identification. He then brought in Professor Colleselli from his cell. Schiffer later reported:

It occurred to me at that moment that Captain Hall might be the American captain about whom the arrested Professor Colleselli had spoken of. . . . I let Prof. Colleselli be confronted with Hall and Colleselli confirmed that Hall really was the American agent who had gotten in contact with him and assigned him, and others, the task of transporting the explosives to Bruneck.

Schiffer also confronted Hall with Tell. Schiffer allegedly paraded his former lieutenant into the machine room.

As Hall knew earlier, his plans to destroy the Brenner railroad tunnel had been blown. Now he faced not only the failure of the mission but also the betrayal of his confidants.

Because Hall refused to talk, Schiffer resorted to his infamous intensified cross-examination. During the swing technique, Hall's wrists were placed in handcuffs and his arms over his knees. Guards inserted a metal bar between his elbows and knees and suspended his balled-up body from the ends of the bar, which rested on the rungs of two ladders. The pain was excruciating.

According to Schiffer, "in most cases, this procedure alone sufficed to make the delinquent confess." In Hall's case, it was likely not sufficient, because he did not reveal all of his confederates or the full extent of his mission. It is likely Schiffer beat Hall with a leather whip, then employed his other method of torture, suspending. The Nazis would have cuffed Hall's wrists behind his back and suspended him between two ladders. And once again he would be beaten severely. It is possible they also subjected him to electric shock using one of Schiffer's devices.

"Usually," Schiffer explained, "the poles of the induction machine were applied to the cheeks of those who were hanging from the swing or were suspended from the ladder."

After enduring days of brutal interrogation and torture, Hall may have admitted he was a member of the OSS who parachuted into Cortina to contact local partisan groups and blow up bridges. Some accounts maintain he never broke and persisted in his claim to be a downed airman. It is also possible Hall revealed part of his plan to destroy the Brenner Pass.

After the torture, Hall was thrown into a tiny, unheated stone cell with a plank bed, in the cellar of the Corpo d'Armata.

Over the next several days, Schiffer fabricated a story that Hall yelled and screamed when Allied bombers dropped their ordnance over Bolzano. According to Christa Roy, around February 16, 1945, Hall sent a note in English to Thyrolf, which stated that Hall wished to contact "the American authorities by wireless to immediately stop the bombing of Bolzano."

It is possible that Hall produced such a note, although it is highly unlikely, given his courage and experience, that he would have stooped to such well-known enemy methods.

During the bombing, Schiffer began spinning a story, asserting that Hall's yelling during the bombing raids showed he had lost his mind. Schiffer was creating a fiction about Hall's captivity, and it was working perfectly.

25

Lover's Lament

HALL'S WHEREABOUTS REMAINED a mystery to everyone except the Germans. On January 26, he seemed to vanish from the world; neither the partisans, the OSS, nor the countess knew what happened to him, as she recalled:

> When Steve disappeared, no one knew it . . . and one day, on going to Belluno to find the Austrian governor [Lauer, the anti-Nazi] who was a great friend of mine, he told me that Steve had been seized by the SS police near Cortina, and would be brought to the military court. I beseeched the Austrian governor to intervene so that Steve might be exchanged for another; that I, myself, would be put up as a guarantee for the success of the exchange; and that Steve was like a brother to me and that if misfortune came to him I would never be able to console myself. The governor, who was a very great admirer of mine, did everything to obtain the exchange of Steve, and everything was going very well. I had informed Joseph Benucci of the capture of Steve—and also our partisans, who still knew nothing, and awaited the return of Steve from day to day—fearing that he had met his end under an avalanche of snow. [Ettore must have had remorse.]

After having returned from his convalescence at Casteldardo, Joe Benucci went back into hiding with Aztec. On February 15, Aztec's radio operator, Sebby Gianfriddo, furtively typed out a message to OSS headquarters over his wireless radio: "Hall captured by Nazis. Held at

Verona. Threaten to shoot him. Willing to exchange for Nazi officer. You must contact Verona immediately. Try to save him. Benucci."

Hall was not in Verona, but Bolzano, undergoing torture and interrogation by Schiffer.

Meanwhile, the OSS attempted to save him, negotiating with the highest echelons of the SS command. In Switzerland, Allen Dulles, the dean of OSS spies and future director of the CIA, had established channels of communication with the top SS commander in Italy, General Karl Wolff. Wolff foresaw the inevitable defeat of Germany and was making unofficial overtures to the Americans. "Arrangements for an exchange were undertaken through Switzerland," recalled an OSS official, "and established contact with the Gestapo. . . . They reported on February 19 that they had started negotiations for the exchange."

Major Schiffer had other plans for Stephen Hall.

26

Rescue

HAVING NO IDEA OF HALL'S whereabouts, Chappell set aside his plans to move north and focused on the Tollot and Mazzini brigades and on bringing in his commando team. A new problem soon surfaced: Tacoma became a magnet for downed airmen. Groups of three and four continually trickled into their base camp.

By February 18, eighteen American airmen and three British POWs attached themselves to the team. The men hailed from a hodgepodge of Allied squadrons, including Lieutenant H. W. Clark of the 99th Squadron, 332nd Group, one of the few exclusively African American air units. Known as the Tuskegee Airmen, the elite unit racked up an impressive combat record, earning them the moniker "Schwarze Vogelmenschen" (Black Birdmen) among the Luftwaffe.

Chappell knew something needed to be done about Lieutenant Clark and the others. OSS orders detailed "rescuing distressed allied airmen and ex-prisoners-of-war" as one of the OG's primary objectives behind the lines. Many of the men had suffered injuries from their jumps and were starving. But capture by the Germans was a worse fate. The Germans sometimes executed Allied airmen even after they surrendered, because they flew the bombers that killed so many German families. Feeding them, caring for their injuries, and getting them out of Italy to Yugoslavia suddenly became a big part of Tacoma's mission.

The needs of wounded airmen and partisans convinced Chappell he was in dire need of a medic. He notified the Brain that he wanted Eric Buchhardt sent in. Buchhardt had become the man in Chappell's OG group most qualified for the position—and he was a good demolitions man.

The Brain radioed back: "Buckhardt [sic] will bring 100,000 lire from Air Corps to be used in caring for pilots. They request names of all pilots and other Allied personnel you have with you. He will come as soon as you give word."

Feeding and caring for the wounded—and hiding the men—absorbed a lot of Chappell's attention, and Tacoma quickly became a mercy mission of sorts. Nevertheless, with characteristic verve, Chappell started devising a series of plans to get the men out of Italy. All of the schemes were fraught with peril, as Chappell explained:

The most popular plan had been to walk to Yugoslavia. However, the snow was too deep at this time, the Germans were too vigilant, and the food supplies were pitifully short. There were long intervals of difficult terrain to move over that had neither food nor partisan aid.

Meanwhile, to alleviate the problem of food and to mitigate the risk of capture, Chappell distributed the Air Corps men among the various partisan battalions. To help the cause, many of the men fought alongside the Italians. The solution for getting them out came from some of the men themselves: build a landing strip. Indeed, several of the mountaintop meadows could make passable landing strips. Chappell described finding a suitable location:

On February 12 we found an excellent landing strip, and we immediately worked to prepare the strip for landings. I had a navigator and a pilot go to the site with me, and they felt certain that it was sufficiently large for a C-47 to make a landing. The snow at this time was three and four feet deep, and we realized that the work of clearing would take considerable time and effort. In all, we had had twenty-one men with us. In addition there were twenty partisans on whom we could count to join the working party. We had twelve mules to clear the snow and logs. We dared not blast the stumps with explosives because we were working about five kilometers from the nearest German occupied town. This necessitated another force of about twenty men to act as guards while work was underway. Work progressed fairly rapidly despite the fact that almost every other day we were alerted by the guards and were forced to take up positions until the patrols would pass.

By the middle of February, Chappell updated the Brain on the progress of the landing strip: "Men working hard to clear strip. Looks like a two week job unless I can find more working equipment. Health of all men not good."

Finding the right plane for the runway was a major concern. The plane had to be rugged enough to land in the rocky pockmarked alpine meadow. It also needed enough power to climb quickly into the air fully loaded with the rescued airmen.

With advice from the pilots on the ground, Chappell recommended a Lysander or a C-47. The Douglas C-47 Skytrain or Dakota served as a workhorse transport plane for the Allies, with more than ten thousand produced during the war. With a crew of three, the aircraft could transport up to twenty-eight troops. Powered by a fourteen-cylinder Pratt and Whitney engine, this plane could evacuate most of the airmen in one trip.

Chappell's other choice, the Westland Lysander, was a lightweight single-engine propeller plane noted for its ruggedness and ability to operate on short, unprepared airfields. The Allied special operations agencies considered the Lysander ideal for inserting and retrieving agents behind enemy lines. Unlike the C-47, the Lysander could only take out a couple of airmen at a time, meaning multiple missions would have to be flown.

The Brain contacted the Air Corps, who determined that the Lysander was too small. Rather than using a C-47 transport, the Air Corps recommended, instead, a Mitchell bomber. Getting the pilots out then became a math problem. The men's extra weight and the strip's length of 2,700 feet would limit the bomber to taking out seven men. Every one hundred feet of additional runway space meant an additional airman would go home. So the men doubled their efforts, still working under the noses of the Germans.

A week later, with only half the field completed, Chappell canceled the work after learning that Schiffer's muscle, SS Major Schröder, was planning another rastrellamento of the area. A week of backbreaking labor had come to naught. One can only imagine the crushing blow this would have dealt to the men's morale.

Chappell shifted gears once again and decided that with the help of partisan guides, the men would travel in teams of three through the rugged Dolomites to the safety of Tito's forces in Yugoslavia.

⁂ ⁂ ⁂

With a rastrellamento looming, Chappell continued training the two new brigades Brietsche assigned to him—the Tollot and Mazzini. "We continued teaching them all we could about the arms, explosives, and other matériel we used," recalled Chappell.

Chappell's partisans soon began putting their training to work, blowing up a bridge near the small town of Savassa, while the Tollot Brigade blew another one at Conegliano. His years of experience training men at Fort Benning began to bear fruit.

In a biweekly report dated February 15, Tacoma's two brigades reported the following death and destruction "personally verified by Captain Chappell":

2 locomotives destroyed

1 locomotive damaged

3 cars destroyed

2 trucks destroyed

6 fascists killed

1 fascist officer killed

1 German officer killed

4 German non-coms killed

18 German soldiers killed

35 German soldiers wounded

3 engineer instructors killed

Tacoma also booby-trapped roads, using the 1940s equivalent of improvised explosive devises (IEDs). Chappell's men wrapped packages of plastic explosive in manure and detonated them with time pencils. They planted the deadly devices on the sides of roads and waited for German convoys to pass. One booby trap killed three and wounded two members of a German patrol.

"[The packages] were placed everywhere, quite often just hidden where they would do more than aggravate and keep German garrisons awake and tense," remembered Chappell. He gave more details in his radio message back to base: "Traffic held up most of the night of Feb. 19. Road to Mel to Trichiana by booby traps covered by manure." Through the manure booby traps, Chappell's men were breeding terror and creating a climate of uncertainty. For the Germans, death was becoming a random event, chipping away at Nazi morale.

✳ ✳ ✳

On the night of February 21, 1945, Eric Buchhardt, Staff Sergeant Egillo P. Delaini, and Staff Sergeant Charles Ciccone hurtled through the air at 120 miles per hour in a matte-black B-24 Liberator bomber. The three men, an advance element of Chappell's OG team, headed to the Azure drop zone outside Trichiana. In the cavernous fuselage of the Liberator, the green light pierced the darkness to signal the group that it was time to drop through the Joe hole.

After a hardy thumbs-up and a grin from the OG's Tech Sergeant Joe Gallech, who accompanied the men as dispatcher, Staff Sergeant Delaini became the first man to drop through the hole and into the cold, dark, Alpine sky. An expert at demolitions, Delaini was slated to train the partisans and take on most of Tacoma's demo jobs.

Eric Buchhardt, who would serve as Chappell's medic, followed Delaini. Last to jump was New Jersey native Charles "Chuck" Ciccone, who would serve as weapons specialist for Tacoma. As the cold air hit his face, Ciccone spotted the five signal fires forming a V burning in the inky blackness. Slowly, the men floated downward. Ciccone grabbed the risers attached to the British X-type harness. Skillfully, he moved the long cords just enough to avoid landing in the fire.

It was a pinpoint landing, compelling Chappell to fire off a radio message to Captain Materazzi: "Buchhardt, Delaini just missed fires, Ciccone burnt pants. Roses to Gallech and Air [C]orps. Practically all containers found 20 minutes after drop. Will receive remainder of my group any time after night of Feb 24."

Tacoma had grown from three men to six, but Chappell was still desperate to get the rest of his OGs to Trichiana. Accompanied by Fabrega, he swaggered over to Ciccone.

"Hello, kid. How about a bottle of good wine?"

27

The Hangman's Noose

ON FEBRUARY 17, 1945, Schiffer summoned his henchmen to his office. Storz, the stocky thirty-two-year-old, entered the room with his comrade Andergassen, "the incarnation of sadism and brutality . . . especially under the influence of strong drink."

Schiffer broke out the cognac, pouring each a generous glass. After they downed their drinks, Schiffer looked at each of his men, furrowing his brow and squinting his eyes.

"Are you ready to carry out the execution?" he asked, pausing to evaluate his underlings' dedication.

"We should do it the same way we killed Dr. Longon," Andergassen replied. Hall's death would be a fake suicide by hanging, as he claimed in a postwar interview:

> I was determined to let Roderick Hall be executed. Regarding this matter, there were directives of the Reich's Chief Security Bureau, according to which the strictest measures were to be taken against members of terrorist bands. I myself, as a persuaded National Socialist, was extremely indignant at the activity of Captain Roderick Hall; furthermore, I knew of the unspeakable misery brought upon German cities by British and American terror fliers. On the basis of this attitude of mine, I became determined to sentence Roderick Hall to death and to let the sentence be carried out.

The next day, after gaining the approval of his superiors, Schiffer, accompanied by Storz, went down to the machine room of the Corpo

Stephen Hall standing behind the lines near the Eagle
Mission Base Camp in Ovasta, Italy, in the Summer of
1944. *(Photo courtesy of Eleanor Lukitsch)*

Captain Howard Chappell, Operational Group Team Leader of the Tacoma Mission, awarded the Silver Star by "Wild Bill" Donovan. Chappell's outstanding heroism arguably qualified for America's highest military decoration, the Medal of Honor. *(Photo courtesy of Howard Chappell)*

Howard Chappell, complete with his signature smile, relaxes after training his commando group on Catalina Island. *(Photo courtesy of Troy Sacquety)*

Albert "the Brain" Materazzi, operations officer in charge of Tacoma and, later, Stephen Hall's Mercury Mission. After the war, "the Brain" set out on a righteous vendetta, relentlessly pursuing German war criminals and bringing them to justice in the proper setting, a war crimes trial. This picture was taken during one of the war crimes trials. After the war, Materazzi became the de facto OSS historian and his basement became a treasure trove of secret files. While researching the book, the author visited this basement treasure trove monthly, while enjoying authentic Italian cuisine and wine with the ninety-three year old spymaster. (*Courtesy of R. Materazzi*)

Wartime photo of the road network feeding into the Brenner Pass, the main supply artery between Germany and its armies fighting in Italy. Hall's mission attempted to sever the secondary supply routes leading to the pass and, later, included a plan to blow up a key railroad tunnel within the pass itself. (*Courtesy of National Archive*)

Major August Schiffer, a brilliant counterinsurgency Gestapo chief. Named the "Evil Genius" by his associates, he ruthlessly hunted Hall and Chappell, as well as other Allied agents in northern Italy. The Nazi officer methodically and mercilessly tortured captured enemy agents to collect intelligence for his counterinsurgency operations. (*Photo courtesy of National Archives*)

Major August Schiffer (right) and the brutal Albert Storz (left), Schiffer's second in command. (*Photo courtesy of National Archives*)

Major August Schiffer.
(*Photo courtesy of*
National Archives)

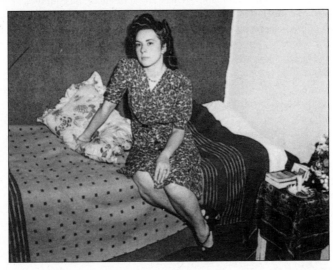

Christa Roy was Schiffer's mistress and stenographer, who
methodically recorded the Gestapo chief's torture sessions, which
she allegedly relished. Schiffer rewarded her labors with luxury
items stolen from captured Jews and Italians. After the war, she
evaded trial, most likely due to her seductive guile in dealing with
the opposite sex. Post-war reports cited that Allied
counterintelligence officers "were unable to distinguish between
their glandular and official functions" when dealing with the Nazi
mistress. (*Courtesy of National Archives*)

The mountainside villa rented by the enigmatic double-agent Countess Isabel de Obligado. A woman of power and influence, the countess possessed a mixture of sugar and spice—she cooked fine sweets and confections at home, while in the field she "could shoot a machine gun and set up bombs." Over sixty-five years later, murals commissioned by the countess still adorn the villa's walls. (*Author Photo*)

Howard Chappell's German OG commandos in formation on California's Catalina Island. A more eclectic group of desperados could not be found: former Luftwaffe pilots, Jewish escapees from German death camps, renegade Poles, and world-class athletes. (*Photo courtesy of Troy Sacquety*)

The author interviewed Mario Rizzardini (left), the former Italian partisan who drove a truck with the Tacoma team hidden in its cargo boxes through a gauntlet of German checkpoints to get closer to the Brenner Pass. At tremendous risk to himself, he bluffed his way past scores of heavily armed SS troops. The author conducted numerous interviews with Italian partisans and civilians associated with the teams while walking and driving the battlescape of the missions. *(Author Photo)*

The dark long corridor in the cellblock of Bolzano Concentration Camp, which was under the command of Major Schiffer. A number of Allied OSS operatives were held in rooms along this shadowy dungeon-like hall, where numerous atrocities were committed against them. *(Courtesy of National Archives)*

The infamous "machine room" located beneath Major Schiffer's office, where he tortured and executed many of his victims. A U.S. soldier demonstrates how his victims were hanged from the valve wheel mechanism. (*Courtesy of National Archives*)

The sixteenth-century Casteldardo was a sprawling villa owned by the beautiful and courageous Contessa Giuliana Foscolo. She selflessly risked her life to aid Allied covert missions in the area, and on one occasion, hiding an Allied spy in her bedroom, directly under the noses of German officers who had commandeered the villa for their headquarters. (*Author Photo*)

RADIO MESSAGE

NAZI PLANS DEFENSE BRENNER FROM MAP
TRACING OBTAINED AUGUST 22 FROM GROUP
ITALIAN ARMY OFFICERS NOW PARTISANS. BELIEVE
SOURCE NAZI GHQ MAP SECTION AT DOBBIACO.
PLOT ON ITALY ONE 100,000 SHEET 4 MERANO
AND SHEET 4A BRESSANONE. GRID REFERENCES
AS ON SHEETS. IN MESSAGE EGG EQUALS
BATTALION, PP EQUALS SMALL ROUND DOT AND
TT EQUALS SMALL RED TRIANGLE.

ON SHEET 4 THE FOLLOWING — one egg
at 025133 PP AT 046226 AND 053224
AND 058225

ON SHEET 4A THE FOLLOWING — TWO
EGGS AT 210990, ONE EGG AT 165040,
TWO EGGS AT 195050, ONE EGG AT 130205,
ONE EGG AT 165223, ONE EGG AT 265053,
TWO EGGS AT 290050, ONE EGG AT 325047,
ONE EGG AT 267085, ONE EGG AT 335147,
ONE EGG AT 315175. Sent Sept 3 1800 hrs

PP AT 101001 AND 116004 AND 151029
AND 152031 AND 153033 AND 154036 AND
126105 AND 193115 AND 187136 AND 187157
AND 268098 AND 250168 AND 272183 AND
274184 AND 318188 AND 318192 AND 346210
AND 342212 AND 334147 AND 150188 AND
152192 AND 144194 AND 108256 AND 073244
AND 073250 AND 075246 AND 076245

Handwritten copy of Hall's September 3, 1944, radio message to OSS headquarters listing coordinates of German positions located around the Brenner Pass. (*Courtesy of National Archives*)

OSS Operatives in northern Italy training for a mission behind the lines. Joe Lukitsch, Hall's best friend, stands third from the left. Lukitsch was known for his integrity and moral courage, successfully executing numerous operations behind the lines. *(Courtesy of Eleanor Lukitsch)*

Interpreter Victor Malispino (left) and Eagle Mission radio operator Joseph "Stan" Zbieg. *(Courtesy of Elleanor Lukitsch)*

On the infamous Marmarole range in the Italian Alps, Hall hiked, climbed, and scaled hundreds of miles with rope and pick-axe. Pushing his body to the limits of human endurance, and his feet blackened with frostbite, he earned the descriptive moniker, "legs of cast iron." *(Author Photo)*

The sheer rock face of Mt. Civetta, near Hall's winter area of operations in 1944-45. (*Author photo*)

Another mountain precipice Hall likely scaled during his sojourn near the Brenner Pass. (*Author photo*)

Winter wonderland near Selva di Cadore, Italy. The Tacoma and Mercury missions operated under similar adverse conditions. Snowfall could easily accumulate to the height of a grown man. Hall launched his final operation under such conditions. *(Author Photo)*

The picturesque town of Ovasta, located in Carnia, in northern Italy. *(Courtesy of Eleanor Lukitsch)*

Caprile, Italy, was located along roads that converged into a choke point feeding the Brenner Pass. The town was near the site of Chappell's final ambush against Nazi forces, and the town's church still proudly displays the white flag used in their surrender.

The impassable gorge at Digonera was located outside Caprile. Here Howard Chappell and Italian partisans trapped and forced the surrender of thousands of SS and German Army troops, including a decimated Tiger battalion, as they were retreating toward the Brenner Pass. Forcing the Nazi surrender with guile and deception, Howard Chappell pulled off one of the most audacious small unit operations of the war. (*Author Photo*)

A column of Italian partisans marching in a post-war celebration in May, 1945. Forerunners to modern day special operations troops, World War II OSS teams helped organize, supply, and train the partisans to be "force multipliers" for the Italian insurgency. As they do today, the various insurgent groups made up an amalgam of ideologies, often with conflicting political views. (*Courtesy of Nick Cangelosi*)

Italian partisans associated with the Aztec and Tacoma teams celebrate victory over the Germans at the end of the war. (*Courtesy of Nick Cangelosi*)

d'Armata. Andergassen led Hall into the dank room full of pipes and gauges. The metal door clanked shut and they rammed the bolt into the lock. Storz and Andergassen pulled Hall's arms behind his back, and Andergassen bound his wrists with a chain and blindfolded him with a gray scarf. Schiffer coldly related what happened next:

> I think that Andergassen then brought a laundry line about as thick as the little finger. This laundry line already had a noose tied on it. Andergassen wound this laundry line around the first regulating wheel and fastened it by means of a knot on the second regulating wheel . . . and placed the open noose of the laundry line over Hall's head, gently upon his shoulders. As Hall turned slightly to the right, Storz pulled his legs away from the floor so that Hall fell directly into the noose which immediately engaged itself tightly around the neck. Andergassen, whose hands were free since the laundry line had been fastened pressed—as far as I know—down on the shoulders of Captain Hall in order to speed up the process of the execution.

The killers let Hall's body hang on the noose for ten or fifteen minutes. Andergassen then checked Hall's vital signs, placing his ear upon his heart and shining light into his eyes with a lit match. Hall was dead.

In a feeble attempt to get away with murder, Schiffer then set in motion the elaborate plan to stage Hall's suicide. First, he asked his trusted friend Hans Butz to walk along the corridor from the machine room to prevent an uninvited person from stumbling upon Andergassen and Storz while they carried the body. Schiffer went in the opposite direction to stop anyone's approach from the other corridor. Schiffer's thugs laid Hall's body across the floor of his tiny cell, near the plank bed he had slept on. Next, Andergassen and Storz positioned his body on the backrest of a chair that was brought into the room specifically for the simulated hanging. According to Andergassen, Schiffer expressed satisfaction with their work. Everything was ready for a uninformed SS guard to stumble upon Hall's lifeless body.

Much to his disappointment, Schiffer made the mistake of relying heavily on the vigilance of his SS guards. He waited for them to discover the "unexpected" prison death, but an entire day went by uneventfully. Peeved, he finally telephoned the guards to "find out how the internees were fed." At that point, the sergeant of the guard reported they had found Captain Hall hanged in his cell in an apparent suicide. Schiffer acted surprised.

Next, Storz and Andergassen brought Hall's body to the Bolzano Concentration Camp so the camp doctor could certify that Hall's death was a suicide. Everything was working according to plan as Karl Pittschieler was stepping out of his office at the concentration camp. The local Italian physician, forced to serve as a doctor for the Nazis, was on his way home when an ominous black Mercedes limousine rolled up.

The Italian internee from Bolzano had no choice but to do the bidding of the Nazis. From 1939 to 1943, the non-Italian speaking people in the Bolzano area were given the option of either staying in and integrating into Italian culture, or immigrating to the Third Reich and losing their cultural heritage. Pittschieler opted to become Italian, opening himself up to suspicion of political unreliability. He was arrested on December 27, 1943, when he was the assistant doctor at a hospital in Brunico, and taken to the Corpo d'Armata. He was held without charges until May of 1944. A kangaroo court sentenced him to detention at the Bolzano Concentration Camp as one of its first inmates. Here he engaged in forced labor, but he was forced to perform medical services because there was no camp doctor. The Germans eventually allowed him to live in Bolzano with his family, but they forced him to remain as camp doctor, and attempted to persuade him to wear an SS uniform and register with the SS.

As the Mercedes rolled into the camp, the bushy-browed Storz and hulking Andergassen stepped out of the car, ordering the young doctor to join them. Pittschieler followed the thugs into the entrance of the cellblock, where a rough wooden coffin lay on the cold cement. Andergassen and Storz then opened the rear door of the limousine and removed a corpse wrapped in a blanket and brought it into the prison cellblock.

"Andergassen and Storz roughly threw the body into the coffin," explained Pittschieler. "The advanced state of rigor mortis made the body difficult to manage. One of the men forced the body into the coffin with his foot."

"See whether he's dead or not," one of the Germans barked to Pittschieler.

The doctor recalled the incident: "I came to the conclusion that the death had taken place approximately six hours previously. During my hurried examination of the corpse, I saw no blood on the body, no marks of strangulation, nor other evidence on which definitely to arrive at determination of the cause of death. . . . I had no thoughts whatsoever of its identity. I answered, 'He's dead,' and proceeded to my house in Bolzano."

The next day, camp authorities ordered Pittschieler to prepare a death certificate for the corpse he had examined the previous evening. He filled out the form, describing "a state-less individual named Holl" who died of "cardiac paralysis." The doctor suspected foul play; however, under the circumstances, he had no choice but to fill out the certificate. Under the Nazis' noses, he had dropped a crucial clue. Cardiac paralysis does not exist as a precise medical term.

Schiffer's henchmen interred Hall's body in a shallow grave in field E, first row, grave seventeen in the Resurrecturis Cemetery in Bolzano. With German efficiency, Schiffer's men filed the death certificate at the town hall in Bolzano.

Before he was interned, Schiffer took Hall's wristwatch "for safe-keeping." As a final touch, Schiffer personally reported to Major Thyrolf that Captain Hall hanged himself in his cell. According to Schiffer, Thyrolf "received this report with a smile."

28

A Cry for Help

THE GESTAPO NEVER INTENDED to release Hall to the OSS. Even after his death, they strung along the Americans. The day after Hall's murder, OSS Switzerland appeared to be making headway, reporting to the Brain in Italy that "the Germans were to give an answer in three days if they would accept the proposition for exchange." They waited over a week, and a message came through their contacts that they were agreeable to an exchange through Switzerland.

Back in Zoldo Alto, the countess was tired of the delays:

> Then, at last, I told everyone of the capture of Steve by the Germans, and I pleaded that someone should go to make the negotiations, but everyone was afraid of exposing themselves in front of the Germans. So I went myself in my name, just as if I had been Steve's sister. The Germans accepted, and waited for new negotiations with the OSS. And I awaited the news from Major Benucci, who was to supply me with the details from the military staff and with the news about Steve. But, instead of that I received a note from Benucci, in which he thanked me for all that I had done for Steve. And for having him freed. I hastened to the governor and thanked him for having obtained this for me and my happiness was great to know Steve [was] in Rome—free—and to be able to see him again soon, safe and sound. But I thought it was strange not to have received this news [from Steve].

✳   ✳   ✳

Back at OSS headquarters in Switzerland, the Gestapo continued to feign negotiations over a dead man. On February 28, the Germans sent a message back to the OSS that they were, once again, agreeable to a prisoner exchange. OSS Switzerland's contacts yielded more information, stating they would like to submit names from within their side for a prisoner exchange. The final message stated cryptically that they "had no details on Captain Hall and needed more information."

To the OSS, it finally became clear the Nazis were "seeking to hide what actually happened to Captain Hall." Nevertheless, the countess and Chappell were not informed.

29

Pitched Battles

IN THE EARLY MORNING HOURS of February 28, 1945, a partisan woke Howard Chappell from a much-needed deep sleep. "About a hundred fascists are moving on our position!"

Chappell nodded and requested that partisan leader Bruno order his men to their positions, which they had set up the day before. In the final week of February, Tacoma was occupied with its own problems, and Stephen Hall had faded from Chappell's focus.

Chappell decided to make a stand at the Passo San Boldo near the Italian town of Cison. The pass, located above the Venetian plains, connects the area with the valley of Belluno by a winding, snake-like road built by the Austrian army in 1917 (with the sweat and toil of Russian prisoners and local women). Several tunnels cut through the mountain faces, making it a perfect place for an ambush.

Unlike a month earlier, when the Seventh Alpini ran from a fight, Chappell knew that this time he was with the right partisan leader: Paride Brunetti. With the nom de guerre of Bruno, Brunetti served as commander of the Mazzini Brigade. Renowned for his lion-like heart, the military leader was described by an English operative as a fire-eater with one plan only: "fight to the last man and to the last shot."

Born in 1916 to a poor family of sharecroppers, "where shoes on your feet were a luxury," as he recalled, Bruno came to hate the oppression of poverty. He became a socialist because "my war, which was a military war, became a social war."

Bruno ran a tight ship and commanded the Churchill Company, made up of escaped POWs. Chappell knew he was in the company of a true warrior.

"As we faced south, there was a sharp rocky decline to the plain below. To the right was a deep ravine, and to the left a very sharp descent laden with snow. To the north was a long sloping decline to Belluno," Chappell later explained.

The Germans and their fascist allies came up the mountain road on the rocky southern side, exposing themselves to fire. The fascist detachments included the Decima MAS, an elite unit of highly trained frogmen and commandos. While Italy was still in the war, the Decima MAS had sunk numerous British ships throughout the Mediterranean. The ruthless fascists, known for their combat prowess, were now fighting on foot.*

Chappell planned to stay and fight a pitched battle similar to his stand with the Seventh Alpini less than a month earlier. He planned to make an Alamo-like stand at the top of the mountain pass.

As the first German-fascist force advanced toward the Mazzini Brigade, Bruno barked in Italian, "Hold your fire." The fascist column crept closer. Unlike the Seventh Alpini, Bruno's men held their position.

"Open fire!" yelled Bruno.

Two mortars, a heavy machine gun, and two Brens ripped into the fascist troops.

Bruno recalled the carnage:

They met our dreadful resistance. Only a few partisans with a few weapons . . . [it was] like shooting clay pigeons. . . . Chappell behaved like a hero. He was shooting like a madman behind a heavy machinegun . . . like God's wrath. A daredevil was he, Chappell!

---

*In September 1943, after the Italian armistice, approximately half of the Decima MAS joined the OSS and conducted raids up the Italian coast; the remainder fought on foot for the Germans.

Charles Ciccone also remembers Chappell's courage under fire: "This is where I saw an American officer show courage, leadership, and one hell of a lot of guts to fight."

With the southern flank sealed off, two hundred fascist troops stormed the flank of the mountain. Bruno's men stopped them cold with machine-gun and mortar fire, pinning the fascist troops down in several stone houses.

Chappell remembered the slaughter: "The effect was devastating, and the fascists were at once completely demoralized." The fascists were not used to a pitched battle. "Their abilities were confined to participation in burning of homes, torturing, and killing of defenseless prisoners!"

The combined German-fascist force, which outnumbered the partisans twenty to one, resumed the attack at noon. A large force tried to hit the south again. Fabrega alternated between a bazooka and light machine gun, devastating the attackers. The Italian partisans grew desperate for ammunition, as many of the ammo bearers were pinned down by two enemy machine guns. Without orders, Fabrega swung into action. He ripped the .30-caliber light machine from its tripod and stood up in exposed position, firing directly on the two German machine guns. "Fabrega began to duel with the two enemy guns, which ended by him driving both gun crews to cover," Chappell recalled.

Under the gray Italian February sky, Chappell spotted more Germans and fascists coiling up the winding mountain road through the pass. Raising the sight on the light machine gun to its highest elevation, Chappell pulled back the trigger of the Browning .30-caliber weapon. The bullets traveled in a three-thousand-yard arc, like miniature artillery rounds, falling downward onto the road. The OSS captain killed three men and forced the others to take cover.

As Bruno recalled: "That day there was a massacre. . . . One machine gun had fired more than a thousand shots."

During the all-day battle on the mountaintop, the machine guns devoured ammunition like mad dogs in a meat shop. Out of mortar shells and running low on belted .30-caliber ammo, Chappell ordered Silsby to radio the Brain back at OSS headquarters to request an emergency supply drop on the mountain.

"In order to make contact," he explained, "Silsby had to stretch the antenna, and while he worked, he was under direct automatic fire . . . bullets whistled through the branches of the tree overhead while he worked."

The lanky operator tapped out the following coded message: "Am in trouble. Can you prepare an emergency drop with A–20 [a bomber outfitted for secret operations]. Need two small mortars and ammo belted for American light machine gun. One light machine gun, Ammo clips for BAR. As much tracer as possible . . . "

The Brain quickly readied the plane.

Finally, the fascists paused to regroup. At dusk, the Axis troops pulled back out of range of the .30-caliber machine guns and formed a ring around the pass. Ominously, they wheeled two cannons into position. Bright amber Axis flares lit up the sky as Chappell saw hundreds of fresh troops move into position around the mountain.

After the fascists broke off the engagement, Bruno went down the hill and seized the wallet of one of the dead Decima MAS soldiers. Inside was a letter addressed from the dead man to a comrade in arms, stating, "We were fighting for Italy's honor." Italy was truly in the midst of a civil war. Fascists, communists, and nationalists vied for power. Bruno later recalled, "These men were my enemies, but they believed in the war they were fighting."

Chappell wisely decided to cancel the supply drop and withdraw to Tacoma's hideout near Valmorel. Tacoma slipped off the mountain and returned to Valmorel before the Germans could mount another assault. The next day, hundreds of SS troops, light tanks, and cannons swept the area.

Chappell later learned Italian civilians were paid to pick up the bodies. Tacoma and Bruno's Mazzini Brigade had killed well over a hundred fascist troops.

Back at his base camp, Chappell thought the moment he had been waiting for all this time had finally come. The rest of his OG team was scheduled to parachute in. However, once again, the Germans foiled his plan by ordering a massive rastrellamento. Over the next two days he authorized and canceled the drop several times because of the pending German offensive.

Before the sweep kicked off, Field Marshal Kesselring paid a visit to Trichiana. The field marshal in charge of Hitler's forces in Italy was a target too tempting—an opportunity Chappell could not resist. Quickly, he organized an assassination attempt: "Fabrega, Delaini, Brownie, and myself started out with personal weapons, one bazooka, and two BARs to try to set up an ambush. We were unable to locate him, however, as he moved from one garrison to another very rapidly, as I later learned from our chain of intelligence."

Chappell's small band on foot could not keep up with Kesselring, who was traveling in an armed motorcade. At four o'clock on March 4, Chappell remembered, "We finally gave up the hunt." Later, Chappell reported the field marshal had moved to Feltre. Exhausted, Chappell and the team retired for the evening in his mountain hideout.

30

Manhunt

HOWARD CHAPPELL PREPARED dinner for Team Tacoma. The muscular operative fiddled with a small pot he was using to brew tea, and tended to the turkey slowly roasting over an open fire in the corner of the team's mountain hideaway. The gentle aroma caressed the men's nostrils and reminded them of their mothers' kitchens. After living on cornmeal for days, they were finally going to eat well that evening.

Rap, rap, rap. A nervous knock on the door quickly put an end to their peaceful thoughts of home. Chappell pulled open the weather-beaten door and beheld a beautiful but terrible scene. The sun was setting behind a stunning young woman whose opal eyes were full of fear. She whispered, "Tedeschi, tedeschi, San Antonio!" (The Germans have you surrounded!)

The village woman had fulfilled her duty to Brownie, who had recruited her to reconnoiter enemy threats. The enemy had entered San Antonio.

"Bury the radio!" Chappell instinctively barked to Silsby. Turning to Fabrega, he snapped, "Put the rest of the equipment in the caves."

As the team hastily buried their one-time-pad codebooks in holes Fabrega had dug a couple of days earlier in tiny caves near Trichiana, Chappell and Benucci grabbed two Browning Automatic Rifles (BARs) and field glasses, bolted through the door, and climbed a nearby rise above the house. Chappell scanned the ridge and quickly zeroed in on a squad of German searchers. The Germans were slowly picking their way along the ridge, just four hundred yards away and coming right for them. Benucci spotted more Germans to the north and east.

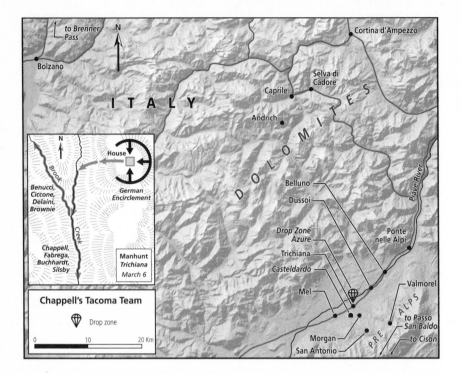

The captain focused on a German talking to one of the locals. "There's a woman pointing out to a German officer our exact location."

Unbeknownst to Chappell at the time, the officer was SS Major Otto Schröder. Schröder, a hulk of a man even larger than Howard Chappell, was in charge of the SS battalion at Belluno. He was essentially Schiffer's muscle. That morning, he was dispatched by Schiffer to lead a manhunt composed of hundreds of SS and Wehrmacht troops. Schröder's orders were to track down the Tacoma and Aztec Teams, while "cleaning up all organized resistance in the entire zone."

The dozen or so soldiers that showed up in Chappell's field glasses were the vanguard of a thousand troops descending on Tacoma's position. The Nazis had them in a tightening noose. Shooting their way out was out of the question.

Believing "it was nearly impossible to escape from the trap," Chappell ordered his men to run for their lives. One escape route still lay open: a creek at the bottom of a ravine running due south from the team's mountain hideout.

Chappell and his five men and several partisans sprinted and stumbled down the muddy, snow-covered slope leading to the creek. As Chappell recalled: "We moved very rapidly down a steep bank, most of us falling a good part of the way."

Brownie led the way. "He was very concerned for Captain Chappell's safety," recalled Ciccone.

Chappell and his men, bruised and exhausted, plunged into the icy, knee-deep creek. With hundreds of Nazi troops hot on their trail, the men desperately lunged downstream. The frigid water seeped into their boots and soaked their pant legs. With their hearts racing, several tripped and fell into the water as they moved down the creek bed, dodging between the snowdrifts.

The creek brought the team through the initial ring of Germans surrounding the house. They managed to move about eight hundred yards before they were spotted and machine guns opened up on them.

"Bullets were hitting the water all around us and bouncing off the rocks," recalled Benucci.

Bringing up the rear of the column, Chappell boldly grabbed a BAR and started firing on the SS.

Brrrp. Brrrp. Chappell depressed the blue gunmetal trigger, shooting any Germans getting too close to the OSS men and the partisans. As he covered the retreat, Chappell also picked up anyone who fell into the water.

"Here again, he displayed amazing coolness and confidence," recalled Salvador Fabrega.

"All this time he kept up his fire with the BAR, making himself a perfect target for Jerry [Germans]. I want to say at this time I don't believe there is another man anywhere with as much guts," recalled Delaini.

The situation looked hopeless. "Buchhardt and Silsby seemed very tired," recalled Chappell. "They were running like hell, but getting nowhere."

Exhausted and lying prone in the water, Buchhardt yelled to Chappell, "Captain, they're going to get us."

Chappell urged him forward. He took the medic's arm and pulled him out of the water, boosting him over a small waterfall.

*　*　*

Chappell's courageous stand with the BAR bought the team a few precious seconds to work out a new plan.

With the SS closing in, their only chance of filtering through the German lines was to split up into smaller groups. Chappell ordered Benucci, Ciccone, Delaini, and Brownie to break away. The groups faced a simple choice that would end up deciding their fates: Continue down the creek, or change direction and go up a small brook? Brook versus creek, freedom or capture. Benucci chose to lead his group up the brook while Chappell, Buchhardt, Fabrega, and Silsby would push on down the creek.

"Now, get the hell out of here! I will cover you!" he yelled. He shot a quick glance at Benucci. "If we are caught, you can still get a message back about us." Chappell considered Benucci to be the most valuable man in the group because, as far as he knew, Team Aztec's radio had not been captured.

Chappell's group didn't get far before the exhausted Silsby collapsed. The lanky radio operator was stretched out on the ground, "apparently unconscious." Chappell looked up to see an SS soldier about thirty yards from Silsby, and another trooper about a hundred yards away.

Realizing the Germans had surrounded him, and hearing the whizzing and snapping of bullets, Chappell shouted his surrender to the Germans, hoping to buy his men a few more seconds to make their escape. "Kamerad! Kamerad!"

Then he barked at Silsby, "Get the hell out of here!"

It was no good. Silsby, who suffered from asthma, struggled to his feet, but "fell down and couldn't get up."

Completely spent, Silsby knew his capture was imminent. He slid his hand into his breast pocket, grabbing his radio crystals and signal papers. He furtively shoved them under a loose rock in front of him.

Thinking his radio operator was wounded, Chappell tried unsuccessfully to carry Silsby out of the firefight. Surprisingly, none of the bullets had found the mark, even though the Germans were so close. Silsby was not wounded, just completely spent.

Chappell refused to leave the helpless man in the hands of the Germans, so he sacrificed himself to save Silsby.

"It was impossible to move him, so I surrendered. I hoped at the time that as soon as he was able to rest a little, we would be able to escape," lamented Chappell.

✳ ✳ ✳

Eric Buchhardt pushed down the creek, moving away from Chappell, Silsby, and Fabrega. The din of machine gun fire pierced the air. Running out of options, Buchhardt scanned the side of the creek. He noticed depressions and crevasses large enough to conceal a man. He quickly ducked into one. He held his breath as a patrol of twenty manhunters passed within a few feet of his hole. A few minutes after the column had gone by, a lone SS trooper tramping through the water happened to glance into Buchhardt's hideaway. Without hesitation, he lunged with the razor-sharp bayonet at the end of his 98k Mauser rifle.

"I could not move more than a few inches, and so I brought up my knees. At this moment, I grabbed the barrel of his gun and pulled. As he tried to pull away from me, I let go. He fell over backwards, giving me the time to get out of the hole to attack him. I dared not shoot for fear of attracting attention, so I hit him over the skull with the butt of my .45 over and over again. I'm certain he wasn't living when I left him."

Buchhardt made a dash down the creek to a nearby village, where he spied a haystack that would offer him cover from the hundreds of Germans swarming around the ridge like hornets.

Covered in mud and exhausted from running, Buchhardt summoned his strength to make a dash for the haystack. Just before he reached it, a partisan yelled, "There's a German behind you!"

Buchhardt looked back just as he reached the stack.

"At the same moment, the Jerry who had followed me took a lunge at me with the butt of his rifle, striking me in the left ear."

The blow from the Mauser nearly stunned him, yet he leaped at the German and wrestled with him with desperate strength, knocking him down. Buchhardt again used the butt of his .45 to incapacitate the German. Not stopping to see whether he had killed the man, he ran farther down the valley. Bleeding and exhausted, he found another hole where he hid and dressed his wounds.

* * *

Several hundred yards down the creek from Buchhardt's hole, Joe Benucci realized he was near a house he once used as a command post. He looked up and saw five SS men standing on a knoll, firing into the brook at the other men who had run ahead of him. "I lifted my carbine and emptied the clip into the group. Three of them fell, one body tumbling off the knoll into the brook," recalled Benucci.

Out of ammunition, Benucci threw away his carbine and frantically searched for a place to hide. He was determined not to let the Germans take him alive. He kept picturing all the partisans who had been captured and impaled on meat hooks in the town square.

Behind the body of one of the dead German soldiers, a cavity where the snow drifted up against an overhanging bank caught Benucci's eye.

"I dived into this cavity, pulled as much snow as possible around me, and curled up. I rubbed clay from the bank on my face and hands and waited, scarcely daring to breathe. In one hand I had my .45 pointed out at the brook. I held the ring of a grenade in my teeth, so even if I was wounded, I could pull it out."

Benucci nervously held his breath. The SS were "so close for a minute that I could nearly touch them."

"Hail Mary, full of grace," he faintly whispered.

An SS lieutenant ordered two of his men to pick up the body of the man near Benucci's hole. Luckily, the men focused on their dead comrade. Several other patrols walked right by the hole, but fortunately, "they kept looking straight ahead." The Italian captain would spend the next seven hours in the frigid, water-filled hole.

✳ ✳ ✳

Running at breakneck speed up the brook, Brownie and Charles Ciccone stumbled into a ditch that Ciccone described as "dry and deep enough to conceal a man unless he stood on the very edge of the top of it."

Both men felt overheated from the sprint and the stress of the fire-fight. Brownie tore off the dark gray scarf wound around his neck. Suddenly, two Germans appeared on top of the ditch, glancing down at them. Nervously, they "leapt back at the sight" of the two operatives.

For a second, the two men froze as they tried to figure out what to do next.

"Follow me," Ciccone whispered in Italian.

Thirty yards to the left was a crevasse obscured by overhanging turf and brown grass. Ciccone quickly estimated that the gash in the earth could conceal two men. He darted for the crevasse, glancing back to see if Brownie was behind him.

"Follow me!" whispered Ciccone again.

Brownie paid no attention to Ciccone. The young Italian scrambled up the side of the ditch with his BAR and disappeared from view, moving to the spot where they had last seen the two Germans. Brownie courageously engaged the Germans to allow Ciccone to escape.

Ciccone heard the distinctive sound of the BAR as Brownie fired half of the weapon's twenty-round clip. A hail of German gunfire replied.

Silence.

"I heard no voices for a couple of minutes. Then two single shots rang out, and then silence again," recalled Ciccone.

The two shots were likely the coup de grâce to kill Brownie. The Germans searched his body and found a letter from his sister. Shortly afterward, she also would be rounded up by the Nazis.

After the two shots were fired, Ciccone climbed into the crevasse and flatted himself against the bottom of the hole.

"The Germans came up the ditch and walked along the top of both sides."

One SS soldier picked up Brownie's scarf, looked at it, then neatly folded it and placed it on a rock at his feet.

"I saw and heard their movements for several hours."

✳   ✳   ✳

Howard Chappell was not so lucky.

"Kamerad!" yelled the blond-haired leader with authority.

"Captain, get out of here. Don't stay with me," murmured Silsby.

Two SS soldiers approached Chappell and ordered him to drop his weapon and help Silsby off the ground. Silsby was too weak to walk, so Chappell supported him as the SS marched the men back to the POW cage in nearby Trichiana.

Out of the corner of his eye, still out of view of the two Germans, Chappell spotted Fabrega about thirty yards away. The Spaniard apparently was about to try to free Chappell and Silsby.

"Raus!" barked Chappell at Fabrega.

He didn't want the Spaniard to be taken by the Germans. Fabrega understood and withdrew into the shadows.

Chappell's shout triggered the suspicion of the guards. One began to search the area, leaving Silsby and Chappell escorted by a single man. Chappell looked straight into the young guard's eyes.

"The war is almost over; let us go and I will give you five thousand dollars." Chappell confidentially stated. "The war is almost over; your house has probably been destroyed. After the war, think about what you can do with all that money." Chappell was not bluffing. He was carrying a small fortune in gold coins and Italian bills given to him by the OSS for just such an emergency.

The guard shook his head, refusing to listen. A nervous expression came across his face, and he started to yodel to attract the attention of his comrades.

"Yodel-ay-he-hoo! Yodel-ay-he-hoo!"

Chappell knew if he did not stop the yodeling, dozens of SS troops would descend on their location and make escape impossible.

With his signature cocky smirk, Chappell started yodeling back. Comically, the men got into a contest of sorts.

"Each time he [yodeled], I would yodel too."

The guard stammered that he would shoot them if Chappell did not stop yodeling.

The argument went on, but the guard stopped yodeling. Chappell's split-second solution, ridiculous in many ways, accomplished his goal and bought him time. He was waiting for the right moment to escape.

With a gun at their backs, the men trekked through the muddy snow for over a mile toward Trichiana. Hundreds of SS troops now garrisoned Trichiana, making escape impossible.

The guard wisely kept his distance. A potato-masher hand grenade dangled from his right wrist by a cord, and he was holding a pistol squarely at their backs. Chappell didn't know whether the cord served merely to carry the grenade or to detonate it as well, so he began to chide the guard to find out.

"I insulted the German grenades in general, while praising our own. He disagreed with me, showing me how the German grenades worked."

This brazen act of manipulation provided Chappell with a vital piece of information: the cord would not detonate the grenade.

Because the grenade was not an immediate threat, Chappell was free to try the direct approach. He boldly pulled a James Bond–like gadget, a Stinger, out of his pocket and pointed it at the guard. "Drop your weapon. If you don't drop it, I will kill you!" snarled Chappell.

The Stinger was a tiny, single-shot pistol that looks like a pen, made by the Rite-Rite Manufacturing Company in 1943 exclusively for OSS agents behind enemy lines. The .22-caliber bullet had a range of two to three yards.

"He did not realize at first what it was, until I threatened to shoot," Chappell said. "Unfortunately for us, he did not lack courage, but backed off about twenty yards, continuing to keep me covered and threatening to shoot."

The guard moved out of the range of the Stinger. Luckily, the guard did not shoot. Chappell knew he was beaten, at least for the time being. He threw the Stinger away. If he was brought into Gestapo headquarters carrying a spy's weapon, he could not credibly claim to be a downed airman.

Chappell continued desperately to plot an escape, as he knew capture likely meant death. His mind flashed back to the atrocities he had seen:

> We all knew about the steel meat hooks at Bolzano. The Germans tied the prisoner's hands, boosted him up, then lowered him so that the two meat-hook points would go into the soft underside of his jaw, just inside the jawbone. His feet are off the ground . . . men could live for a couple of days [until] the jawbone snaps and the prongs can go on up to the brain.

The march to Trichiana continued. After reaching a familiar bend in the road, Chappell knew time was running out.

"We need to make a break for it soon," Chappell whispered to Silsby.

As they rounded the bend, Chappell spied a stable. The main door was open, facing them. As he looked closer, he saw daylight through the back door, which led to a ravine and possible freedom. It was their best chance for escape. Chappell quickly hatched a plan: "I told Silsby, when we reached the house, to make a break through the stable and I would go through around the house."

When they were at the nearest point to the house, Chappell whispered: "I'm going to make a break." He bolted toward the door like a racehorse. Chappell ducked through the door and sprinted into the ravine.

Instead of running away, Silsby staggered toward the guard.

"He was too far away to jump him in the condition I was in, but it did take his mind off Chappell."

The guard pointed his Luger at Silsby.

"I thought I was dead," recalled Silsby.

Instead, a miracle occurred. The guard pulled the trigger, but there was no bullet in the chamber.

Silsby did his best to distract his captor as the German recocked a round into the Luger's chamber. His actions allowed Chappell to escape. Chappell dashed through the stable without looking back. Filled with adrenaline, he scrambled down the ravine, running about four hundred yards. Out of sight of the SS guard, he slowed to a brisk walk.

Silsby resumed the march to Trichiana.

"I stopped rather stupidly, turned around and walked down the road in the direction we had been going and the guard followed. That was how I left the Tacoma Mission on the morning of 6 March."

Shortly after reaching Trichiana, Silsby was joined in captivity by Fabrega. He had been run down by a group of German soldiers after a gun battle.

"The enemy kept firing at me and got as close as about twenty yards from me. There was too many for me to attempt to continue to fight them. . . . I accordingly surrendered to an SS Lieutenant and a squad of six men," Fabrega said.

Fabrega and Silsby ended up in captivity, but Chappell, Benucci, Buchhardt, Ciccone, Delaini, and the Aztec Team were still in the fight. Brownie was dead.

31

Hiding

Avoiding the SS patrols, Chappell moved along the snowy ridges of the rugged Italian mountainside. However, near the small village of Morgan, half a dozen SS troopers spotted him and fired a few shots.

"One of them ricocheted and hit me in the calf of my left leg." Sixty years later, Chappell's scar was still noticeable.

Avoiding capture once again, Chappell kept running. After breaking contact, he hid behind a snowbank until darkness fell. The howls of the SS rottweilers pierced the darkness.

Chappell crept back into the town of Morgan to find shelter. He located a friend, a partisan named Cherbro—the same partisan Chappell saved from imminent death weeks earlier as they were being attacked by Nazi troops on the side of the mountain.

During that incident, Chappell put the man in a fireman's carry, avoiding a hail of bullets as he brought him to safety. Chappell placed the man on a sled, gave him his pistol, and had another partisan bring him to a doctor. Now, Cherbro returned Chappell's pistol and the favor. The partisan informed Chappell that Silsby, Fabrega, and five partisans were captured. Chappell also found out the SS had killed Brownie. The partisan incorrectly informed him that Brownie had been wounded and taken to San Antonio, where an "SS officer had cut off his hands and gouged out his two eyes."*

---

*Years passed before Chappell finally found out Brownie had died in a firefight with the SS and was not mutilated. However, on March 6 he had no reason to doubt the partisan's version. He had told him that Brownie had been tortured. It was yet another reason to hate the SS.

Later, Chappell would reveal his feelings regarding this episode in a letter to Brownie's sister:

His death was a serious blow to me, even in death I would like to think of him as being whole. . . . We all loved him so much. . . . One thing that I will always remember, Brownie never did it for anybody else but me. When we had eggs, he would take three or four eggs and beat them until they would rise up in the bowl. Then he would add a little sugar and milk and give it to me to drink. It was kind of a tribute to me that he would work so long and hard to beat the eggs. Perhaps what distressed [me] most about the death of Brownie was the fact that his loyalty to me caused it. He could have stayed at where he spent the night [where the Aztec team was hiding].

✳   ✳   ✳

Joe Benucci crept out of his watery hole, his entire body aching after spending hours in the damp hiding place. Benucci walked down the brook, crossed the stream and crept toward the house where he hoped his team was hiding. The house was shrouded in inky blackness, the door closed, snow and cold weather creating an eerie silence.

"Of all the houses in the area, I didn't know one where I would be safe. Finally driven by hunger, I decided to make my way to my command post, where I knew we had buried some food and vitamins. There, I might find some bodies, or at least some indication of where we stood."

Benucci moved closer to the house and heard someone talking. He could not believe his ears. The voice belonged to First Sergeant Nick Cangelosi. Cangelosi and Sebby Gianfriddo, Aztec's intrepid radio operator, had been hiding in the house all day.

"All day long the enemy passed up and down before the house where the men were hiding, behind it, beside it. Yet for some strange reason they did not enter the house, where the men were geared to fight to the end."

In retrospect, some of the men viewed it as true divine intervention, as hundreds of Nazis had searched every house in the hamlet save theirs. Cangelosi recounts:

Our hearts raced. Sweat was pouring down my face. All day, the SS passed by our house. Miraculously, they never looked in ours. I remember the worst moment when Sebby had the detonation cord in his hand. Basically, there was a self-destructive bomb in the radio. If he pulled it, the entire house, including us inside, would have been dead.

He looked at me closely and asked, "Should I pull it?"

"No," I said.

The OSS issued each agent L-pills, lethal cyanide tablets. Seconds after ingestion, they would cause death. Briefly, both men's thoughts lingered on the dilemma: take the pills or pull the cord. Fortunately, circumstances prevented either. The SS passed over their house.

* * *

Slowly, Benucci walked up to the door of the safe house and whispered the password. He rapped on the hardwood with his knuckles.

"They all came tumbling out—the whole bunch of them, every single one of them safe! They started to pound me on the back," remembered Benucci.

"But we thought you were dead!" exclaimed Nick Cangelosi. Relief and adulation swept over them.

After they briefly traded the stories of their ordeals, Benucci ordered several partisans to get news on the situation. A short time after leaving, they reported that most of the Seventh Alpini had escaped the rastrellamento and were hiding in a valley known as Valmorel.

Most importantly, Aztec's radio operator had survived, equipment intact. Aztec's radio was Chappell's last lifeline to headquarters.

* * *

Back in Morgan, while Cherbro tenderly bandaged Chappell's leg, Chappell arranged to have four partisan girls on bicycles start gathering information on the whereabouts of Buchhardt, Ciccone, and Delaini.

The impromptu human intelligence network achieved its purpose. The girls returned, reporting Buchhardt, Delaini, and Ciccone had escaped and were in hiding. Chappell's first message was to Buchhardt: "Sit tight."

Shortly thereafter, he sent similar messages to Ciccone and Delaini. After hearing that Benucci was safe, Chappell sent word that he was alive. Though still on the run, Chappell was calmly and methodically putting together the facts and hatching a plan.

The partisan girls also reported contradictory rumors that Silsby had escaped and also that the SS was holding the lanky radio operator and Fabrega at the local schoolhouse. Chappell decided on an audacious plan: a jailbreak.

With the pistol Cherbro had returned to him, he snuck into the town of Trichiana. The Germans had imposed a curfew. Chappell spent more than three hours moving around buildings and eluding German patrols. The Nazi soldiers were covering the town like a dark cloak.

Chappell finally made it to the schoolhouse, where he peered into a blackened window. The building was empty—no trace of Fabrega or Silsby. The SS had already moved them to Gestapo headquarters in Belluno. Discouraged, he returned to the foothills outside Trichiana.

Tramping through the snow, Chappell cocked his head vigilantly and scanned the nearby ridgeline. In the frigid air, his breath appeared as a plume of vapor pulled from his chest, the last shreds of perseverance and drive dissipating. He succumbed to exhaustion, the pain from his left leg forcing him to rest. He found what appeared to be a deserted stable. Upon entering the wooden structure, he was greeted by ten Italian civilians.

"They assured me that the Germans would never find this place. I laid down in the hay and fell asleep immediately."

An Italian man woke Chappell at six a.m., informing him that the Germans were approaching. The civilians peered through cracks in the flimsy wood, eyeing the German troops as they passed.

"A patrol of about thirty Germans passed by the stable, seemingly neglecting to search it. Amazingly, the Italian civilians began laughing at their stupidity. One of the Italians opened the door slowly and poked his nose out."

Brrrrp. Brrrp. A stream of crossfire ripped into the stable.

"The civilians started running out and I saw two go down, and a few others were hit. I waited inside to see where the fire was coming from and then slid out of the door and edged around the back of the building."

As Chappell slid out the door, he tiptoed around the corner of the stable, and backed right into the barrel of a Mauser. The thirty-man patrol was a cunning diversion, while another group advanced to the rear of the building. The Nazi forced Chappell to disarm and marched him at gunpoint in the direction of his commanding officer. Foolishly, the lanky SS youth did not inform his comrades of the capture of the OSS team leader.

The area was swarming with hordes of Germans. "I estimated that there were about seventy, although that figure is purely a guess," recalled Chappell.

Between their position and the SS lieutenant was a ravine, which provided a fleeting degree of cover. As they moved across the ravine together, the SS trooper unwisely moved too close to Chappell. The captain had been an instructor for young paratrooper recruits at Fort Benning, and he had taught how to disarm a rifle-wielding captor. The training was muscle memory for him.

"You suddenly grab his pistol wrist, bend over, give just the right quick pull and he goes rolling over your shoulder, dazed, onto the ground. . . . In doing so, I believe his neck was broken. I then stuffed him into a culvert."

The only possible hiding place was a lonely Italian mountain house at the edge of a nearby field. The problem was getting there. He had to cross the open field in plain view of the Germans.

Though his adrenaline was pumping, Chappell suppressed the instinct to run. Rapid movement would catch the attention of the SS. However, if he slowly moved along like the other searchers, he might blend in and not catch their attention. His only chance was to walk.

"It appeared impossible to hide from them. So, I [straightened] my hair some and tr[ied] to appear as German as possible [while wearing English battle dress]. I walked across a large, snow-covered field, taking my time though I wanted to run like hell."

Chappell knew the Germans were looking at him, so he kept glancing to his right and left "as though I were a member of the German search party." The SS seemed ubiquitous. With ice in his veins, he nonchalantly walked within twenty yards of the SS sentries. "I was lucky and passed fairly close to them without being questioned."

Miraculously, he made it to the house and opened the front door "as if I were billeted there."

"Sitting by the fireplace were an old woman and two young girls, spinning wool by hand. When I told them I was an American captain looking for a place to hide, they went right on with their spinning as though American captains dropped in for breakfast every morning. They hard-boiled some eggs, gave me bread to stuff in my pocket, and then a girl led me to a ravine where she thought I would be safe."

Chappell found another overhanging ledge and hid under it until nightfall.

32

Captured

SILSBY'S WAR SEEMED OVER. The radio operator could only guess at the horrors Hall had endured. He recalled the atrocities committed by Nazis when partisans were captured.

The guard brought him to the German bivouac area, where they searched and interrogated him. Over and over, he calmly reiterated the shot-down airman story. Remarkably they treated him with respect, considering many of the cities they hailed from had been destroyed by Allied aircrews.

"I was treated decently by these troops. They were mostly youngsters of seventeen and eighteen. The one guarding me could speak English. They fed me and I sat under a tree until about six o'clock."

✻ ✻ ✻

Less than a mile away, Salvador Fabrega began the fight of his life. The Germans held the Spaniard in the schoolhouse in San Antonio, packed to the gills with captured partisans and civilians rounded up in the rastrellamento. While the Germans coerced the civilians to identify the combatants, the brazen Fabrega stuck out like a sore thumb in his American uniform.

Horrifically, Fabrega received what the Gestapo dubbed special treatment. They isolated the Spaniard, placing him in a small room for interrogation.

"They applied electric wires to my tongue and ears," he explained, "and tried many other savage methods, such as beating me unexpectedly from somewhere in the circle they formed around me. They threatened to shoot me as a partisan if I did not speak freely."

Though knowing only poor English, Fabrega courageously insisted he only knew the foreign tongue. The savage beating continued for hours, but the resilient Fabrega did not crack, reiterating the downed airman story.

Not knowing what to do with the Spaniard, the Germans loaded him into a military truck packed with captured partisans. The lorry rumbled down the road and stopped at the bivouac area where they held Silsby. The radio operator clambered into the back of the truck. Much to his joy, he found himself beside Fabrega. Stealthily, as the truck lumbered down the road to Schröder's headquarters, the two men whispered to each other in order to synchronize their downed airmen story. They even memorized their respective squadrons and bases.

✼ ✼ ✼

Schröder had set up his SS headquarters in a seventeenth-century stone church in the heart of Belluno. The Germans placed Silsby and Fabrega in a "room of thirty or so partisans" and demanded their names, ranks, and serial numbers. Both gave fake aliases. Silsby told the men he was a staff sergeant who served as a tail gunner on a B-25 Mitchell bomber before being shot down.

The Gestapo ordered both into a room containing a single peephole embedded in a closed door. Silsby saw an eye appear at the hole.

"Stretch," someone croaked (Silsby's nickname to the team and partisans). According to Chappell, it was likely a partisan with the nom de guerre of Victor.

"They brought in two of our partisans they had captured—Porthos and Victor. Porthos did not talk, but Victor revealed all of our identities. He even led them to the cave where we had buried our equipment. After he talked, they hanged him and Porthos," remembered Chappell.

After they were exposed by Victor, the SS threw Fabrega and Silsby into a five-foot by eight-foot hole infested with "ten thousand lice," Silsby revealed.

"Don't talk, it's probably skillfully wired," Fabrega whispered to Silsby. With their stories straight, the two men mentally prepared to face the SS interrogators.

On the evening of March 7, they dragged Fabrega out of the cell first. Once again, the torture process began. According to Chappell, "They tortured Fabrega . . . with an electrical device run by a hand crank. After a while, they put the electrodes on his wrists and ankles. Fabrega said the worst was when they put one up his nostril. They also used whips. But they couldn't break down his story." Fabrega would not crack. Roughly twenty-four hours later, he passed Silsby in the hallway, a pivotal moment. Handcuffed and exhausted, he shuffled by, whispering, "They know you're the radio operator." He also warned Silsby to maintain his silence. An SS guard then led Silsby down the dark hallway to a room with an aging SS sergeant behind a typewriter. Silsby explained:

> The old boy could speak broken English. I didn't know the story Fabrega had given, so I faked misunderstanding until I knew what Fabrega had said.
>
> They seemed very stupid and the story was this: We had been airmen shot down and, upon making our way to Yugoslavia, we had received word from base—in Bari—through a British mission in the area that we were to stay and set up a mission to help other airmen get out. It was a very weak tale, but it seemed to satisfy these characters.

The story had some grains of truth, as Tacoma's mission had indeed mushroomed into rescuing airmen shot down behind the lines. Whether or not the SS bought the story is another matter. Silsby and Fabrega remained separated. Each man was eventually taken to Gestapo chief Major Schiffer's headquarters in the Corpo d'Armata in Bolzano. Silsby was the first to meet the evil genius and remembered the ordeal when he arrived at Bolzano:

> From 8 o'clock to 1 o'clock, I was visited by five SS soldiers. This was not an interrogation [but] merely sport for the "supermen."

They all thought I was a pilot, and most of their ravings went as follows:

"Why are you in Europe?"

"You will kill no more babies."

"What do you fight for—money?"

"—Scheisse!"

Next, Silsby got a dose of what Fabrega endured for days. "It didn't go so bad, until they brought in a rubber hose. I never saw these men again, and I was finally taken to SS Major Schiffer for interrogation," remarked Silsby.

Andergassen and Storz likely softened Silsby up before Schiffer's surgical interrogation. The SS officer calmly greeted the battered and bruised radio operator. When he finally met Schiffer, the officer apologized: "Sorry for what happened. The men will be punished."

Silsby was escorted into Schiffer's office, where he was greeted by the plainclothes Gestapo and Christa Roy. Silsby was shocked, but maintained his bearing. Before him lay Tacoma's radio sets, a Eureka (used to guide in planes for parachute drops) and the team's radio containing all of its message files and fire plans. At Schiffer's side, Christina Roy took notes on the interrogation.

Schiffer had Silsby in checkmate. With all the team's radio messages in hand, he knew almost everything Tacoma had accomplished. Now the maniacal counterinsurgency expert had Chappell, his nemesis, in his sights. Nevertheless, Silsby initially stuck to the downed airman story.

"I continued the same story as told in Belluno until they confronted me with the messages and said they dealt with several OSS teams. They knew more than I did about the outfit. In fact, one Gestapo agent in civilian clothes said he knew Captain Materazzi personally and he was on my side!"

With Tacoma's radio messages and the information gleaned from earlier coerced interrogations with Hall and the partisans, Schiffer's knowledge of the team's operations proved extensive. During the interrogation, he even slid a picture of Captain Hall across his desk.

"They asked me where the base was. I told them Bari. Also when we dropped, where we operated, and what type of work we did. I answered these straight because they cross-checked them with the messages."

Schiffer was merely toying with Silsby, using him to confirm what he already knew. He was closing in on Chappell.

*　*　*

Back in the cell in Belluno, Fabrega endured over a week of torture. The SS played mind games, insisting "Captain Chappell and the rest of the boys had been killed," and that he might as well talk.

"They brought partisans before me who had actually operated with us and tried to get them to identify me. Some of them did identify me as a member of the mission. But, I continued to insist that I was a downed airman." Sette, the mole at Gestapo headquarters, appeared several times, telling him to stick to the story.

Schiffer ordered the headquarters at Belluno to transport Fabrega to Bolzano. They handcuffed Fabrega in the back seat of the car. Sette talked his way into driving the vehicle. They made their way up the winding mountain roads to Bolzano.

"Now's our time," Sette said. "I'll give you a chance to escape. I'll open the door and we'll both run into the hills and join the partisans."

"You're much more valuable to us here in the Germans' headquarters than you would be in the mountains," said Fabrega.

Sette delivered Fabrega to Bolzano, where Major Schiffer interrogated him repeatedly. From the mountain of radio messages and Silsby's interrogation, Schiffer now knew Chappell led the Tacoma mission. He became determined to get him.

In the next few months, a duel would ensue, pitting Schröder and Schiffer against Chappell. As Chappell and his men tried to outlast the Germans, continuing to target strategic routes, the Brenner Pass was taking on more importance. For the Germans, this once vital route for supplies and troops into Italy was becoming their only route of escape back to Germany.

33

On the Run

CHAPPELL RETURNED TO CHERBRO'S HOUSE in Morgan following his failed attempt to break the men out of the schoolhouse in Trichiana and his narrow escape from the SS patrol. The Germans searched Cherbro's small house numerous times, and he knew he couldn't stay there. Ingeniously, he returned to the same stable they had captured him in the night before. Rather than sleep inside the building, he slept on the ground just outside, realizing that he would be safer in the brush beside the barn. As he curled up into a fetal position, exhaustion set in. Freezing under the stars, Chappell fell into a deep slumber.

The shrill bark of rottweilers jolted him out of sleep. Four German soldiers checked the stable with their war dogs. Chappell left quickly. He recounted his escape: "Hopping into a creek, I [waded through] the water for about two miles. . . . The snow was too deep to walk on. Then I ducked into a hole and stayed there until dark."

Eventually, Chappell crept back toward Morgan and started to make plans for re-forming his team. The mission had gone awry. Both the Brenner plan and the mission to transport the rest of the German OG team into the Dolomites were blown. Nevertheless, he remained focused. The welfare and survival of the team dominated his thoughts. Once they regrouped, there was still damage to be done to the vital routes feeding the Brenner.

✳ ✳ ✳

After running for their lives for the past two days, Delaini and Ciccone both found their way to the headquarters of the Seventh Alpini. The partisans hid the men in the mountains outside of Belluno. Staff Sergeant Delaini remembered his escape and his reunion with Ciccone, and what happened next:

> They hid me in a stable and the following morning I was mighty happy when they brought in Sgt. Ciccone. We spent the day talking. He didn't know how the others had made out. We now heard that Jerry was coming back in strength and so we again prepared to leave. It was decided that the brigade would split into squads. Ciccone and I took off with one of the squads for a place about a mile from Belluno. We spent the day resting and drying our clothes which had gotten wet crossing the river.

The men holed up in a partisan safe house, "losing all track of time," and waited for contact from Chappell. During the day, Germans surrounded the house, making venturing out impossible. But food was scarce, so at night the men would don civilian clothes and travel into the nearby hamlet. Pangs of hunger drove Ciccone and Delaini on one of their more audacious and humorous excursions. One evening, they boldly walked into a café run by the partisans and sat down at a table, ordering a bowl of pasta. In an adjoining room of the café, separated by a thin wall, a German patrol entered and began to dine. Unbeknownst to the Nazis, their quarry was drinking wine and eating pasta within earshot. Behind the lines, life and death were often separated by only a few feet.

✳   ✳   ✳

Eric Buchhardt's life on the run was also saved within a hair's breadth of capture several times. In vain, the medic searched for Chappell. Suffering from the leg wound sustained from his brush with a German bayonet, Buchhardt found another hole the following evening and hid for most of the night. Eventually, he made his way to a farmhouse, where a farmer gave him eggs and milk. He stayed with the man until the early hours of the morning, departing when the man pleaded with him to leave "because he was afraid the Germans would come searching."

Avoiding German patrols, the medic walked more than a mile along the ridge near Trichiana. He made his way to San Antonio, where he met a friendly hotelkeeper. Chappell had told him to meet with the man if the mission did not go as planned. Buchhardt recalled:

> It was dark by now, and I took the road, being very careful, since I did not know whether the Germans had left the town yet. I reached the town and as I saw no Germans, I went to the hotel. Here, they greeted me warmly, gave me clean bandages and civilian clothes, and told me that Fabrega and Silsby had been captured. They did not know of the others, but said they would try to locate them for me. I slept that night and all the next day in this hotel, and about 5:00 a.m. on 9 March they awoke me, telling me the Jerries had come back. I left and had found a ditch not far off in which I hid for four hours. I heard women crying, and when I went to see what the trouble was I saw the Germans had hanged [several] civilians just a short distance from me. The last one was just being hanged with the rope about his neck and his toes barely touched the ground. It took about three or four hours for them to die by this method. I returned to the ditch and remained there till nightfall when the hotel owner came up to me and told me to hide in the hayloft at his place. On March 10, I received a message from Captain Chappell.

Buchhardt had witnessed atrocities committed at the hands of Major Schröder's men. The Nazis had rounded up several local civilians who had nothing to do with the partisans, including Brancher "Ezio" Gioacchino, Mario "Fressina" Grassadonio and four brothers with the last name Schiocchet.*

Chappell contacted Buchhardt through his human intelligence network, and the two reunited. Chappell, with Buchhardt at his side, began to rebuild the mission and plot his next moves against Schröder and Schiffer.

---

*A plaque in the town square of Trichiana honors the innocent men who died at the hands of Schröder's SS.

34

Camp

SILSBY STARED AT THE GRAY CONCRETE WALL topped with rusty brown barbed wire. The Gries Concentration Camp on the southern outskirts of Bolzano became his new home. The camp housed captured partisans as well as political prisoners of the Nazis. Among the prisoners were also transient Jews who were being transported to Nazi death camps deeper in the bowels of the Reich. The site served as a way station for what the Nazis deemed as human cattle.

Once through the main gate, Silsby noticed that the buildings formed a rough quadrangle on the east side of the compound. Sections divided the so-called blockhouses, identified by letters of the alphabet. The buildings served as human warehouses. Silsby learned that blocks A through K housed political prisoners, captured partisans, prostitutes, and the other undesirables of the Reich. Blocks D and F were designated for prisoners requiring "rigorous treatment" and were surrounded by barbed wire and additional walls. Cellblock L was designated for Jews, a temporary home for them on their way to the hell of death camps such as Auschwitz-Birkenau.

"The camp was a medley of Europe and the war. There were babies, old men, cripples, French, English, Poles, Czechs, Russians, Yugoslavs, and Italians," recalled one internee.

"The evil of these buildings was how they were used," a postwar report recounted. The Nazis packed inmates into the buildings like sardines. They lined the windows of the blocks with iron bars and metal screens so the inmates could not pass messages back and forth. To restrict light and ventilation, the SS placed reinforced wooden frames outside the window.

Under the command of Major Schiffer, SS Lieutenant Karl Tito, a "stocky, fat North German," administered the Gries Concentration Camp. Not especially brutal—some described him as rather a weak character who "merely carried out the orders of his superiors"—Tito had blond hair, tightly combed straight back, accentuating his extremely high forehead. The meek Tito left all the heavy-duty brutality to Johann Haage, the senior noncommissioned officer of the camp—Haage was the camp enforcer. Haage brought with him his mistress, Hildegard "Hilde" Lächert, a member of the SS auxiliary corps. Lächert, known for her extreme brutality, was in charge of the women prisoners.

Named the Tigress by the prison inmates, Lächert was a tall, buxom woman with thick brown hair. She "enjoyed striking male and female prisoners with a whip." Even the coldhearted Christa Roy described Lächert as a "brutal sadistic bitch," but one whom Schiffer held up as a model Nazi woman, exhibiting "necessary firmness." According to one account, the Tigress beat with a metal rod the hands of women caught stealing food. Always armed, the SS woman boasted she was a sharpshooter with a pistol. Lächert often ran through the camp shouting like a demented demon, delivering slaps to any man who did not remove his hat when she passed.

Two Ukrainian SS soldiers, Otto Sein and Michael Siefert (known as Misha), served as muscle for the Tigress. Uniquely, the two Ukrainians were both inmates and guards, sentenced by the Germans to work and live in the camp for brutalizing a teenage Italian girl. Otto had several aluminum crowns on his front teeth, which revealed themselves with a sinister sneer. His dental work was complemented by a voice that was squeaky "like a eunuch." Otto's comrade was the fair-haired and muscular Misha, a hunched man with a low forehead and a hooked nose that gave him a "repulsive face." Twelve other Ukrainians were also employed as camp guards.

All Gestapo prisoners in the camp fell under the authority of Major Schiffer. Soon the captured OSS operatives came under his purview—and his wrath. Fabrega soon joined Silsby. The day he entered the camp, two other POWs also entered with him—Captain Ross Ruger Littlejohn and Corporal Joseph David Crowley of the Special Air Service (SAS), a British special operations unit equivalent to the OGs. Ironically, Crowley and Littlejohn were also going after the Brenner Pass. The two served as part of a twelve-man ski team known as Operation Cold Comfort that parachuted behind the lines to block, via landslide, rail lines through the Brenner. The plane mis-dropped them, and they remained constantly on the run. Like it had Silsby and Fabrega, Schiffer's dragnet swept up Littlejohn and Crowley.

Camp life was miserable, each morning beginning with a mass roll call. Silsby, Fabrega, and the SAS men woke at five in the morning as the entire camp was lined up in the predawn darkness in front of their cells. This assembly occurred every day—rain, sleet, or snow. Every prisoner stood at attention, bareheaded for over an hour as an internee was designated to take roll call. The Germans also took the roll, and the two reports were compared for accuracy in order to ensure no one had escaped in the night. In the unheated cells, the internees slept on bare planks and lice-infested wet blankets. They were fed spoiled bread and a thin gruel.

Crowley and Littlejohn soon suffered Schiffer's wrath. Schiffer told Silsby the British operatives were being removed to a "jumper's camp" in Germany. Both men were removed from the camp but were actually taken to the Corpo d'Armata. There, in the machine room below Schiffer's office, they were subjected to all of Schiffer's "special treatment."

Christa Roy, the "female without feelings," recalled: "I remember Captain Littlejohn in the beginning showed himself very obstinate and took the view he was a soldier of an enemy unit, and therefore should merely be taken prisoner and put in a POW camp."

Lieutenant Parker, an Air Corps pilot, soon joined the SAS men in special treatment. Schiffer tortured all of them, repeating the same torture regime Hall had received: the swing, beatings, and electricity. Eventually, Thyrolf told the men, as he had Hall, that "they should talk with complete freedom" since nothing would be revealed to the Allied authorities. If they disclosed the full details of their mission, they would be taken to a "special" POW camp. Schiffer first placed them in the swing, and then they were beaten with whips by Storz and Andergassen. As a final method of coercion, Schiffer used the electrical apparatus on them. They returned to beating Littlejohn after he said something in Gaelic to his comrade. The Germans did not understand the comment and intensified the abuse. Sweating and bloody, the men started to talk and revealed some details of their objectives.

One witness, a Gestapo official, it is alleged, privately confronted Schiffer after the torture. He chided Schiffer, asking why captured enemy agents were always transported to a "camp for special prisoners." The deep natural crease in Schiffer's forehead furrowed as he scoffed: "How can that be done in these circumstances? I shall simply kill them."

Nevertheless, the men bought Schiffer's deceptions. Clinging to a thread of hope, Crowley and Littlejohn believed they would now be transported to a special camp.

But Schiffer's words were hollow. He revealed his thoughts later in a postwar deposition: "It came to light they belonged to a special English organization, I believe that the name was the SAS, which was charged exclusively with terrorist assignments. . . . [By] order of the Führer . . . SAS members, being terrorists, were subject to 'special treatment.'"*

---

*Schiffer was referring to Hitler's Commando Order, which ordered that captured commandos, saboteurs, or enemy agents, uniformed or plain-clothed, receive special treatment. They were to be handed over to Nazi security services and executed. This order was a direct violation of the Geneva Conventions and generally accepted laws of war, but it was interpreted differently by various German commanders. Andergassen recalled that Schiffer told him "the so-called 'illegal Führer order' came directly from the Führer or from the Reichsführer of the SS, Himmler." Schiffer's subordinates also understood that his interpretation of the order meant that any execution carried out was to be done without leaving any evidence. Hence, Schiffer went about meticulously plotting each execution as he did Hall's.

Schiffer had also captured American pilot Charles Parker, who had bailed out along with three of his fellow crewmen about twenty kilometers over Bolzano when flak hit their plane on a return trip from a bombing run over Germany. Schiffer hit Parker, tortured and beaten, with a hook that dropped him to the floor. Wounded, he felt the full force of Schiffer's wrath. Schiffer later explained his actions to postwar interviewers: "Around this time I have heard about the most complete destruction of German cities and I was also familiar with the terror raid on Dresden. Consequently, I saw these bombardiers

(*continues*)

(*continued*)
not as soldiers of an enemy army, but terrorists whom I believed one had to fight with terrorist methods. Prompted by this idea, I let Charles Parker . . . and his comrades . . . be shot."

To ensure their compliance, Parker and his two companions, Littlejohn and Crowley, were told that they were being taken to a special camp in Germany for their safety. Soon thereafter, a black Mercedes pulled up, driven by the muscle-bound Andergassen and Storz. Camp guards escorted the prisoners to the six-passenger car. Schiffer's henchmen had orders to drive toward the Brenner, pretend they were having trouble with the car, and pull over. They would invite the prisoners to stretch their legs and then shoot them as though they were trying to escape.

Storz later recalled:

We compelled the three to take their seats in the car and took the connecting street to the police transient camp into the Neue Meraner Street. Just before one of these side streets which branched off to the right at a little distance I had a breakdown. The left tire was flat, doubtless a blowout from picking up a nail. This breakdown was favorable for us for we bade the three of them to get out of the car. They were induced to proceed along the side street. Andergassen and I followed them for a short distance, I on the right and Andergassen on the left. After about 50 steps, Andergassen asked me whether I was ready to fire, which I acknowledged, whereupon he gave the order "ready."

We shot at the same time with our Italian MPs [machine pistols] which we had brought along, with prolonged bursts of fire. The three Englishmen [sic] in front of us fell silently to the ground. All three lay face down on the ground. Andergassen stepped up to the victims and gave each of the three a finishing shot to the head from his MP.

Storz went on to say, "The order for shooting of the two English officers and the English NCO without any doubt was given with the knowledge of Kommandeur Thyrolf and especially of Fritz Kranebitter and Gruppenführer Dr. Wilhem Harster." Storz's testimony demonstrates that the Gestapo chain of command had knowledge of the murders of Parker, Littlejohn, and Crowley. This makes it all the more likely they had knowledge of Hall's murder as well. In other words, Schiffer was not acting alone. His entire chain of command was complicit in the war crime.

The two henchmen returned to Schiffer's office that evening and gave their boss a full verbal report. Schiffer quickly responded, "Good, you did the job bravely, and you did it for Germany."

Later, Schiffer turned on Parker's fellow aircrew members. Schiffer reported to Thyrolf that he was going to shoot the airmen. He said later that Thyrolf, "received this report without comment . . . [he] only smiled." This was the green light Schiffer needed to liquidate his quarry.

Schiffer decided to use the by now well-oiled "shot while trying to escape" method of murder on the airmen. Schiffer also suspected that one of the airmen, Medard Tafoya, was a Jew. Once again, Storz and Andergassen received the call to pick up three airmen—Hammond, Narran, and Tafoya—in the black Mercedes.

In order to make the escort on foot understandable to the three flyers, I [gave] Andergassen and Storz the order to pretend having trouble with the functioning of the vehicle. Andergassen and Storz were further directed by my order to bring the corpses of the

Under Schiffer's thumb, Silsby and Fabrega were marked men—it was only a matter of time before the two would face his wrath. Both men had witnessed Schiffer's tactics on other prisoners, as Silsby reflected later:

> It was the same routine each time. Major Schiffer and his Gestapo men would ask their base, number of missions, etc., and when they wouldn't talk, they (Major Schiffer . . . I saw personally) slapped them around, then took the pilot away—came back with the information, and took the rest of the men to a "POW camp."

Meanwhile, life inside the camp was getting more miserable as the two Ukrainian SS men, Otto and Misha, "beat an untold number of prisoners to death in cells." Silsby was, sixty years later, "still haunted by the screams at night." Otto and Misha unleashed a reign of terror:

---

three executed flyers to the Air Base Command and report that they had been shot trying to escape, while being escorted.

Storz and Andergassen took the airmen to the outskirts of the airbase, feigned mechanical trouble, and urged the men out of the vehicle. As before, everything went like clockwork. The men fired their machine pistols and killed the airmen. Or so they thought.

That same evening, March 24, 1945, Storz and Andergassen returned to the Villa Polacco. Schiffer's entire gang of underlings were present, including his boss, Major Thyrolf. Inebriated, Schiffer overheard Thyrolf bark to Andergassen, "I want your full report on this."

It was reported to Thyrolf that, unexpectedly, Medard Tafoya was only wounded and had managed to escape the execution. The bloody airman had stumbled into the arms of German authorities, who then summoned Thyrolf. The wounded flyer was returned and placed in a cell at the Corpo d'Armata.

Furious at the botched execution, Thyrolf stammered, "Do I have to go or do you want to go to get rid of him."

It was all the two stooges needed to make a beeline for the cell. Schiffer was drunk and retired to his quarters, thinking the matter resolved. However, on Monday morning it was reported to him that the wounded flyer was still alive and "it was only in the late afternoon hours Storz had finally liquidated him by a shot in the head."

It was probable that Tafoya, the man Schiffer knew to be a Jew, survived not one but two executions and, Schiffer later said, "[one] can only assume that neither Andergassen nor Storz had the courage to report to me or Thyrolf that the final liquidation of Tafoya was again unsuccessful."

Almost every night while I was there I heard the screaming in ad-joining cells in the cellblock. I also heard what sounded like blows being struck with a steel whip. During the daytime I saw coffins being carried into the cellblocks which were apparently removed at night by the jailer who had charge of my cellblock. These coffins were used for the bodies of Italians confined therein, who had either died of beatings or been strangled during the night by the SS men as-signed to the beatings.

Silsby and Fabrega's luck, however, was about to change. OSS head-quarters held secret negotiations with the commander of the SS in Italy, General Karl Wolff. Subsequently, pressure was put on Major Schiffer, preventing him from executing the two OSS operatives. Schiffer buck-led to pressure from his superiors and Silsby and Fabrega were released into the general prisoner population at Bolzano Concentration Camp, where they enjoyed freedoms they had not tasted since their capture. They were now allowed to mingle among the cellblock inmates. They soon met many internees, including a man who had once sheltered Stephen Hall. They also met Brownie's sister, whom Schiffer had cap-tured and tortured after the letter addressed to her was found on Brownie's body when he was killed.

Yet Schiffer's and Schröder's hunt for Chappell was not over, despite the fact that the OSS captain always seemed to be one step ahead of them.

35

Regrouping

By MID-MARCH, THE PLAGUE of Schröder's rastrellamento appeared to be over. Using the partisan human intelligence chain, Chappell established contact with the remaining members of Tacoma in hiding. In case of an emergency, Chappell had designated several caves at the small Italian village of Dussoi as their rallying point. One by one, Chappell regrouped his team. His first contact was with his medic, Eric Buchhardt, and so he sent a guide to Buchhardt with instructions to meet him in the grottos at midnight.

That bright moonlit night, Chappell made his way to the secret rendezvous. On the way, he passed a small osteria, and out staggered a German lieutenant. Nimbly, Chappell stepped off the road and hid in the shadows, letting the drunken SS officer pass him. Chappell described what happened next:

> When I was sure he was alone, I stepped in front of him. I was in an American officer's uniform. He stopped abruptly and stared at me. We were at least three hundred miles behind German lines. Everything went quiet. I could see he couldn't believe he was looking at an enemy officer. I would give a hundred dollars to know what was going through his mind.
>
> But I didn't have time to take chances. If a patrol came along I was sunk. I had a ski pole, which I was using for hiking in the mountain paths. I swung it on him and he went down with a broken neck. I reached inside his pocket and took out his papers. . . . [He] was a Lieutenant Mueller attached to the same outfit that murdered Brownie.

After killing the SS officer, Chappell made his way to the caves. It was a joyful reunion. Chappell fondly remembered the meeting:

> We were so happy to see each other again. I was sorry I had been unable to take better care of my men. I will always have an undying admiration for their courage and coolness in the face of danger. It is men like these who make an officer proud to say, "These are my men!"

The joyful gathering was short-lived. Chappell moved into action, plotting their next moves against the SS. After shaking hands, the medic noticed the OSS captain limping. At first, Chappell refused to allow Buchhardt to examine him:

> He would not permit me to examine him at first. However, I insisted, and found he had been hit by a bullet in his left leg. The bullet had grazed the left shin. I dressed the wound, and for a week I tried to keep him from being overactive, though he insisted on carrying on.

For Chappell, the mission and his men came first, and he would not let a flesh wound affect him. But a plan to link up with Ciccone and Delaini had to be set aside. Both men were located on the other side of a river and hard to reach. Then Chappell contacted Bruno, the same warrior who stood shoulder-to-shoulder with Tacoma at the winding mountain pass outside San Boldo, killing numerous fascists.

"When Bruno arrived with over a hundred partisans and Gigi, an Italian radio operator to replace Silsby, we were ready for business," recalled Chappell.

Chappell needed to reestablish radio contact with the Brain back at OSS headquarters in order to resupply the partisans and resume the Brenner mission. The partisan operative Gigi became the link that brought Chappell into contact with headquarters.

Luigi Feltoni, a.k.a. Gigi, came from the OSS Portland mission. Portland was part of the intelligence division known as SI (Secret Intelligence), whose mission it was to go behind the lines to gather intelligence.

The intelligence Gigi gathered ended up revealing more than they expected, thanks to Gigi's womanizing partner and mission leader, a man code-named Toni. In his postwar mission after-action report, Gigi recalled their mission:

> On February 7 Toni and myself left by plane on a mission and were parachuted in the Belluno zone. My drop from the plane was effected too far away from the dropping, so that upon landing, I had to walk two hours before reaching [the] destination. . . .
>
> In the zone where we were dropped, Toni was [already] well-known; besides, he was easy in talking with the women, and he must have told them everything, as everybody knew that I had a secret radio station. I was warned in time by a partisan messenger, who informed me that at Mel the Nazi-fascists were looking for a radio [man] and a parachutist. Therefore, I took both the radio and the encoding books, and joined the Mazzini Brigade in the mountains. Here I met Major Chappell.

Chappell described Toni's exploits more bluntly: "[Gigi's] commander [Toni] almost caused [his] capture due to an overfondness for women, wine, and song."

Regardless, Chappell now had a radio operator who could communicate with base. Using Gigi, Chappell's first radio message to Materazzi was sent March 16. Problematically, Gigi did not have proper command of the English language. Back in Siena, the Brain received the garbled message:

> Howard Wheeler Chappel to Materazi [sic]. Fabrega Silsby captured. In Belluno last info All others safe including Benucci. Buckhardt srxwht [untranslatable] wound in safe wpjcyzx [untranslatable] Chappell captured twice but safe now. Have lost all. Resupply urgent. Zone Axion. Phase Molten [sic] eve. No Signal from plane. Ground Signal T. My Signal J. Small fighter diversion attack in zone at same time drop requested. Am using Portland radio. Believe Tacoma radio captured intact. Will use my middle name in future msgs.

Chappell's use of his middle name signaled he was not transmitting under duress. Known as the *funkspiel*, or the radio game, Germans who held captured agents, usually at the point of a gun, made them play back their radios while under their control, with the hope of deceiving the other side and gaining information. The Allies did exactly the same thing—all German agents captured in England were similarly played back to the Germans. In this spy game, information, some of it true, would be sent over the air to make it appear the agent was operating independently when in fact he or she was under enemy control. Deception operations and a host of other schemes could then be attempted by the side that controlled the phony playbacks. Regardless of Gigi's garbled message and the suspicions it may have raised, Chappell still needed to get a supply drop and the radio was his only means of communication.

Toward the middle of March, Chappell finally linked up with Ciccone and Delaini. Reunited, the team stayed on the run. Unfortunately, Schröder struck again. Tacoma and Bruno's men ran into another rastrellamento. This time Schröder employed a smaller force, although the SS troops were likely armed with the intelligence Schiffer had gleaned from his interrogations and Tacoma's captured radio messages.

"They were apparently trying to secure the entire zone for good," Chappell recollected, "but were using a much smaller force because they did not expect to find any resistance."

Chappell planned to meet the Germans head-on: "We were fortunate again in having gained good points in defense and were able to keep them at long range with two Bren guns. On the morning of [March 18], about forty partisans arrived from near Vittorio Veneto, and after a great deal of firing in which no one was hurt, the Germans withdrew."

The forty added partisans helped swing the momentum of the battle, another unique situation where Tacoma and Bruno's men fought a pitched battle rather than the typical insurgent hit-and-run tactics.

✳ ✳ ✳

On the run, the team was running out of safe houses. Chappell, placing himself in his enemy's shoes, realized the most unlikely place the Germans would look was right under their noses. He had used this type of stealth before. This time, Chappell hid his headquarters directly on Major Schröder's mortar range—the same range where the booby trap a year earlier led to the violent reprisal from Schröder that had left ten partisans executed. In the middle of the night, Chappell and the partisans dug a hole ten feet long, eight feet wide, and five feet deep. They put logs over the roof and then covered them with sod, camouflaging the hole so well the team themselves had trouble getting back to the spot. For ten days, the men plotted their moves under the constant drumbeat and nerve-rattling thunder of mortar rounds detonating nearby. "They were the kind of days that were made to bring on war nerves," Chappell recalled. "Occasionally, a short one would land nearby and rattle the dirt down on us."

"The hole was about 150 yards from the main road," recalled Ciccone, "and German motorcycles and troops would pass by us every day. We were right under their noses."

36

Blow the Bridge

BY THE MIDDLE OF APRIL, only three major bridges remained open around the Belluno area. After the Air Corps destroyed one of them, only the Vidor and Busche were left. The Vidor was then destroyed by Chappell and the partisans, leaving just the Busche. Composed of nearly a thousand feet of stone arches, the Busche formed part of a vital supply artery. Down that highway and over the Busche flowed German soldiers and tanks to the front lines farther south. Traveling north, the bridge would be critical as a means of escape back to Germany. Tacoma put it in their crosshairs.

Miraculously, the Busche had seemed impervious to US Air Corps bombs. Bombers had tried to knock it out on several occasions, but their payloads never found their mark, although several had barely missed the bridge. Precision-guided munitions were still decades away, and so a single target in World War II often needed hundreds of bombers to ensure its destruction. Chappell reasoned that the only way to take it out was sabotage from the ground.

From his underground lair at Schröder's range, Chappell readied for the mission:

> Our nearest explosives were twenty miles away. We didn't have time to go get them if we were to halt the supplies the Germans were sending over the bridge. I learned that there were two dud bombs near the bridge as a result of an attempt by our bombers to destroy it. I decided to use these. . . . Intelligence reports showed there were twenty-four guards in a barracks two hundred yards from the bridge and two on duty at each end of the bridge.

Chappell audaciously planned to assault the bridge with two dozen of Bruno's partisans. Emblematic of his leadership style, he personally led the attack. Normally, a three-to-one advantage is required when assaulting a fixed, fortified position. "There were two dozen of us as we approached the bridge. I sent one crew across the river to booby-trap the road to stop reinforcements. Another group was sent against the barracks, and a machine gun crew approached each end of the bridge," Chappell recollected.

The captain hoped that proper planning, surprise, and speed would win out. After the assault team killed the main body of guards with bazookas and machine gun fire, the four remaining guards on the bridge "sniped at the partisans."

"Two of the guards scampered to the middle of the bridge as Bruno and I moved in on them with machine guns blazing. They jumped over the side and were killed in the fall. We killed the other two with gunfire."[*]

Inside ten minutes, under Chappell's and Bruno's leadership, the partisans killed all twenty-eight guards. The men were rolling one of the five-hundred-pound Air Corps bombs onto the Busche bridge when "two armored cars full of Germans" counterattacked. Chappell coolly ordered Bruno's partisans off the bridge in the event the bomb detonated, and the men hit the cars with bazooka fire, destroying them. The surviving Germans engaged the partisans and fired upon Chappell as he prepped the bomb for detonation.

I inserted some Composition C [plastic explosive] in the fuse hole of the bomb and also a ten-minute time pencil. I saw one of the armored cars blow up—a bazooka shot did it—as I moved off the bridge.

The ten-minute wait was one of the longest I have ever had. Then there was a terrific hissing sound and the sky flared out for a few seconds as the bomb burned out—it failed to explode.

---

[*]Chappell's citation for the Silver Star described his courage under fire: "With complete disregard for his own safety, Captain Chappell advanced with his sub-machine gun, engaged the guards, killing two of them and the other two jumped or fell in the ravine many feet below."

Remarkably, the men held the Busche Bridge for an hour and re-pelled a counterattack without the loss of any partisans. Even though Chappell had failed to blow the bridge, it was a remarkable small-unit action that demonstrated his hands-on leadership and derring-do.

"Full of disappointment," Chappell and Bruno's men withdrew from the bridge, now "more determined to blow it," recalled the OSS captain.

Chappell soon came up with another, more daring plan, this one re-quiring perfect timing. His first order of business was to send Bruno's partisans north to recover Tacoma's explosives from their hole on the mortar range. Chappell then waited for the perfect moment to pounce.

"I figured the Germans would guess that we were out of explosives and would try to remove the other [unexploded Air Corps] bomb. If they did that, they probably would evacuate the personnel until the salvage of the bomb was completed. I figured this would be the strategic moment to blow it."

It took Chappell's men three days to get new explosives ready. Just as Chappell had figured, the bridge was evacuated so the Germans could destroy the remaining dud bomb. On April 14, following Chappell's plan, the men mined the bridge, and the Busche was soon blown sky-high, without "the loss of a life."

With the bridge down, all the roads leading up to that point became choked with German vehicles and troops. They made juicy targets for American fighter-bombers. As Chappell recalled: "The next night, planes lit the area with flares and caught the roads chock-full of German equipment and men. They bombed and strafed it, killing several thou-sand Germans and wrecking hundreds of vehicles."

Though unaware of its details, Chappell was accomplishing Hall's plan to block the routes leading to the Brenner. He would complete the plan with the help of the countess.

37

The Trial

WAITING FOR HER CONTACT to arrive, the countess stood in the gardens of Piazza Campitello in Belluno, wearing "a beautiful scarf and a wide belt." With her flowing copper hair and statuesque figure, Contessa de Obligado commanded attention. A young woman strolled by, striking up a conversation. They spoke of local affairs, even mentioning German officials of influence. Seemingly from nowhere, several men in civilian clothing descended on the square and surrounded the two women at gunpoint.

Throughout the war, the seductive spy had walked a tightrope between the partisans and the Germans. Now, she had fallen into a trap. The talkative stranger, who had struck up the conversation, was, in fact, the seventeen-year-old Rosanna Vedana, and she had accomplished her mission—delay the countess and give partisan police the opportunity to make an arrest.

The partisans drove the countess to Ceresera di Limana—a tiny hamlet nestled on the left bank of the River Piave, three and a half miles from Belluno—and brought her into a villa inside the hamlet. To her dismay, a special court was in session. The partisan police of the Seventh Alpini were executing the orders of the Comando Zona, which was part of the partisan high command.* The Comando Zona planned to charge her and others with treason for helping broker a truce between the Val Cordevole Brigade and the Germans a month earlier. If found guilty, they would be executed.

---

*The Comando Zona oversaw the communist-led Garibaldi Divisione Nannetti and Divisione Belluno, plus the four autonomous brigades created in the fall.

Entering the court, she glanced across the room. She noticed Ettore, leader of the Val Cordevole Brigade, and a key lieutenant among the accused. Remarkably, considering they were behind the lines, the partisans permitted them to retain legal counsel.

The trial revolved around the events of March 22, when Lieutenant Georg Karl, head of the Gestapo in Belluno, which fell under the command of Majors Schiffer and Schröder, picked up an Italian noble in his private car. The two men drove from Belluno to the countess's house in Mareson, where they met Dr. Lauer, the German prefect of the region. They made arrangements for a truce between the partisans of the Val Cordevole Brigade and the Germans. The agreement was essentially a "live and let live" policy, assuring a cease-fire between the Germans and the Val Cordevole. This assured that the Val Cordevole's area of operation would become a free zone. As a result, German troops would not fight the brigade. Considering the war was nearly over, it is unclear why the countess, a French agent, would broker such a deal with the Nazis.

Several theories exist to explain her actions. One maintains that the countess's only motivation was to protect the civilians of her town against reprisals from the Germans. Another theory asserts that the countess, acting as an agent of France, was operating in her country's geopolitical interests, hoping to establish the region as a buffer between the countries.

Another concern of both the French and the British was the strength of the communist partisan movements in northern Italy. After the war, a communist takeover of the entire Italian peninsula was possible. Perhaps the purpose of the truce was to give the Val Cordevole Brigade breathing room to deal with the communists, in preparation for the postwar period. In fact, the CIA, in its first major postwar operation in 1947, would give millions in hard cash to the Christian Democrats, who "formed a government that excluded communists." Throughout wartime Italy, similar nebulous truces existed.

✳ ✳ ✳

As the court assembled, the counsel for the accused, Rafael Daval, a member of the intelligence service of the Comando Zona, instructed Rosanna Vendana to find Howard Chappell and Joseph Benucci. He knew the Americans would be the best weapon for the defense. The young Rosanna sped off on her bicycle to a beautiful Italian villa down the road. The estate belonged to a family of nobles hiding the Aztec and Tacoma teams as guests in their home.

She met Benucci inside the villa. "It was not easy to convince him to intervene. I was under the impression he was trying to stall," recalled Rosanna.

It is likely Howard Chappell broke the deadlock:

"[The trial] was such an obvious scheme to place communist leaders over non-political brigades that Benucci and myself summoned the commander to squash the whole plan," he recalled. Both men diplomatically presided over the trial. For Chappell, it was a strange twist of events that came full circle: "These two people had worked with Captain Hall . . . and had been in contact with me in January when I wanted to move north."

Without consulting the Brain or OSS headquarters, Chappell put the full authority of US missions in the area behind suspension of the sentence:

Piave Command Area
25 April 1945
Declaration:
American missions invite Command Area suspend the criminal proceedings against the commander and commissioner of the Brigade "Valcordevole" [and] the Countess De Obligado, assuming absolute responsibility.

Howard W. Chappell
Major, U.S. Army
Tacoma Mission

Chappell's intervention worked, giving Ettore, his lieutenant, and the countess their freedom. Most importantly, having secured the release of the countess and Ettore, Chappell obtained a ticket north. He quickly resurrected the scheme he had formed back in January, when he planned to take the team into northern Italy hidden in a vehicle. With a truck procured by the countess, Chappell could now travel through the German lines, getting closer to the Brenner Pass, which, in the closing days of the war, remained so difficult to reach.

38

Ticket to Ride

THE AGING WOOD-BURNING TRUCK sputtered along the winding mountain road carved and blasted into the sides of the sheer Dolomites. Snow covered the highest crags. Danger tainted the bucolic drive. A wrong turn or patch of ice could send the truck careening over the side of the mountain. It drove through a treacherous area infested with hundreds of German troops. The truck carried hidden cargo—Chappell, Buchhardt, Ciccone, Gigi (the radio operator), two radios, batteries, and their personal equipment and weapons were crammed like sardines in a tiny cavity. It was an all-or-nothing venture. The Germans planned to move into mountain positions farther north in Austria. By going north and blocking off the routes that fed the Brenner Pass, the team could cut off the main supply routes of the Germans, as well as the roads they would need in retreat.

"My main worry," Chappell explained, "was that the German retreat would reach the Alpine defenses [above the Brenner] which they had prepared and which would have been impregnable had they been manned even by a small force. Following the capture of Captain Hall, there had been no Allied officer north of the Prealps to provide resistance. I also realized it would be next to impossible to get missions near the Alps in Brunico, Cortina d'Ampezzo, Bolzano, Dobbiaco, or anywhere in that zone once the Germans manned it as a defense line."

Chappell's suspicions were well founded at the time, as the Germans were reputedly making preparations and building some fortifications in an area of the Alps they dubbed the "Alpine Redoubt." Although most of these "defenses" were nonexistent, the Nazis fed the Allies with propaganda intended to conceal their real strength. Nevertheless, it was here that the Nazi high command had plotted to make a last stand.

Stephen Hall's whereabouts still remained unknown to Chappell, and he did not know that Hall's original plan also targeted the roads around the Brenner. Sharing Hall's sharp military instincts, he was attempting to accomplish elements of that same mission. He notified Materazzi to ready the remainder of his section and prepare them to jump into Hall's old drop zone near Fontanafredda, called "Beast."

Their journey had begun on the night of April 25, 1945, in the middle of a downpour. Chappell, Ciccone, Gigi, and Buchhardt arrived at the centuries old villa, Casteldardo. In the middle of the night, a striking woman holding an umbrella greeted the men. She escorted them down the long winding road that led to the entrance. Months of being on the run led Ciccone to be suspicious of their beautiful guide: "I kept one hand close to my .45 the whole way down the road."

Upon entering the beautiful estate, the woman introduced herself as Contessa Giuliana Foscolo. Months earlier, she had nursed Aztec's team leader Joseph Benucci back to health. Through her brother, she had come to know the Contessa de Obligado. She explained that a truck would be waiting in her courtyard in the morning, and it would transport them north to Contessa de Obligado's villa in Mareson.

The team rose to the aroma of ham and eggs and ersatz coffee. Chappell's men smoked their last cigarettes and boarded the truck at five in the morning. Mario, an organ maker by trade and now a partisan working with Ettore, greeted the men. (Mario would one day become the mayor of Zoldo Alto.)

In the front cab of the truck, just behind the driver's seat, a trapdoor concealed a small hole. Chappell's men squeezed through it into a cavity made up of boxes nailed to the bed of the truck, each about three feet square.

"Chappell was a monster," Mario remembered. He couldn't believe such a man could fit through the tiny opening. Somehow, they all contorted their bodies to fit into the space.

Chappell recalled the moment: "We were fortunate that it was a dark, cloudy, rainy day. The fear of being strafed by our Air Corps was absent, leaving only the partisans and the Germans to worry about. I say partisans because it was quite possible they had booby-trapped the route we were using and might shoot, thinking it was a German vehicle."

About a half hour into the journey, the truck pulled up to the first roadblock. With ice in his veins, the driver eyed a nearby machine gun manned by a platoon of gray-clad Nazis. The corporal of the guard stepped into the road.

"Halt! Papers!"

Mario held out the documents.

"Our hearts went into our mouths," Chappell remembered, "as we heard the driver hand out his papers and say that he had been sent to Belluno to get the month's cigarette ration for the German road laborers but, finding no tobacco there, he was returning with empty boxes." If the boxes had been loaded with tobacco, the Germans may have demanded their cut and uncovered the team. The guard waved them through.

The truck creaked along the roads and approached the next roadblock. Calmly, the driver repeated the process. Handing the guards his papers, he convincingly repeated the cover story. The guards contented themselves with reading his papers and pounding the sides of the truck, waving them forward. The vehicle moved along for miles, and the icy mountains rolled by, almost frightening in their grandiose whiteness, their sheer faces sharp and frosted with snow.

Wedged between the wooden crates, Chappell looked around to check on the spirits of the other members of his team. Only one more roadblock and they were home free. The final one was at Mezzocanale, where the Germans had a small garrison of troops and a Todt construction unit building defenses. They were only a few miles from the countess's villa in Mareson. The process was once again repeated and the truck was allowed to pass.

"When we passed the third roadblock, we thought it was the last and were beginning to breathe easy," Chappell recalled.

Mario slowly put his foot on the accelerator and the truck lurched forward a few feet.

"Halt!" Machine pistols and guards surrounded the truck. In German, one of the guards barked, "Take off the tarp. We want to have a closer look."

"We lay as still as death," remembered Chappell. "We could hear the creak of the ropes as the driver untied them, then the swish of the canvas as the tarpaulin was dragged off. The chill drizzle of rain pattered down on the boxes."

"The boxes have to come off," yelled one of the guards.

Shooting their way out would be impossible for the OGs, with their arms and legs numb from sitting in the cramped space. The guards clambered aboard the truck, and one started wrestling with a box on top of Chappell's head. Several of the boxes tumbled off the back. Fortunately, the one over his head was nailed down tightly. Miraculously, a gust of wind suddenly turned the drizzle into a downpour.

"Verdammter Regen!" (Damned rain.) the corporal complained.

Chappell recalled: "We could hear the sentry jump off the truck and the crunching of the gravel, as with the previous roadblocks, [the guard] walked over to the shelter house a few yards away."

Ignoring the impulse to hit the gas and make a hasty exit, Mario calmly got out of the cab, grabbed the tarp, and nonchalantly tied the cords.

"By the time he was back in his seat and we had started slowly up the road, it seemed to be late autumn of 1946," said Chappell.

The truck rumbled up the road and within half an hour arrived at Mareson, where they pulled up to a nearby inn. Numb, yet relieved to be alive, the men crawled out of the vehicle and walked inside. Ettore and the Contessa de Obligado greeted them.

Ciccone remembered: "[Ettore] was quite a guy and the partisans worshipped him. Their spirit was very high and it was all because of [him]." Most of them were young, barely over the age of eighteen.

Ettore settled the team in their new quarters.

"It was the first time I had slept in a feather bed in months. It felt so good," Ciccone remembered.

Gigi set up the team's radio in the building's attic. As they got settled, Ciccone witnessed a ritual the partisans performed every night: "They brought down a large cask of wine and started singing Italian songs while sitting on nearby rocks. It was beautiful."

During the performance, Ettore turned to Chappell and said, "I don't have any right to tell you what to do. I'm only an enlisted man; you are an officer."

Ettore respected Chappell, not only for his rank, but also for his presence and leadership abilities. It is likely that he also felt beholden to Chappell, considering Chappell had recently saved him from execution.

The next day, Chappell and Ciccone began additional weapons training for the partisans. They were preparing for an attack on the German outpost they had just passed at Mezzocanale.

The night before the attack, Chappell ordered the partisans to take up concealed positions on the high ground above the German outpost. Their position was reinforced with several hundred men. Sensing the war was nearly over, the civilians in Mareson had also bravely taken up arms.

"As we moved down the road," Chappell explained, "all types of civilians with all types of weapons including pitchforks, hammers, and even big rocks, followed in our wake. They were anxious and eager at long last to retaliate for the murders and other outrages that had been perpetrated against them for so long a time. While it was inspiring, it was pathetic to think of these people coming to grips with a trained and skilled enemy."

Mercifully, Chappell ordered Ettore to keep the band of civilians at a safe distance. "Their courage put a lump in my throat," recalled Chappell.

When the time came, Chappell and Ettore gave the order to attack. From their concealed positions, scores of men of the Val Cordevole opened fire on the Germans. Although the German garrison outnumbered the partisans, "it soon became apparent between the fire [from the high ground and our roadblock] that the enemy was pinned in." Sensing the hopelessness of the situation, the Germans surrendered. The partisans marched them to a large "sanitarium" and placed them under guard.

With Ciccone, Chappell moved south to Selva. Buchhardt and Gigi stayed behind at Mareson with the radio. That night, Chappell received a report: "A large German force was moving north."

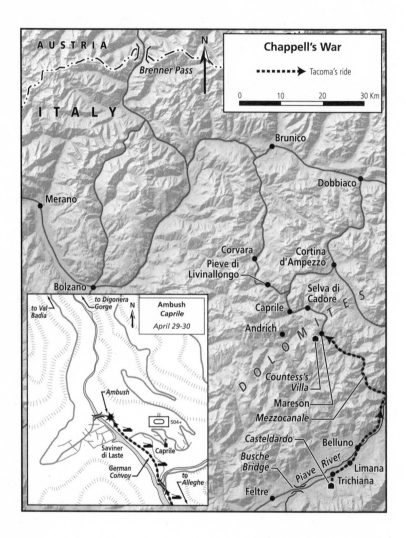

Chappell's War

------> Tacoma's ride

0   10   20   30 Km

AUSTRIA

Brenner Pass

ITALY

Brunico

Dobbiaco

Merano

Corvara
Pieve di
Livinallongo

Cortina
d'Ampezzo

Bolzano

Selva di
Cadore

Caprile

Andrich

D
O
L
O
M
I
T
E
S

Countess's
Villa

Mareson

Mezzocanale

Casteldardo

Belluno

Busche
Bridge

Piave River

Limana

Feltre

Trichiana

to Val
Badia

to Digonera
Gorge

N

Ambush
Caprile
April 29-30

Ambush

504+

Saviner
di Laste

Caprile

German
Convoy

to
Alleghe

39

Ambush

On APRIL 30, NEW ORDERS arrived by radio from the Brain:

Allies have reached the Piave. Your mission is now: an all out effort on
main route, which appears to be enemy's route of withdrawal. Cut road
in as many places as possible. Go get 'em boys. Can't be long now.

This was the kind of order Chappell lived for. If he was now ordered
to blow up the Brenner routes, why not take out a few Germans as well?

It wasn't long before Chappell had set the perfect trap for an ambush, concealing dozens of Val Cordevole men behind large boulders situated hundreds of feet above the impassable gorge of Digonera. The
gorge lay northeast of the small town of Caprile, not far from the Brenner Pass. The traffic on the road, which was cut into the mountain crags,
was painfully slow as it negotiated hairpin turns, steep grades, and rocky
obstructions. A sheer wall of dark, volcanic rock loomed above the site
of the ambush, sixty yards from a bend in the road. The partisans positioned themselves perfectly atop this natural bottleneck. Further com-
plicating troop movement north of the gorge, the route went over a small
bridge crossing the river that cut through the Val Cordevole, the name-
sake of the battalion. The tortuous route made vehicles and personnel
completely vulnerable to an attack from the high ground.

Atop the gorge, 180 feet above the road, Captain Chappell knelt by a
large boulder. He scanned the panorama below with his field glasses:
troops on foot, trucks, light tanks, and half-tracks towing the notorious
88mm antitank guns snaked their way in a column more than half a

mile long over the winding mountain roads of the Dolomites. Cobbled
into a makeshift fighting group, the men represented the remains of several of Germany's finest units: a heavy Tiger battalion, German mountain troops, and the notorious SS. The bedraggled soldiers had spent the
last several days fighting northward toward the Brenner and the perceived safety of their crumbling homeland. The Brenner, once a lifeline,
had become an escape route. Snipers, strafing Allied fighter-bombers,
and all-out combat with partisan bands now made the mass retreat back
to the Reich a journey through hell.

Field glasses in hand, Chappell primed for battle. Though he had never
read the details of Hall's plan, he was executing a fundamental element of
Operation Mercury, sealing off one of the routes feeding into the Brenner.
"We moved down the road and blew up a small bridge north of Caprile . . .
[and] set up a roadblock under the command of Ettore. . . . At this time, I
sent [another] battalion partisan commander to set up a roadblock at Alleghe about eight kilometers to the south," Chappell recalled.

As a final defense, ten of Ettore's troops held positions on the north
side of the bridge.

In the north, Ettore's men blocked the German advance outside of
Caprile. In the south, the partisans blocked any retreat by cutting the
road at Alleghe. Before they could escape through the Brenner, the Germans would have to capture the gorge and repair the bridge. The ambush represented the final resistance they faced on the ground: their
final obstacle to freedom.

The Germans were advancing into an elaborate trap.

A bony finger depressed the gunmetal trigger of an Italian Breda machine gun. With a maximum cyclic rate of over 450 rounds per minute,
the weapon spat bursts of flying lead with deadly fury. "Two skinny kids"
from the Val Cordevole did most of the damage. Sitting behind ideal
cover—huge boulders—they worked as a team, feeding one belt after another, cutting down Germans like a scythe through a wheat field. More
than 130 of Germany's elite mountain troops died within fifteen minutes.

Chappell described the carnage he and the partisans dished out:
"When we pinned the Germans down at these points, it was impossible

for them to do more than one of two things. They could fight and die, or they could surrender. When the convoy moved into the trap, they did both. As they reached our roadblock, they tried to fight. One hundred thirty of them died in fifteen minutes, and the rest asked for a truce shortly afterwards."

Ciccone remembered: "The area was littered with large boulders. It wasn't like the westerns where they could shoot you from behind the boulders . . . and when *we* shot, our bullets hit."

At last, Chappell had the Germans in checkmate. But a familiar face emerged from the convoy to try and wrench victory from Chappell and Ettore's grasp. The face belonged to the man Chappell had seen in his field glasses before the SS descended on his mountaintop hideout on the morning of March 6. Major Otto Schröder started issuing orders.

Chappell described the unfolding scene: "Looking down from the crags above, we saw the SS dragging [scores of] civilians from their houses and herding them into the [town] church."

Shortly thereafter, a German command car flying a white flag of truce appeared up the road. (The same flag still hangs in the town church today, sixty-three years later.) The car contained the town's priest and a German sergeant. The sergeant came with a message from Major Schröder, who thought he had figured a way out. The man who had hunted Chappell for the past several months, and captured Fabrega and Silsby, was delivering an ultimatum. Dumbfounded, Chappell instantly recognized the name on the message. The conniving SS officer attempted to turn the tables with a threat: "If you do not permit all German military personnel to pass, all civilians in Caprile will be executed."

Ettore looked straight at the Nazi sergeant and said, "If any of the civilians are bothered in any way, we will refuse the Germans any chance of surrender."

The priest stood nearby, weeping. He begged Ettore to change his position and spare the townspeople.

"Ettore wouldn't budge, which took a lot of guts," Chappell recalled. "I backed him up."

The command car returned to the village with Chappell's and Ettore's rebuff. Playing his final card, Schröder sent back a request for a conference. Seizing the initiative, Chappell made a quick decision.

"I'm going down there to talk to them," Chappell told Ciccone.

Chappell walked toward his beat-up German motorcycle and sidecar. Grinning, he turned to Ciccone. "Get in."

It was an audacious decision, a memorable moment, and it was classic Chappell. Their motorcycle did not carry a white flag, just Chappell and Ciccone with their .45s strapped to their legs. Chappell gunned the engine, riding down the winding path to Caprile. In the town they moved past a parked column of half-tracks, 88s, and troops. Approaching the first soldier they saw, Chappell barked in perfect German, "I want to know where your commanding officers are. I want to talk to them."

One of the men pointed to a building, the Hotel Albergo Posta. As they approached, Chappell repeated the same order. Two NCOs peeked around the threshold of the front door. Surprised to see an American officer, one said, "What can I do for you?"

Chappell repeated the request. Caught off-guard, the sergeant looked at him. "Go right in."

As usual, Chappell was fearless.

Sixty years later, Ciccone reflected on the moment: "All they could do was kill me. After everything we had gone through, I didn't give a shit if I died."

Chappell and Ciccone entered the main lobby of the hotel. Several officers stood inside, wearing smart, black panzer tunics adorned by epaulets lined with rose piping. In spite of their recent defeat, they still maintained the military bearing and discipline of German officers.

A hulk of a man approached Chappell. At six foot three, powerfully muscled with a barrel chest, Major Otto Schröder cut an impressive figure.

"I couldn't take him," Chappell recalled over sixty years later.

The OSS captain instantly recognized his formidable opponent, the German who chased him for the past several months, whose men had captured him twice. His opponent, however, did not make the same connection. The SS major, flanked by other officers, boldly sported an

American M1 Carbine. The two foes stood face to face. "I couldn't keep my eyes off him," Chappell remembered.

Chappell glanced down at Schröder's weapon, recognizing it as Brownie's carbine.*

Time stood still.

As Chappell let Schröder do the talking, he "remembered all the partisans his men hanged in the public squares on meat hooks."

Confronted with imminent defeat, Schröder asked: "What are your terms?"

"There are none. Surrender unconditionally or be annihilated," Chappell sternly responded.

In his "customary pleasing character," Schröder repeated the threat that all the civilians of Caprile "would [be] kill[ed] if the convoy was not permitted to pass unharmed."

Chappell sternly looked at Schröder. "If a single civilian is harmed in any way, we will accept no surrender."

To drive home his point, Chappell pulled out his own wild card, bluffing that an American parachute battalion blocked their advance beyond the mountains.

Breaking the stalemate, a tall, ruggedly handsome officer stepped forward. A large battle scar creased the side of his face. In English, he introduced himself as Captain Herbert Heim. At twenty-seven years old, he was the well-educated, intelligent commander of Schwere Panzer-Abteilung 504. Through battlefield attrition, he had become the ranking officer of a Tiger battalion, one of the war's most powerful units.

At full strength, Heim's battalion possessed forty-five Tiger I Es, one of the most feared tanks of World War II. At over fifty-six tons, it possessed formidable frontal hull armor with a thickness of 100mm. The Tiger I was armed with the awesome 88mm KwK 36 L/56 rifled cannon capable of piercing the armor of any Allied tank. A handful of Tigers manned by expert German crews could stop an entire Allied offensive, as German tank

---

*It is likely Brownie carried a carbine most of the time, but he was killed when he was using a BAR.

ace Michael Wittmann had proven at Villiers-Bocage in Normandy. Tiger battalions had plugged holes in the line all along the Russian front.

A member of the battalion since its inception, Heim fought during the invasion of Sicily, heroically firing upon American landing craft as they invaded the beaches at Gela. Later, he led a counterattack against the beachhead. Since the middle of April, the 504th battled throughout Italy. They launched one counterattack that pushed over seven miles into American lines, rescuing an encircled German parachute unit.

When the 504th crossed the Piave River they were mauled by a relentless aerial bombardment, losing all but one of their Tigers. Heim and his survivors had linked up with Schröder's SS unit in Belluno a few days earlier, and they began the journey north to the Pass.

Heim interjected: "We would like nothing better than to give you a good fight. But we are almost out of ammunition and food." He explained he could not see his men killed without the ability to fight back. Though outranked by Schröder, Heim exerted great moral courage: "As far as my unit is concerned," he said, "we are placing ourselves in your hands." The other officers concurred with Heim. Recognizing the war was over, he likely wanted to prevent further bloodshed on both sides.

Schröder was furious at Heim's capitulation. Not only had he surrendered the 504th, he had decided the fate of Schröder's SS troops. Grudgingly, Schröder admitted defeat. He turned to Chappell.

"Before I agree to surrender, I must know who I am surrendering to."

Chappell paused. With a sardonic grin, he replied, "Captain Howard Chappell of the OSS."

Absolutely stunned, Schröder now realized who he was dealing with. Schröder knew his prey had turned the tables. In an attempt to curry favor, he changed his tone, complementing Chappell on his Aryan looks. He said Chappell appeared Prussian with his height, blue eyes, and blond hair: "I've often heard about your bravery, and I will be happy to surrender to you personally because you are an officer and a Prussian and therefore a man of honor."

AMBUSH

Schröder stated emphatically he knew "[Chappell] would treat him and his seven SS officers exactly how they would have treated [him] had [Chappell] been captured [by Schröder]."

Chappell responded with the faintest hint of sarcasm: "This you can be completely sure of."

With Schröder's capitulation, Chappell ordered that the Germans were to be "reformed into organization[s]." All arms and matériel were to be placed in one area. Heim and his officers then returned to their troops, issuing orders to surrender.

That day, Chappell, Ciccone, and the rest of the Tacoma team, including Buchhardt, began disarming the entire group. An amazing scene unfolded, as the units formed into parade formations, feeding into endless lines that snaked through the streets of Caprile. Hundreds of men turned over their arms and munitions. The scent of oil and gunmetal permeated the town as stacks reached over six feet high. Machine pistols, grenades, machine guns, and other implements of war piled up.

In a sign of respect for his captured enemies, Chappell allowed the officers to keep their sidearms. Nevertheless, Captain Heim gave Ciccone his field glasses as a gift, saying, "Better you have them than the partisans."

Heim asked Ciccone, "How old are you, thirty?"

"No," he replied. "I'm only twenty-two."

The war had taken its toll.

*   *   *

Both sides retired for the evening. The German officers were kept together in the house of a lady who spoke German and cooked a "fine dinner" for them. One officer, who spent two nights with the SS, recalled the SS commander: Schröder the "sea dog" was a "merry man, very talkative, spinning his yarn," and "making card tricks." In an attempt to disguise their SS affiliation, the SS donned the black tanker battle jackets of the Tiger battalion.

The next morning, Heim and his men requested to be separated from Schröder and his SS officers. The regular German army officers did not want anything to do with Schröder and his ilk. It is likely they feared for their lives and wanted to be separated from the fanatical SS, which had committed numerous atrocities against the Italians.

The matter was settled by Sette, the Italian mole in the Gestapo. Ever the opportunist, he surfaced during the surrender. He lived in a village close to Caprile, and it is not known whether he was part of the advance or roaming freely due to his position in the Gestapo. Described by Ciccone as a businessman, he proceeded to identify more of Schröder's SS men in the convoy. Eventually, Sette sorted out and separated six of Schröder's SS and one unnamed SS from the army officers.

After talking with the German army officers and Heim, Chappell called in Major Schröder. "We became quite friendly and even joked about how they had once captured me. We drank a little wine and I learned the name of the spy who had disclosed my location prior to March 6. We laughed about the fact that some of my equipment had been captured and was in his and some of his officers' possession. He told me at this time that neither he nor any of his officers had ever committed any outrages and that they regretted some of the brutalities that other Germans had committed."

Schröder mentioned Fabrega and Silsby's capture: "Of course we treated them well!"

Chappell gritted his teeth. *They tortured Fabrega with electrodes.*

Schröder then smiled and said that he and his men had discussed suicide, but felt it was their duty to "go back and build a better Germany."

Chappell also smiled.

That night, all of the SS officers were reported killed trying to escape.

When he stayed at the countess's villa, Chappell had likely heard about the prisoner exchange deal the countess thought she had successfully arranged for Hall's release. He was now determined to find out what happened to Hall. However, before he could do that, he and the team could still cut off additional German units. And so, he left Caprile for Cortina.

Farther to the north, Chappell's other foe, Major August Schiffer, was trying to make his own escape through the Brenner Pass.

40

Schiffer's Run

WITH THE ITALIAN FRONT on the verge of collapse, Schiffer knew time was running out. Germany and the Nazi party, the wellsprings of his existence, lay in ruins. All hopes of catching Chappell had evaporated.

Schiffer, the hunter, had become the hunted. He knew the Allies wanted him captured and brought to justice as a war criminal. His only hope was to bury his recent past and return undetected to his family.

To escape the Allies, Schiffer had made an elaborate plan involving a man by the name of Hermann Matuell.

Matuell, a captured German noncommissioned officer trained by the OSS as a secret agent, had parachuted into Austria in April with a mission: "To organize, in Innsbruck, a few small groups of approximately five men [each] who were anti–National Socialists and who would, during the occupation of Munich by American authorities, assist in arresting party officials and other leading personalities of the party and state."

Unfortunately, Matuell's mission had a disastrous start. During the parachute drop, he lost a haversack containing some of the parts for his radio. Because he could not communicate with base, he attempted to make a prearranged rendezvous with Allied agents in Milan. After he crossed through the Brenner, German troops captured him and turned him over to Schiffer. The resourceful Schiffer saw an opportunity. He sent the Allied agent, with an armed escort, in search of the lost haversack. They found the radio parts. Schiffer then coerced him, at the barrel of a gun, to work the radio game, *funkspiel*.

In the closing weeks of April, Schiffer moved Matuell to Innsbruck, where he set up his radio in Hans Butz's apartment. Matuell went on the air and contacted the OSS. Schiffer recounted how they made the scheme realistic and plausible to the OSS: "It was agreed with Matuell that he would organize in Innsbruck, as he had been ordered, a few resistance cells which, however, I would infiltrate with my confidantes. I intended originally to use Andergassen, Hanz Butz, and Storz for this purpose. Matuell agreed."

The collapse of the German lines in Italy forced Schiffer to abandon the scheme. Days later, with the full knowledge of his superior, Dr. Wilhelm Harster, Schiffer returned to Innsbruck and attempted to hatch a more nefarious plot. With a final roll of the dice, the evil genius planned to stage a fake defection from the Gestapo in front of Matuell.

"Schiffer and another Gestapo agent, in the presence of the radio operator [Matuell], would have a fake argument which was to result in Schiffer saying that he wanted no more to do with the SS and Gestapo. That he would pass over to Matuell's side. Matuell was to be convinced that Schiffer had completely changed his mind and did not want any more to do with the SS, the police, or the entire Nazi clique," recalled Christa Roy.

During the final days of the war, the winds of the Cold War were beginning to blow, and many SS and Gestapo intelligence officers possessed skills in great demand by the Allies. Both Russia and the United States made a grab for these individuals. In one of the more shameful episodes of history, both sides secretly employed war criminals against each other. Schiffer thought he could curry favor with the OSS through the fake argument. Matuell raised Schiffer's hopes by lying and informing the Gestapo chief that his mission was to recruit Gestapo officers to fight the Russians after the war. Schiffer bought Matuell's story, perhaps hoping to demonstrate his anti-communist credentials.

Unfortunately for Schiffer, Matuell had just received an order over the radio from headquarters to stop all further activities and wait for American troops to arrive. The war was nearly over.

Abandoning the complex scheme and realizing that his only hope now was to leave Italy, Schiffer donned a single-breasted, dark-blue suit with "very thin white stripes." He fastened Stephen Hall's wristwatch to his wrist, "for safe keeping." "Always well furnished with money," Schiffer put on a belt that contained sewn-in secret compartments for gold pieces and banknotes. Finally, he grabbed a briefcase with twenty new thousand-lire notes. Embracing his mistress one last time, he climbed into a black Mercedes with Storz and Andergassen. With Storz at the wheel, on April 30, the men drove through the Brenner Pass. Despite all the efforts of Hall and Chappell to close the Brenner, their hated enemy had now made good his escape through the pass.

Arriving in Innsbruck, the men went into hiding.

41

Freedom

BEFORE FLEEING THROUGH the Brenner Pass, Major Schiffer made one final visit to Fabrega in the cellblock.

"You are to be removed to Innsbruck for your safety," he told the Spaniard.

The savvy Fabrega immediately "suspected that [he and the other operatives] were to be executed and [he] requested [to] be allowed to remain there." Somehow the Spaniard convinced the SS major that the operatives were not worth his time. Why Schiffer left for Innsbruck without harming the OSS operatives remains unknown; perhaps he was preoccupied with saving his own skin.*

Nevertheless, over the past several weeks, the prisoners had prepared for the worst. Through Chappell's contact, Sette, they smuggled "half a dozen pistols into the camp." They further organized prisoners in the event the Germans attempted a mass execution. Considering the fate of Captain Hall and Schiffer's other prisoners, such a move seemed inevitable.

The day after Schiffer left a miracle occurred. Fabrega learned that the Red Cross had offered to take over the camp with the Germans' permission, and they had agreed. Many other camps farther north, inside Germany, had no such luck. Horrifically, the Nazis relocated and executed concentration camp prisoners even as Allied armies approached within miles.

Fabrega appealed to the Red Cross delegate, Jaac van Harten, and "he interceded with the Germans for us and on April 29 succeeded in ef-

---

*It is possible that the OSS's backdoor negotiations with the SS high command prevented Schiffer from killing Fabrega and Silsby.

fecting our release." The Red Cross began to relocate the prisoners of the concentration camp to Merano, a few miles north of Bolzano. The former apple-packing plant included a large warehouse surrounded by a fence. The first day, the Red Cross evacuated a hundred Jews, and on the following day, a thousand more prisoners were taken to the plant. The mass exodus included several British POWs Schiffer had captured in April. The site was "supposedly a stopover before going to Switzerland." Fabrega, Silsby, and even Brownie's sister were finally on the verge of tasting freedom. Unfortunately, their troubles were far from over.

In the chaos of the closing days of the war, a random German patrol happened upon the warehouse. "They heard we were using the warehouse for partisan purposes," recalled Fabrega. To dispatch this perceived threat, the Germans fired their automatic weapons into the plant, though it "was clearly marked with a Red Cross."

Silsby remembers the drama:

> We saw a patrol of Germans coming toward us with full weapons. The three [British POWs] and I ducked around a corner to wait out their intentions when they started firing. They couldn't see us, so we made a break around the building and tried to conceal ourselves along the base of a wall when they spotted us. They fired on us and threw a grenade, killing [one of the Brits and wounding two others].

The British prisoner had endured Schiffer's wrath, only to receive a glimpse of freedom and be cut down by the random misfortunes of war. During the firefight, an old Jewish man courageously stepped forward, pleading with the Germans that "the building was under the protection of the Red Cross." Mercifully, the Germans stopped firing and withdrew. At that point, Fabrega calmed the evacuees inside, calling for medical aid. Dr. Pittschieler, the same man who had signed Hall's fake death certificate, appeared on the scene.

The war in Italy was drawing to a close as Howard Chappell moved north from Caprile.

42

Chappell's War

ON THE LAST DAY OF APRIL, snow still choked the roads and passes of northern Italy. In some places, the snow reached eight or nine feet. Nevertheless, Chappell set out for Cortina, Hall's original objective and the site of German HQ in the area: "In the company of two partisans, I went close to Cortina d'Ampezzo to see if it was possible to take the town. We observed much movement in the town. But because of the deep snow and the mountain passes, we were unable to move by vehicle, and so could not bring up any sizable force to accomplish this."

Chappell returned to his base at Caprile and organized "two battalions of the Val Cordevole Brigade to move north on Brunico." Meanwhile back in Caprile, Buchhardt sent the following radio message to the Brain: "Have about 1,800 prisoners and materiel being stored. Chappell now at Caprile. Road blocked at Alleghe to Caprile and of Agordo [sic]. This road can be used for Allied advance to Cortina. Request you send Hall into this zone as soon as possible."

Hauntingly, Buchhardt had requested that headquarters send in a dead man. Hall's disappearance was a mystery to the entire team, though Chappell may have thought Hall had been set free in the supposed prisoner exchange that the countess described.

On April 30, Chappell reiterated his desire to bring in his OG team, even as the war was coming to a close: "Am moving to Cortina, please get my section in quickest . . . send me gas for my motorcycle."

Chappell was on a roll. Within days he had effected the surrender of thousands of German troops. As one of the only Allied officers deep in northern Italy, the Germans gladly put their fate in the hands of an American rather than the hands of the partisans, whom they had been hunting, capturing, torturing, and hanging for the past two years.

As Chappell moved north, the Brain sent him a message with a reminder not to exercise frontier justice: "Use your influence with partisans to prevent summary execution of war criminals, asking partisans to keep them locked up until they can be properly tried. No sense sending section [Chappell's OGs] now. Would like to get German cipher machine intact. See what you can do in Cortina when it is taken. Hall not available. Your job not over when overrun. You will have to help AMG [American Military Government] disarm the partisans."

Chappell first hit Pieve di Livinallongo, where he accepted the surrender of the German garrison there. Following Materazzi's order to capture a German cipher machine intact, he surprised the German outpost at Corvara. The Germans kept a reserve officer pool and "the central telephone station" in this small northern Italian town:

> Six partisans and myself broke into the hotel and surprised a Colonel Fabian and about sixty officers at breakfast. This was before the armistice, but apparently they knew the war was about over in Italy and did not resist nor attempt to destroy any of their equipment.

However, Corvara's greatest prize also included an enormous treasure. Chappell captured the payroll for the Todt construction workers in the area. After the Nazi garrison surrendered, Chappell discovered nine metal boxes loaded in trucks. Each box contained tens of millions of lire, equaling nearly one million dollars in cold hard cash. In today's dollars, the hoard easily exceeded fifty million.

Corvara also yielded the signals intelligence bonanza requested by Materazzi: three German cipher machines, serial numbered A17204, A15407, and A2638. Chappell's handwritten notes detail the booty he acquired from several raids, including military information on every German officer who had come into Italy, money, cipher machines, and some Nazi propaganda booklets.

The men were also starting to accumulate vehicles. Chappell found a blue '39 Chevy convertible and a brand-new Fiat truck with only five kilometers on the odometer.

Meanwhile, the Allied offensive was pushing deeper into northern Italy. On May 1, Chappell learned that American forces had entered Feltre, a town twenty miles west of Belluno. He decided to link up with them in his newly liberated blue convertible.

* * *

On May 2, 1945, OSS Switzerland, under future director of the CIA Allen Dulles, effected the surrender of all German forces in Italy. The surrender negotiations had taken a month, and a great deal of skullduggery to accomplish. Beginning in early 1945, the OSS master spy contacted the SS high command in Italy and arranged for their secret surrender. The effort was nearly derailed on several occasions by the Soviets, who feared the agreement would be a separate peace with Nazi Germany rather than unconditional surrender of all German forces. Dulles finally finished up negotiations with the SS in April. A Russian general was brought in, and Russia's fears were allayed. The surrender went forward and the armistice took place on May 2. Remarkably, all German forces in Italy laid down their arms a week before the official surrender of Germany. Perhaps these early backdoor negotiations at Allen Dulles's OSS station in Switzerland had also kept Silsby and Fabrega alive.

Chappell and his men sped south to link up with Allied forces. At Mas, they encountered the vanguard of the German 26th Panzer Division. The German unit was spread along the road: vehicles, men, and tanks "for about ten kilometers with no organization. . . . They were in a state of confusion. They did not know if they were to fight or surrender." Even Chappell did not know of the armistice at this time.

Bravely, Ettore, Ciccone, and Chappell tried to repeat their successes at Caprile, Pieve di Livinallongo, and Corvara. They passed through the ranks of the division and found the command post. As he had done in Caprile, Chappell negotiated their surrender: "We learned that they had been in contact with American forces at Feltre, so after acquainting them with the fact that the roads were impassable and that there were large forces of well-armed partisan forces north of them, we left them with the understanding that they would stay where they were, intact."

Once again, Chappell's bold action persuaded thousands of heavily armed Germans to lay down their arms. With the German 26th Panzer Division out of the war, Chappell continued his journey south to link up with the Allies. The OSS operative sent a garbled message back to the Brain: "26th Armor Division surrendered three miles south ADOR [sic] Fabrega, Silsby with International Red Cross. Chappell have three cipher machines. Have huge number of materiel and weapons . . . have trouble turning him [sic] to proper authorities."

Moving south in his "borrowed" convertible, Chappell drove to Belluno. The journey was dangerous. Bands of Germans who did not know about the surrender were still roving the area, and the vehicle he was driving could be mistaken by the partisans as a German car. On May 3, he reached the 339th Infantry Regiment of the US Army, informing the commanding officer that the road from Belluno to the Austrian border was held by partisans waiting for him. "I told him they would need chains for his trucks because of the deep snow, and [gave him] other intelligence." Chappell was not finished.

At 9:00 a.m. on May 3, Chappell reached the 85th divisional headquarters, the main Allied unit in the area. With one hand on the wheel and Ciccone in the passenger seat next to him, he confidently rolled up to the checkpoint. Curious to see who was entering their perimeter, an ornery captain approached the blue convertible sedan. Chappell, bedraggled, his last haircut five months ago, "looked more like a partisan than a soldier." With classic Chappell bravado, he pretended to be a major, and with an oak leaf concealed under his lapel, he nodded at the captain.

"Why are you not saluting there, soldier?" the captain asked.

With his characteristic smirk, Chappell nonchalantly flipped up his lapel, revealing his shiny gold oak leaf. Flabbergasted, the captain smartly saluted and waved them into the division's makeshift headquarters.

Upon arriving, Chappell removed his fake rank insignia, demoting himself back to a captain. Chappell requested to see the colonel in charge of the division's G-2 (the intelligence section). He was directed to an olive drab pyramidal tent filled with the hustle and bustle of a busy headquarters. He explained his business to the sergeant in charge and requested to see the colonel. Like Rip Van Winkle, Chappell returned to the world he had left five months earlier. To catch up with that world, he sat down and picked up a copy of *Yank Magazine*. Suddenly, a powerful presence entered the room, the 85th's commanding general.

"What the hell are you doin' in here, and who in the hell are you?"

"Captain Chappell, sir, of the OSS."

"Are you a soldier? Stand at attention! Get out of this office!"

Chappell stood up, insulted. He had just spent months in the field going above and beyond the call of duty. The OSS operative turned, ready to move back north and on with the mission. Fortunately, as he was leaving the command tent, the colonel in charge of G-2 entered. The situation was rectified, as the colonel recognized the value of the captain's firsthand knowledge of the goings-on in the field.

Chappell returned to his car and began the trip back up the mountains, to attend to the unfinished business of his operation and reunite with his men.

On May 7, Chappell sent a message to OG headquarters: "Have turned about four thousand prisoners [over] to 88 Div. in Brunico. Have large supply deposits under guard all along road from Agordo to Brunico. General Michahellem commander of Todt and one thousand Todt workers turned over Brunico. Have about 80 million lire. What is the ruling about the money that partisans captured?"

Upon returning to Corvara, Chappell doled out a final order to Ciccone. The captured money had to be returned to the Italian government.

Neither Chappell nor any of the team members kept any of the money. Sixty-five years after the war, he lamented how he could have been a rich man, but "that would have been against the law." Referring to his career after the war as a drug enforcement agent: "I could have used the money to set up an effective sting."

Nevertheless, the money had to be returned.

Chappell approached Ciccone and said, "Chuck, you're going for a little drive."

"Where?"

"You're going to Siena."

Accompanied by a single man from the Val Cordevole Brigade and armed with just two Marlin submachine guns, they made the arduous trek through the mountains in the Fiat truck. Money in war-torn Italy was scarce, and the Fiat was a bank on wheels. They traveled through partisan-controlled territories, braving patrols of diehard Nazis who disregarded the German surrender and rousing bands of partisans who, had they known the contents of the truck, may have been tempted to seize it. Though new, the truck's carburetor was not calibrated for the mountainous terrain, and several breakdowns occurred. Yet somehow, the wheezing Fiat made its way back to OSS headquarters in Siena. Ciccone placed the chests of money in Captain Materazzi's office for safekeeping, until the OSS shipped the money to the Allied Financial Agency, which transferred it to the Italian government.*

Mission accomplished, Ciccone took a deep breath and pondered: "at which time I learned that the war had ended. When I fully realized the significance, I took a good shower and had a long, comfortable sleep."

---

*A receipt found in the archives obtained from the Allied Financial Agency by Col. John Riepe, Commanding officer of 2677th states: "Official count of the money 45,649,591 Metropolitan Lire and 18,000,500 in bank checks." After the war, investigators from the Italian government approached Riepe, alleging some money was missing. He produced the receipt, stating: "I'm a West Point officer and the first thing they teach you is always get a receipt." The matter was dropped. Sixty-three years after the war, the Italians have a different take on the situation. One official close to the story opined that some Italians in the area suddenly became rich.

43

Trapped

BACK IN INNSBRUCK, time was running out for August Schiffer. With the tables turned, he suddenly found himself in the same position Stephen Hall had been in months earlier—on the run with few places to hide. In an unusual end-of-the-war episode, Frederick Mayer, an OSS agent trained by Howard Chappell, persuaded the Germans to surrender Innsbruck to the Allies.* Before Allied boots occupied the city, however, members of the Austrian resistance took over. Mobs scoured the city in a hunt for Nazis. The resistance cornered Schiffer like a rat, hauled him to the local police station, and threw him behind bars.

"I made an attempt to commit suicide," the defeated Schiffer recounted, "by cutting my arteries on both wrists with a piece of glass from a bottle I found in my cell. . . . Later in the evening, I was found in my cell, bandaged. My wrists were stitched in a hospital in Innsbruck."

Over the next several days, Allied troops transferred the major from one prison to another. Finally, they transferred him to a POW camp in Ulm, Germany. Still suffering from his wounded wrists, he was admitted to a hospital in Göppingen under his real name. Using his new location to his advantage, the Gestapo major methodically plotted his final escape.

---

*Mayer had parachuted into Innsbruck months earlier and during early May convinced the Gauleiter of the area, Franz Hofer, that he could protect Hofer from war crimes prosecution if he surrendered the entire city to the advancing Allies. The bold scheme worked, and Innsbruck surrendered to Patton's army. It is also the topic of the author's next book.

44

Vendetta

ALBERT MATERAZZI AND SALVADOR FABREGA briskly pushed past rows of headstones and an old mausoleum. They moved deeper into the Resurrecturis Cemetery, adrenaline pulsing with each step as they searched for field E, row one, plot number seventeen. The tall, thin officer spotted a little white headstone engraved with a freshly chiseled *seventeen*. The Brain glanced at the forlorn Spaniard. Since Materazzi last saw him, he had sprouted a few gray hairs and developed lines of age.

Enraged, they looked down at the shallow grave.

When they investigated further, cemetery records confirmed their find. Roderick Hall's body had been hastily interred at this site. However, he did not rest in peace. Mysteriously, the grave keeper also mentioned that "the previous day two SS officers had been there to examine the grave."

Materazzi sternly looked into the custodian's eyes and issued strict instructions the grave not be touched except by proper United States military authorities. One word summed up the Brain's feelings at this moment: "Vendetta." The rage still lingered for the ninety-three-year-old veteran after sixty-three years: "I wanted to command the firing squad that executed the men who did this."

Their journey to the cemetery in Bolzano occurred during the first days of May, when Materazzi rolled out of OSS headquarters in Florence as part of the Livermore mission. Colonel Russell Livermore, commanding officer of the 2677th, was in charge. Their official objective was to represent 15th Army Group, prior to the arrival of the regular army, and protect the interests of the partisans. As the war ended, the

Allies had to deal with the many complex and sometimes overwhelming issues of an occupation. They needed to disarm the Germans and partisans alike, while simultaneously covering civil and military issues before the American Military Government (AMG) and Italian government arrived. For the Brain, the mission was personal. He wanted to find Silsby, Fabrega, and Hall.

After a two-day delay, they finally departed on May 4. The mission muscled its way up to Bolzano, using two tanks from the American 85th Division, a Dodge command car, and a few other soft-skinned vehicles.

Materazzi and Livermore rode up the winding mountain roads to Bolzano in the Dodge. They passed several Allied checkpoints and witnessed firsthand the death and debris left behind by battle. The war in Italy was over, but fighting still raged in Germany, just twenty miles north. The official surrender of all German forces would occur a few days later, on May 7.

After a four-hour trip, they arrived in Bolzano and were greeted by an officer in the US Army's 339th Infantry Regiment, the same unit Chappell had spoken with a couple days earlier at Feltre. The officer escorted them to their sleeping quarters. Ironically, they found themselves in the very belly of the beast—the drab brick barracks of the Corpo d'Armata, Schiffer's former headquarters. Over the next several days, Materazzi handled the affairs of the partisans. The young officer had a personal stake in finding the whereabouts of Captain Hall.

The mission's first success was Materazzi's reunion with two of his men. Working their way back from the Red Cross camp in Merano, Silsby and Fabrega arrived in Bolzano and greeted the Brain with a handshake and a hug. He ran into Chappell a few days after. Not surprisingly, the Brain discovered Mr. Fabrega was running the entire Red Cross operation. The two men were happy to be alive and together. The tall, lean operations officer continued to look for Hall.

The first clue in his search came from Oliver Silsby, who told Materazzi that Major Schiffer had shown him a photograph of Hall while interrogating him. With this puzzle piece, Materazzi pressed the Wehrmacht and SS headquarters in Bolzano for answers.

On May 11, the SS responded that they had "no information." However, they added, "some time in February, a 'stateless' individual known as 'Holl' had been arrested and subsequently committed suicide in prison in Bolzano." With that information in hand, Colonel Livermore personally confronted the SS high command, relating Silsby's story that Schiffer had showed him a picture of Hall. The SS dodged the issue and stated dismissively "that they would continue the investigation."

Meanwhile, Materazzi received a message from Hall's original boss, Company D commander Major Suhling, reporting that a French mission stated categorically that "Holl" was in fact Roderick Stephen Hall.

The key clue had come from a French agent—Contessa Isabel de Obligado.

The countess had survived the war by walking a fine line. Living a double life, she had been an Allied agent and also a German mayor. She had been accused of treason, but through Howard Chappell's intervention was now a free woman.

The countess was also determined to find out what had become of her lover Hall. As an Allied agent of the French, and as a woman of power and influence, she had contacted a French delegate by the name of Major de Michel when Allied authorities first liberated the area. She had urged the major to investigate Hall's disappearance.

The French officer, who served as chief of a "special French military mission," used his influence to launch an investigation. Using contacts in the SS, he uncovered the facts of Hall's murder. The French then cabled OSS headquarters and Major Suhling, clarifying that the "stateless individual" known as "Holl" was indeed Captain Hall.

Suffering the agony of a broken heart, the countess, unfairly, held herself responsible: "After the arrival of the Allies, I sent a messenger to the house of the commanding officer in order to know about Steve, and in that way learned that the OSS base had given false information to Benucci, and Benucci had transmitted it to me. I insisted no more with the Germans for an exchange and they, on seeing nobody occupied with Steve, killed him, as you know."

* * *

Back in Company D headquarters, the news of Hall's death came as a devastating blow to the survivors of the Eagle mission who had fled Italy in November and December. Joe Lukitsch, who had just returned from his second mission behind the lines in Italy, was devastated. He wrote to his future wife, Eleanor: "I lost my best friend."

Knowing that Hall was dead, Materazzi decided to search for a death certificate in the Bolzano City Hall archives. To push through bureaucratic red tape, he brought in an Italian OSS agent from the Norma mission. The agent, a lawyer by trade, knew the inner workings of the Italian bureaucracy. Combing through the records, they found what they were looking for—the death certificate leading them to the Bolzano cemetery.

* * *

The French then turned the SS against themselves. De Michel ordered Arthur Schoster, a forty-six-year-old career detective from Graz, Austria, to conduct the investigation. During the war, Schoster was a member of the Kripo, or the German state police, similar to the FBI. He knew Schiffer, Thyrolf, and Roy personally. Most importantly, he thought he knew who murdered Hall.

Schoster was a career police officer, but the Kripo came under the authority and direction of the SS when the Nazis rose to power. Though a civil official, he was ordered to wear the uniform of the SS. As a member of the Kripo, Schoster had spent most of his life cracking cases: his knowledge and expertise "were purely in the field of civilian criminology."

Schoster was ideally suited for the job, in his own words, he possessed the "knowledge of the German police system in this area and of the principals most likely involved in killing Captain Hall."

Schoster's motivations for investigating Hall's killers are unknown; however, it is possible that Schoster needed to work for the Allies in order to avoid criminal prosecution. And so, in one of the most ironic detective stories of the war, the French had unleashed an SS man, a human bloodhound, to track down Schiffer and the others responsible for Hall's death.

✳ ✳ ✳

Back in Bolzano, the Brain continued to piece together Hall's final days. The day after they found Hall's grave, Fabrega brought the camp doctor, Karl Pittschieler, to the Brain's makeshift office in the Corpo d'Armata. He was the same Dr. Pittschieler who had treated the wounded British POW shot by the Germans at the apple-packing plant in Merano on the last day of the war in Italy, and who had signed Hall's death certificate. Fabrega escorted the doctor to the Brain, vouching for his integrity, explaining that he had treated the inmates at the camp well and that he had been forced to serve the SS at the concentration camp. In Materazzi's drab office, Pittschieler brought to light several key details surrounding Stephen Hall's murder.

Pittschieler explained that he had created material evidence implicating the principal murders. On February 20, he explained, Nazi officers had approached him at the concentration camp with Hall's body, asking him to determine whether he was dead. In accordance with Italian law, the doctor needed to record a cause of death on the certificate. In a stroke of genius, the doctor had "invented 'cardiac paralysis' as the cause" in order to highlight foul play for any future investigators. There was no such thing as cardiac paralysis, he explained.

Materazzi collected all of the information he had gathered and rode back to OG headquarters in Florence to pass it along to OSS officials investigating the case.

✳ ✳ ✳

Fifty miles east of Bolzano, late spring snow was melting in the hamlet of Andrich, revealing the gray-green bottles Hall had hidden months earlier. Howard Wheeler Chappell looked down at the bottle in his hands. Uncorking the vessel, he unrolled a letter from the man for whom he had searched for so long—the impetus of his mission. The letter, written by Hall to his father, was clearly written by the young soldier under extraordinary circumstances. He might have known that these would be his last words.

As Chappell read about the mundane work of occupation duties, disarming partisans, handing out medals, and organizing parades, it all seemed unimportant. Yet he needed to know what happened to this brave brother officer in the field. More importantly, he needed to know who was responsible for his disappearance. Since arriving at the countess's villa in Mareson several weeks earlier, Chappell had interrogated anyone with any possible connection to Hall and the events that led to his disappearance. The countess likely revealed the misinformation she had received through Benucci and the Germans, namely, that Hall was released in a prisoner exchange. The priest who rescued Hall from hypothermia, the partisans, the downed airman who saw Hall off on his final mission—each gave Chappell pieces of the puzzle. Chappell had left no stone unturned. Ciccone remembered, "We even interviewed the Germans. No one knew where he was." The contents of the bottles provided the first significant break in the case. But before tackling Hall's disappearance, he received word that Fabrega was in Bolzano, though Silsby and Delaini had already left for Siena.

Chappell did not waste any time driving up to the Corpo d'Armata in his commandeered blue convertible. Arriving in Bolzano, Chappell tracked down his war-weary but proud comrade. With a slap on the back and a joyous glint in his eye, he exclaimed, "Mr. Fabrega!"

The two warriors triumphantly rode back to Cordova. Driving down the winding mountain roads, Fabrega discussed his ordeal at the hands of Major Schiffer. They arrived at the makeshift base. Smiling grandly, Chappell pulled up to Ciccone in the convertible. "Chuck, look who I got."

Fabrega got out of the car and kissed Ciccone on both cheeks, giving him a big bear hug.

"It's so good to see you!" Ciccone said to Fabrega.

Chappell turned to Ciccone. "Hungry?"

"No, I'm not hungry."

VENDETTA

Chappell then looked Ciccone straight in the eye. "Give me your .45."

Ciccone untied the lanyard and gave him the pistol and web belt, along with two clips of ammunition. Chappell and Fabrega disappeared. Chappell, who was looked upon as a demigod by the partisans, now seemed to morph into an avenging angel.

What occurred will never be fully known. However, armed with knowledge from sources such as Sette—and haunted by the letter in the bottle—Chappell scoured the Italian countryside with Fabrega, looking for anybody who had anything to do with Hall's death.

On May 14 he found his quarry. He sent a message to OSS headquarters, an update on his administrative duties in the area, with a cryptic twist:

> The enemy spy who turned in Captain Hall [was] captured 12 May. . . . I was taking him to Feltre when he tried to escape and was killed.

Chappell's handwritten notes, dated two days later, shed greater light on the interrogation of the "enemy spy who turned in Captain Hall":

> [Tell] captured by Germans in hotel in Caprile. [Germans] Used electric treatment to make him identify pictures. Germans had real names of 13 men and he [Tell] supplied battle names. He did not give location of four men who he knew. He then told Germans to hunt for these men. On 22 November, captured 12 men. 26 November captured two more prisoners. After this, Germans took him to Belluno also looking for Hall. But Hall escaped. First time Germans did not know about Hall, but second time he [Tell] gave info and led Germans to where Hall was at. But Hall was not there [November 22]. He [Tell] admits that he gave Germans all this information. Hall had escaped to Fonta[naf]redda, but Tell declared that Hall had been living in the house. House and owner were not disturbed for reason unknown. From November 26 till December 25th, he was sent to Cortina. Till February 27 at Cortina, worked in prison during this

- 229 -

time. During this time he [Tell] was helping Germans find [partisan] ammo dumps in mountains. Also took Germans where he knew Hall had been three times.

Chappell and Fabrega returned to the camp in mid-May, and Chappell was not done. He continued his mission, searching for information on anyone else with Hall's blood on their hands, including the forester who had turned in Hall while he was recovering from hypothermia in the priest's quarters in Cortina.

※　※　※

Meanwhile, the Aztec and Tacoma missions were "turning in prisoners, equipment, and information to the proper authorities."

Chappell sent several radio messages back to base requesting the remainder of his section. Two of his men came via truck, along with a new radio operator to replace Gigi, the Italian operator borrowed from the Portland mission. He sent one final piece of information regarding Hall back to headquarters: "Tell, former aide to Hall and later traitor, killed night of April 17. Have complete info on all of Hall's movement. Including death."

Chappell did not want his war to end. When Materazzi ordered him to bring his team south to OSS headquarters, he requested a two-day extension.

Materazzi shot down the request, later adding: "I practically had to threaten him with court-martial to get him out of there."

Tacoma's final radio message from Materazzi was blunt: "Your request for a two day delay is not approved. You will leave there no later than Tuesday morning, May 22." Additionally, Materazzi sent another surprising message: Chappell's exploits had reached the Man himself. "Donovan wants you to be prepared to give full story." The head of the OSS was interested in Chappell's story, which would later become very significant to the future of the spy organization.

Meanwhile, the survivors of the Tacoma and Aztec teams loaded a truck full of champagne. Before departing, Chappell said good-bye to friends he had forged in battle. He shook hands with Ettore and Bruno. He also gave the partisans some of the captured money to build a memorial for Brownie, who had given his life for Italy and the mission.

Before boarding the truck, Chappell made one last gesture. He said good-bye to the countess, making sure she possessed the means to start a new life. Shortly afterward, she disappeared in the same mysterious manner in which she had arrived in 1942.

Victorious, the teams rode back to OSS Headquarters Siena in their truck loaded with champagne.

45

War Crimes Case #36

BACK IN FLORENCE, Materazzi, Tacoma, Aztec, and the other OSS operatives savored victory in Europe with wine, women, and song. Chappell, Fabrega, and Benucci toured Venice. It was a nice break from the war, but for many of the men, internal conflicts still raged below the surface. Like most soldiers who have tasted battle and loss, a part of them remains where they fought.

Sometime in the first week of June, following a directive from Donovan, Chappell and the other members of the Tacoma team spent days preparing a report of their activities. While the memories were fresh, they relived the mission in their own words, putting the details to paper. Hundreds of the team's radio messages, memos, and plans went into the files, where they remained classified for decades.

Nevertheless, Hall's murder investigation continued. The Brain compiled a report of his findings. Chappell also completed a report and gave the war crimes investigators all the evidence he had found, such as Hall's letters and diary from the bottles. The evidence, combined with Kripo investigator Schoster's work, became the heart of War Crimes Case #36.

First, the prosecutors identified the key suspects, putting together what amounted to an all-points bulletin for Schiffer, Storz, Andergassen, Thyrolf, and Christa Roy. Allied counterintelligence agents scoured the camps and POW cages holding former soldiers of the Reich. Several of the larger fish such as Thyrolf and Harster seemed to vanish. Ukrainian camp guards Otto and Misha, and the "Tigress" of the Gries Concentration Camp, Hildegard Lächert also disappeared.*

---

*Hildegard Lächert was later apprehended, tried, and convicted. More recently, the camp guard incarcerated at Bolzano for brutally raping an Italian woman, Misha, was

The Allies cast a dragnet across the territory occupied by the US, British, and French forces. One by one, Counter Intelligence Corps (CIC) agents started hauling in Hall's murderers. The 206th CIC Detachment snared the first, Heinrich Andergassen, on May 8 outside Innsbruck.

As the suspects were apprehended, authorities brought them back to Bolzano, where Kripo investigator Arthur Schoster interrogated each one in turn. In their own words, without being tortured, they revealed what happened in February 1945 in the Corpo d'Armata. Schoster asked the right questions, and each story was cross-checked. He eventually obtained signed confessions spanning scores of pages.

Stephen Hall's final days were beginning to emerge, and the Allied dragnet was closing in on August Schiffer.

---

extradited from Canada to Italy, where he began serving a life sentence for war crimes.

46

On the Lam

AUGUST SCHIFFER RELAXED in his hospital bed, pondering his next move. Hospital staff periodically handed him questionnaires regarding his service in the Nazi party. As an expert interrogator and spy handler, he knew how to deceive. With exceptional guile, he gave a series of half-truths, stating he merely held the position of a German police captain. With a clever flick of the wrist, Schiffer changed the year of his entry in the Nazi party from 1925 to 1937.

"I knew," Schiffer explained, "that in the case that I would give my real profession and correct date of my joining the party, I would be interned immediately. . . . I wanted under any condition to go see my family, even if I counted on being interned sooner or later and so I put everything on one card and tried, even by making false statements, to be discharged after my convalescence. I succeeded in this because on September 6, 1945, I was discharged from the hospital in Göppingen with a regular discharge paper bearing my own name."

Before he left, the SS officer had sewn sleeping tablets into his socks. He preferred death over capture. Walking and hitchhiking, Schiffer made his way back to his hometown of Bad Hersfeld, near Kassel, where his wife and children were waiting. The joyous reunion, however, lasted only a couple of days. He was arrested on September 9, 1945, by Allied counterintelligence agents. Shortly after his arrest, Schiffer unwrapped the lethal dose of sleeping pills he had concealed in his socks. In a final attempt to escape justice, he swallowed the pills.

47

Home

AFTER TURNING IN COPIES of Hall's letters and diary for the case, Howard Chappell reverently placed the originals in his musette bag. While the war still raged in Japan, the team was ready to go home. Chappell, Silsby, Fabrega, Materazzi, and the rest of the OSS teams traveled to the port of Naples, where they boarded a troopship for the long journey to America. In mid-July, after several boring weeks at sea, they arrived in Norfolk, Virginia, exuberant to have survived history's deadliest war. Upon disembarking, one of the men joyfully kissed the ground.

The OSS operatives boarded trains for Washington, D.C., where most received passes to go home on leave. Chappell, however, received orders to report to San Francisco.

In a forgotten bit of history, he began training a Japanese American operational group to drop behind Japanese lines. With the atomic destruction of Hiroshima and Nagasaki in August 1945, Japan surrendered and the need for a Japanese special ops team thankfully vanished. After more than four years of service, Howard Chappell was finally going home—but not before being summoned to Washington, D.C., Chappell, Stephen Hall, Lloyd Smith of the Eagle mission, Joe Lukitsch, Oliver Silsby, and Salvador Fabrega were about to be decorated by General Donovan.

✻ ✻ ✻

Though the dark cloud of the Cold War hung ominously on the horizon, America was disarming. Divisions demobilized and plants stopped producing weapons, as America reverted to a peacetime economy. The OSS, also faced disbandment as World War II drew to a close.

The Cold War would largely become an intelligence war, fought between spies and special operations units, but the sources and methods painstakingly learned in the OSS were about to be thrown out the window.

Regardless of the valuable experience OSS operatives had accumulated, the OSS had become a political football. Particularly problematic were the known communists who had operated within the agency during the war. Several of Stephen Hall's operations officers, who were not active communists—yet worked with communists in the Italian resistance—were soon standing in front of a congressional committee. Ominously, Hall and Smith had exposed some of the problems that would be faced by the Allies who were working with the communist resistance.

Due to an extremely negative report from US Army Major General George Strong and some backbiting by FBI director J. Edgar Hoover, the OSS was soon on the verge of being disbanded. The OSS fought back through the media, releasing bits and pieces of its secret history. The American public needed to understand what the OSS accomplished during the war and why a Central Intelligence Agency was needed to fight the Cold War. The OSS would also recognize some of its greatest heroes.*

---

*Harry Truman issued Executive Order 9621, disbanding the OSS, on October 1, 1945. Nearly two years passed before the CIA was created.

48

Atonement

SCHIFFER'S BID TO END his life failed. Allied authorities arrested him and brought him before Schoster, who put him under an interrogatory knife wielded with the precision of a brain surgeon. In most cases, the SS officer truthfully answered the questions, claiming the obligations of duty and orders. Displaying a measure of loyalty, he refused to implicate his superiors, claiming he acted alone when he killed Hall and the others.

Schoster, the OSS, and the office of the US Army Judge Advocate carefully built War Crimes Case #36. The investigation stretched on for several months.

One by one, they brought suspects into an office building in Bolzano. Most of the individuals involved with torture and murder at the concentration camp came under interrogation, plucked from the area around Bolzano. Others were apprehended in Germany. Although the dragnet had captured most of the suspects, Schiffer's superiors Thyrolf and Dr. Harster could not be found. Even some of the smaller fish such as individual Bolzano camp guards were never found and would vanish for decades.*

---

*During the waning days of the war, Thyrolf and Schiffer participated in discussions regarding the Werwolf movement in the Bolzano area, which developed into a postwar German guerrilla organization composed of fanatical Hitler Youth and die-hard SS troops. The organization continued the fight against the Allies even after Germany officially surrendered. Various secret underground Nazi movements persisted, transporting the SS and Gestapo men out of Germany and finding them refuge in South America and Middle Eastern countries such as Syria and Egypt. The most famous of these secret Nazi organizations, Die Spinne, was founded by Hitler's SS übercommando Otto Skorzeny. Notably, Die Spinne also took advantage of the Brenner Pass, using a series of secret safe houses to spirit wanted Nazis out of postwar Germany to "escape either to Rome by land or Genoa by water." It is not known for certain whether he used Der Spinne connections to escape, but Thyrolf vanished without a trace.

After they apprehended Christa Roy, she gave a statement running approximately twenty pages. During the interrogation, she attempted to manipulate Schoster, stating she was under orders and was now a reformed Christian. The OSS official documenting the case noted:

> Apparently, Miss Roy is willing to tell everything she knows without reservation. Her own reputation in Bolzano, however, was far from savory, and she is reported to have been the 'Queen of the Gestapo.' She is very shrewd and, according to Schoster, a dangerous woman. I myself have seen that her physical attractiveness and physical charms have in several cases had the power of confusing certain American officers and operatives in this area to the point where they were unable to distinguish between their glandular and official functions.

It is more than likely that Christa Roy used her powers of seduction and deception to connive her way out of prosecution.

On January 9, 1946, August Schiffer, Heinz Andergassen, Albert Storz, and Hans Butz were brought to trial in Naples before a military commission. Hall's diary and letters became material evidence in the case. Hall had devised the Brenner plan in a letter, and now his letters were used to condemn his murderers. All pleaded not guilty to the charge of violation of the law of war. Specifically, they were charged with having "wrongfully, and contrary to the law of war killed summarily Captain Roderick S. G. Hall, an officer of the Army of the United States who had been captured and was a prisoner of war, by causing him to be hanged by the neck until dead." The same charges were leveled against the accused for the unlawful deaths of flyer Charles Parker and SAS officers Roger Littlejohn and David Crowley, as well as American airmen George Hammond, Hardy Narron, and Medard Tafoya.

All the men claimed they were following orders. Schiffer claimed he was following Hitler's Commando Order. Andergassen and Storz would later make appeals to the commanding general of the Mediterranean Theater and to Pope Pius XII.

The trial concluded on January 15, 1946. The accused were found guilty and sentenced "to be hanged by the neck until dead." Only Hans Butz, Schiffer's "lifelong" friend, received life in prison.

Andergassen and Storz stated they were following the orders of the "Secret Reich Operation," claiming the following:

> In the submitted case the subjects are saboteurs and terrorists who should not be regarded as prisoners of war or dealt with as such. The Supreme Command orders their execution. You well know that saboteurs and terrorists are to be executed. What I ask you to do is no crime. What you are ordered to do, you do for Germany. Since we have no other possibilities and the order was a "Secret Reich Operation," to shoot them on their way to escape and then deliver them to the Wehrmacht for burial.

After exhausting their final appeals, Andergassen, Storz, and Schiffer were brought to the gallows in Livorno, Italy. They were hanged on July 26, 1946.

49

Full Circle

SEPTEMBER 22, 1945, turned into a sunny day. Twenty-seven members of the OSS's finest gathered for an awards ceremony, standing in front of the Q building in muster formation. Smartly dressed in khaki uniforms, the men were called to attention. Before them, the figure of Major General "Wild Bill" Donovan appeared, walking ramrod-straight in his four-pocket green dress uniform. He spoke briefly to the men, congratulating them for their outstanding heroism behind the lines. In formation they revealed no emotion, stoic with military bearing. Chappell, a striking and muscular figure in his service khakis, dwarfed the larger-than-life Wild Bill. The general pinned the Silver Star on the pocket of his barrel chest. The medal had been downgraded from the Distinguished Service Cross, though Chappell arguably merited the Medal of Honor.

The OSS awarded Fabrega the Distinguished Service Cross. Silsby, Ciccone, and Lukitsch, Hall's best friend, received the Bronze Star. Eagle mission leader Lloyd Smith received the Legion of Merit. The OSS posthumously awarded Stephen Hall the Legion of Merit.

After the ceremony, the men of the missions parted ways. Ciccone and Chappell remained lifelong friends, but Fabrega and Buchhardt disappeared.

Chappell refused to discuss the mission with anyone, including his family, for the rest of his life.*

---

*After the war, Materazzi and Chappell became best friends. Only through Materazzi's arm-twisting did Chappell agree to speak with the author, one of the few people with whom he ever discussed the war.

Before departing for a long overdue leave, Howard Chappell made a phone call to the resident of 2301 Columbia Road, Washington, D.C. He arranged to meet Stephen Hall's father, Ray, at the Statler Hotel. Ironically they met at the very hotel where Hall, Lukitsch, and Eleanor enjoyed their rooftop farewell celebration. They sat at a table in the hotel restaurant. Without a word, Chappell reverently opened his musette bag. Reaching in, he pulled out copies of Stephen Hall's letters and gently placed them in Mr. Hall's hands.

"Your son was a hero," he said.

With a tear in his eye, Hall's father nodded. "I know."

50

Sunrise

The countess returned to where it had all begun. The villa stood exactly as it had during the war. Tucked into the side of the mountain in the tiny hamlet of Mareson, two comrades in arms from the Val Cordevole met the countess. The first light of Christmas day 1945 peeked over the gray-faced mountain.

The group stood in front of an ancient larch where Hall had leaned his skis before entering the house. A plaque rested gently in her hands. The circular brass disk, fashioned from a six-pound cartridge, was elegantly engraved with an inscription:

CAPTAIN STEVE HALL

FROM WASHINGTON

FALLEN FOR HIS COUNTRY

CHRISTMAS 1944

They carefully fixed the plaque to the trunk of the great tree, facing east. Their thoughts drifted back to Hall. One at a time, the countess and each officer took turns firing twenty shots each, the carbine raised to the heavens.

"Sixty shots, all in honor of Steve," the countess said.

Walking away, she turned and looked back at Hall's tree, "which bears at its heart the great plaque facing the sun—rising in his memory."

CAST OF CHARACTERS

Andergassen, Heinrich "Heinz," Gestapo henchman to August Schiffer. He was hanged from the gallows, July 1946.

Benucci, Joseph "Joe" "Capo," Captain, OSS, Aztec Mission Commander. He died after a long postwar career as postmaster in Newark, NJ.

Brunetti, Paride "Bruno," partisan commander, Mazzini Brigade. After the war, he enjoyed a successful career in Italy, living in the Milan area.

Brunner, Karl, SS Brigadeführer. He eluded prosecution after the war and was never heard from again.

Buchhardt, Eric, Technician Fifth Grade, OSS, Medic, Tacoma Mission. He was last seen by his comrades in 1945.

Chappell, Howard Wheeler, Captain, OSS, Tacoma Mission. After the war he became a leading drug enforcement agent for the Federal Bureau of Narcotics (FBN). Fearlessly pursued leading mafia kingpins such as Mickey Cohen.

Ciccone, Charles "Chuck," Staff Sergeant, OSS Weapons Specialist, Tacoma Mission. After the war, he worked for a major telephone company and raised several children.

Davare, Ettore, partisan commander, Val Cordevole Brigade. He died in 1948, most likely of a heart attack.

de Obligado, Countess Isabel, Mayor of Mareson, possible double agent and spy in the service of France. After the war, she mysteriously disappeared. Her last known address: Buenos Aires, Argentina.

Fabrega, Salvador, Technician Fifth Grade, OSS, jack of all trades, swindler, and master scrounger. He was last seen by most of his comrades in 1945. He allegedly carried with him a large and heavy chest on the homebound ship, which he guarded carefully, and then disappeared. He is buried in Texas.

Hall, Roderick Stephen Goodspeed, Captain, OSS, Mercury mission.

Harster, Dr. Wilhelm, lieutenant general and superior to August Schiffer, in charge of SS and Gestapo in northern Italy. He was captured May 10, 1945, and was sentenced in 1949 to twelve years, serving only four. He was convicted again on other charges in 1967 and was sentenced to fifteen years but was pardoned two years later. He died in 1991.

Karl, Georg, lieutenant in charge of Gestapo in Belluno. He was captured May 8, 1945, but was never seen or heard from again.

Lächert, Hildegard "Tigress," Bolzano camp attendant. In 1947 she was sentenced to 15 years for her war crimes at Auschwitz and Plaszów, and in 1981 she was sentenced to 12 years for her war crimes at Majdanek. She died in 1995.

Lukitsch, Joseph, Lieutenant, OSS, Eagle mission and Stephen Hall's best friend. After this war, he went on to have an illustrious military career, including service in two more wars. He became a successful teacher and father and died in 2005.

Materazzi, Albert "The Brain," Captain, Mission Operations Officer, OSS Headquarters Italy. After the war he entered the cartography business, working for defense intelligence agencies. He became a historian of the OSS missions in Italy and has helped countless researchers and academics. He died in March 2008. In the final weeks of his life, he was tirelessly researching World War II, trying to find the countess, and writing a final article.

Palman, Aldo "Brownie," partisan, killed fighting for his country in March 1945.

Roy, Christine "Christa," stenographer and mistress to August Schiffer. After the war, she successfully eluded prosecution, using her powers of seduction, and disappeared without a trace.

Schiffer, August, Major, Bolzano Gestapo. Hanged from the gallows, July 1946.

Schöster, Arthur, Kripo investigator who helped to take down Schiffer and his henchmen. He later became part of Germany's post-war police force.

Schröder, Otto, Major, Gestapo. He was reported shot trying to escape in 1945.

Seifert, Michael "Misha," camp guard. In 2008, he was extradited from Canada to Italy to begin serving a life prison sentence.

Sette, Italian policeman, driver and mole within the Gestapo. After the war, he disappeared from the Bellano area and moved south to Tre Viso, where he served as a policeman.

Silsby, Oliver M. "Stretch," Corporal, OSS, radio operator, Tacoma mission. After the war, he became CIA station chief for the Middle East. He died in 2006.

Storz, Albert, Gestapo henchman to August Schiffer. He was hanged from the gallows, July 1946.

"Tell," partisan commander and one of Stephen Hall's confederates. He was reported shot trying to escape in 1945.

Thyrolf, Rudolph, SS Major. After the war he eluded prosecution and was never heard from again.

NOTES

The genesis of *The Brenner Assignment* began more than seven years ago. Combing through dusty files at the National Archives, I found an original copy of the wartime exploits of the Tacoma Mission, written primarily by Howard Chappell. Instantly, I was drawn into the document and what happened behind the lines. This book is written from thousands of documents that come from the National Archives, private collections, and scores of oral histories with the original participants. First we will identify the primary sources and their locations, and then use abbreviations throughout the endnotes that identify their location.

TACOMA MISSION FILE (TACOMA)

The first large group of documents comes from Tacoma, located at the National Archives and record administration in College Park, MD. The Tacoma files include all the incoming and outgoing radio messages sent by the team, as well as individual accounts written by Tacoma team members Howard W. Chappell, Oliver Silsby, Chuck Ciccone, Salvador Fabrega, and E. Delaini. In an almost biblical manner, each account buttresses the other while telling the individual's own perspective. National Archives Record Group 226, Entry 99, Box 45.

MERCURY/EAGLE MISSION FILE (MERCURY)

The file is broken down into two major portions: The original Eagle Mission report, located in National Archives Record Group 226, Entry 190, Box 136. Large portions of the file are also located in Record Group 226, Entry 154 and Box 52. This section contains the majority of the Eagle and Mercury plans and after-action reports, written by Major Lloyd Smith.

WAR CRIMES CASE #36 (WC#36)

War crimes case #36 is located at the National Archives and was an extensive case file used to bring the Nazi war criminals who executed Stephen Hall and other Allied agents to justice. This section contains literally thousands of other documents. The heart of the book comes from the section that includes Stephen Hall's original diary and letters, which were entered into evidence against Gestapo chief August Schiffer and his henchmen. The letters are also located in the director's file maintained by William Donovan located at the National Archives as well. The testimony and depositions that span hundreds of pages provide us the German viewpoint in their own words. War Crimes Case #36 is located in Record Group 492, Entry 246, Box 2059.

AZTEC MISSION REPORT (AZTEC)

The Aztec Mission Report includes a detailed summary of the Aztec Mission and all incoming and outgoing radio messages. The report is located at the National Archives, Record Group 226, Entry 143, Box 10.

MATERAZZI PAPERS (MATERAZZI)

This book would not be possible without the help of my good friend the late Albert "the Brain" Materazzi, who spent decades amassing thousands of documents on the missions that he personally coordinated and oversaw as the Operations Officer. His collection included copies of Hall's original letters, letters from the Countess about Hall, and correspondence from him to his best friend Howard Chappell. His files also contained correspondence with Charles Ciccone, Eagle Mission leader Lloyd Smith, and numerous letters from Italian partisans who worked with the Allied missions recounted in this book.

ORAL HISTORIES (OH)

Over the past six years, I interviewed every surviving member of the Tacoma Mission. Beginning in 2000, I interviewed Howard Chappell. Telephone interviews typically spanned no more than twenty-five minutes and abruptly ended with, "Well, we'll talk about it more when you come here one day." It was a polite brush-off. I finally took him up on his offer in the Summer and Winter of 2006, and spent several days at his home interviewing him—even on (I did not know at the time) his deathbed. Remarkably, Howard's memory was clear and he confirmed many details of his incredible exploits behind the lines. His memory also jibed with the original

Tacoma Mission report and all of the radio transmissions that accurately recorded to the smallest detail some of his most incredible exploits. I also spent a delightful and long weekend with "Chuck" Ciccone, at his home near Cape May. Chuck's incredible memory fleshed out many of the team's experiences during the final ambush. Furthermore, I spent many hours with Tacoma's radio operator Oliver Silsby, who confirmed Chappell's heroics.

For the Aztec mission, I interviewed First Sergeant Nick Cangelosi extensively over a six-year period of time. Overarching the entire Tacoma and Eagle Mission reports were my monthly interviews with Albert Materazzi, who understood the big picture as well as minute details on the missions.

Partisans who served with Chappell and Hall behind the lines were also consulted. I went from village to village in the mountains of Northern Italy, gathering their stories and filling in the Italian viewpoint. I also consulted several historians in the area who are experts on the missions.

PROLOGUE

The contents of the prologue come from the author's extensive interviews with Howard Chappell. Interestingly, details of the note being found in the bottle are also contained in a list of evidence "Letter found in a bottle" contained in the extensive files of War Crimes Case #36 (WC#36). A deposition from the women who found the letter is also located in (WC#36)

CHAPTER 1: LETTER TO DESTINY

1   "Letter to Destiny" Hall's original letter to the OSS is located in the "Wild Bill" Donovan's "Directors File." Interestingly enough it can also be found on the CIA website.

Hall's bio was taken from his original personnel records located at the National Archives in St. Louis.

The author also located his grades and other personnel information from the staff at Andover prep school.

I gathered details about Hall's exploits with the 270th engineer battalion from oral histories of the surviving members of the 270th S-2 shop who ran into Hall during the war. Background on the OSS comes from an oral history I wrote on the OSS: Operatives, Spies, and Saboteurs (New York: Simon and Schuster, 2004).

7   "Big league professionals in shadow warfare" Richard Dunlop, *Donovan: America's Master Spy* (New York: Harper & Row, 1968), 276.

7 "The OSS undertook and carried out more different types of enterprises" OSS, *Assessment of Men: Selection of Personnel for the OSS* (New York: Rinehart & Company, 1948), 10.

7 "Sabotage, Fifth Column activities, and other forms of subversive action." OSS *Organization and Function.* (June 1945), NA: Record Group 226, Entry 141, Box 4.

8 "Instruction of agent personnel recruited for infiltration" *War Report of the OSS.* (Walker and Company, New York: July 1975.) The publisher nearly printed verbatim the original OSS office's report on the OSS's activities behind the lines.

All quotes on Hall's activities and hand-to-hand combat come from original OSS training documents used on pages 1–14 in my book *Operatives, Spies, and Saboteurs.*

11 "A strong, quiet, confident looking man, a man with a mission." Oral history interview with Eleanor Lukitsh, who also provided details on Joe Lukitsch and Stephen Hall's last days before leaving for the war.

CHAPTER 2: "LOOKING FOR TROUBLE"

All quotes in this chapter come from the author's oral history interviews with Howard Chappell and were confirmed by hundreds of other paratroopers the author interviewed for his prior works. Chappell's bio comes from the National Archives in St. Louis.

CHAPTER 3: ODYSSEY

18 "During the general quarters alarm, you will clear the decks … Calisthenics, close-order drill, and hikes" V-Mail letters from Joe Lukitsch to his great love Eleanor Lukitsch. *(Letters courtesy of Eleanor Lukitsch)*

CHAPTER 4: DESPERADOS

21 "The whole bunch were the craziest people I've ever met in my life" Oral history interview with B. Stevens.

22 "Aggressiveness of spirit and willingness to close with the enemy" Kermit Roosevelt, War Report of the OSS, Vol. 1, p. 224. This is an official history of the OSS produced by President Roosevelt's son, Kermit, and other former OSS personnel shortly after the war. The study (in two volumes) remained classified for decades, and is now available in the National Archives.

All quotes regarding Salvador Fabrega or the German Operational Group (OG) come from oral history interviews with Howard Chappell and were confirmed with oral history interviews with Chappell's fellow teammates.

26 "We called him Fuck-Up. He was very good as a radio operator." "Soldier let me have it" From oral history interview with B. Stevens.

CHAPTER 5: THE PLAN

29 "[That he] could block the Ampezzo Highway and [the Brenner] railroad beyond." From *Letter to Destiny*, Hall's original letter to the OSS.

29 "the project had to be drafted as carefully" From Hall's letter behind the lines. (WC#36 and MATERAZZI)

30 "tough," "a man of complete confidence" From oral history interview with Frank Monteleone.

30 "Philo-communists," "some of OSS's most dedicated operatives" From Materazzi oral history interview conducted by the author.

30 "If you don't risk, you don't win" Oral history interview with Fred Mayer.

31 "In future, all terror and sabotage troops" Hitler Directive on execution of allied agents.

31 "all military aspects of the proposed operation," "go ahead and do it." Memo on SO operation in CORTINA d'AMPEZZA to Lt. M. Jiminez. 9 July 1944. (MERCURY)

32 "prime responsibility [was] the organization of the partisans," "the attack upon the communications route" Original Eagle Mission report. (MERCURY)

33 "maps, sleeping bags, foreign money, climbing gear" Proposed SO operation, 2677th Regiment OSS. Written by Stephen Hall to Riepe. (MERCURY)

All of the equipment and supplies, including "balloons" for the Eagle Mission come from the original manifests and quartermaster acquisitions found in MERCURY.

34 "Dear Captain Suhling, Our operation against that certain supply route" From Hall Letter to Suhling dated July 31, 1944. (MERCURY)

CHAPTER 6: BOONDOGGLE

Description of the journey comes from Howard Chappell interview as well as interviews with Steinmetz, B. Stephens, and other German OGs.

Quotes regarding specific details on Fabrega come from Howard Chappell interview and are confirmed through other OGs.

CHAPTER 7: THE JUMP

41 "We sweated rivers and froze later ... It was bad news for me ... With a full moon, the tumbled hills below looked small and eerie ... opening with a crack ... sailed past like a shot out of a cannon ... two wicked spikes of limestone" From Hall's letter behind the lines. (WC#36 and MATERAZZI)

44 "Somewhere safe," "friendlies" from *Debriefing of 2nd Lt. Joseph Lukitsch.* (MERCURY)

45 "They set up a collection point between a large oak" From Hall Diary and also *Debriefing of 2nd Lt. Joseph Lukitsch.* (MERCURY and WC#36)

45 "We felt that we had been granted a miracle" From Hall Diary. (WC#36)
        Description of partisan movement from extensive interviews with Italian partisans and ISBREC.

46 "Osoppo numbered approximately two thousand men ... politically unbiased, pro-democratic and anti-communist ... All leaders, including company and platoon commanders" All quotes are part of Eagle Mission report. (MERCURY)

48 "We went fishing, to try to get fresh meat" From Hall Diary. (WC#36)

49 "Joe and I placed charges. one-hundred and fifty pounds of dynamite." (WC#36)

50 "Wonderfully received ... being my birthday, I drank to my health with milk at 12:01 a.m." From Hall Diary. (WC#36)

51 "I scrambled upstairs just in time ... walk through the town ... black as a hat" From Hall Diary. (WC#36)

51 "Crawling on slimy wood ... very tired and sore" Hall Diary. (WC#36)

52 "Yellow peril ... I could have reached over the edge of the open attic and touched them" Hall Diary. (WC#36)

52 "Although cloudy, could see all major roads." Hall Diary. (WC#36)

53 "Tolmezzo is being strengthened daily." From Eagle Radio File. August 15, 1944. (MERCURY)

54 "Firebrand" Hall Diary and Hall Letter. (WC#36 and MERCURY)

54 "Stayed up till 12. *No drop.*" Hall Diary. (WC#36)

54 "They were accusing me of not supplying them with arms." Hall Diary. (WC#36)

54 "Hall states, rock fall" From Eagle Radio File. (MERCURY)

54 "From Smith, to whom it may concern" Eagle Radio File. (MERCURY)

55 "Partisans ready to block all minor roads through the Alps." Eagle Radio File. (MERCURY)

55 "Waited in bushes until 5-30" Hall Diary. (WC#36)

55 "Are you Captain Hall? … They hung on me like glue" Hall Diary. (WC#36)
56 "Brenner defense plan of maximum importance" Eagle Radio File. (MER-CURY)
56 "General celebration. Reviewed all radio messages" Hall Diary. (WC#36)

CHAPTER 8: "NO"

57 "Had finally found a home." Chappell oral history. (OH)
57 "Belly to belly" Materazzi oral history. (OH)
58 "Fourth Arm" OSS History
59 "The Brain" Materazzi oral history. (OH)
59 "I don't remember … I made short shrift…pain in the ass." Materazzi oral history. (OH)

CHAPTER 9: BRIDGES AND MOLOTOVS

60 "Nearly ate my clothes off." Hall Diary. (WC#36)
60 "Clear evening sky" Hall Diary. (WC#36)
60 "A clear brilliant blue sky" Hall Diary. (WC#36)
60 "I said not to kill them" Hall Diary. (WC#36)
61 "They were shot that evening" Eagle Radio File. (MERCURY)
61 "Boom dust," "Aunt Jemima" Hall Diary. (MERCURY)
61 "Heard a scurry of running feet" Hall Diary. (MERCURY)
61 "Adventurous," "boyish charm" Dozens of interviews with Italian partisans and Hall's teammate L. Smith. (OH)
62 "I asked all civilians for wine bottles" Hall Diary. (MERCURY)
62 "looked over just as Nazis drove" Hall Diary. (MERCURY)
62 "After interrogating Nazi prisoners" Hall Diary. (WC#36)
63 "10,000 white Russians. (Cossacks)" Eagle Radio File. (MERCURY)
63 "Air force will not take action on targets" Eagle Radio File. (MERCURY)
63 "Disheartening. Bad news all around," "solid overcast," "all tobacco gone." Hall Diary. (WC#36)
64 "Routes 50, 51, and 52 completely" Eagle Radio File. (MERCURY)
64 "Quarreled with Nemo" Hall Diary. (WC#36)
64 "Climbed to plateau" Smith letter to Materazzi. (MATERAZZI)
65 "Germans answered with a sustained" Hall Diary. (WC#36)
65 "Two German soldiers…Perfect Detonation" Hall Diary. (WC#36)
65 "Hell of a time" Hall Diary. (WC#36)
65 "Get intelligence teams to Brenner" Eagle Radio File. (WC#36)

65 "Very tired." "Decision: yes." Hall Diary. (WC#36)

CHAPTER 10: BORED IN SIENA

67 "Not to vorry, I vill get you de chicken." Interview with B. Stevens. (OH)

67 "A real pain in the ass." Interview with Materazzi. (OH)

CHAPTER 12: THE MOUNTAINEER

74 "I made up my pack and started out" Hall Diary. (WC#36)

74 "The threat never leaves you" Hall Letter. (WC#36, MERCURY, MATERAZZI)

74 "A pair of legs of cast iron." Hall Letter. (WC#36, MERCURY, MATERAZZI)

76 "No food, very hard climbing, tiny breakfast." Hall Diary. (WC#36)

76 "Climbing 2,000 meters, on foot, Right foot frozen" Hall Diary. (WC#36)

76 "Local representatives" Oral history with Italian partisans and Italian historians. (OH)

77 "Even if smiling in front" Oral history with Italian partisans and Italian historians. (OH)

77 "Message to base on Brenner biz" Hall Diary. (WC#36)

77 "Hall can blow the Brenner" Eagle Radio File. (MERCURY)

77 "It was a great thrill all around" Hall Diary. (WC#36)

78 "Cossacks" numerous documents at ISBREC were consulted plus oral histories from those who lived through their reign of terror.

78 "The Republic Alpine patrol" Eagle Mission Report. (MERCURY)

79 "The partisan of Friuli" Eagle Mission Report. (MERCURY)

   All messages on the communist involvement behind the lines comes from the Eagle Radio File and Eagle Mission Report. (MERCURY)

81 "Lukitsch is coming" Eagle Mission Report. (MERCURY)

81 "Officers and non-coms knew" Hall Diary. (WC#36)

82 "We watched the tracers" Hall Letter. (WC#36, MERCURY, MATERAZZI)

82 "Scarlet Pimpernel from C" Hall Diary. (WC#36)

CHAPTER 13: THE COUNTESS

During my trip to Italy, I met Judge Giuseppe Sorge, an expert on the activities of the partisans. He wrote an excellent article on the Countess entitled, *Apetti di Convivenza e di Belligeranza tra Partigiani ed Autorita Locali: Isabel de Obligado, La Contessa di Zoldo.* The judge granted me permission to use the original interview he had

N O T E S

with the countess's housekeeper, who had an intimate knowledge of the countess's activities in WWII, including her use of a covert radio and a room filled with arms and ammunition. The article was printed in the #5 quarterly issue of "Protagonisti," published by the *Istituto storico bellunese della resistenza e dell'eta contemporanea. (ISBREC)*. I also interviewed two Italians who were children during the war and acted as aids to the countess.

The countess's letters to Hall are also revealing and provide many details about their relationship and were given to the author by Albert Materazzi. Direct quotes in the countess's own words come from the letters. (MATERAZZI)

Additional details on the ountess's appearance were found in an article written by a partisan commander Giuseppe Lande.

84 "Tea and Talk," "Bits and pieces" Hall Diary. (WC#36)
84 "great admirer of mine" Countess Letter. (MATERAZZI)
84 "Dr. Lauer used his position" CIC Letter on Lauer. (MATERAZZI)
85 "She could . . . set off bombs" Chappell interview. He clearly admired the woman yet also stated he sensed she "played both sides of the fence."
85 "Bound together" Countess letter. (MATERAZZI)

CHAPTER 14: GREEN LIGHT

86 "Materazzi spliced two objectives" Oral history interview with Materazzi. (OH). (TACOMA)
87 "Howard wanted to go through the Brenner" Interview with Ciccone. (OH)
87 "Liberating the concentration camps" Interview with Stevens. (OH)
88 "Chappell team coming next" Aztec Radio File. (AZTEC)

CHAPTER 15: MISSION IMPOSSIBLE

89 "Inform Hall. Narrow gauge railroad" Aztec Radio File. (AZTEC)
89 "To disable the Cortina Railroad" Italian oral history interviews. (OH) IS-BREC
91 "Mop-up," "the effect of the theatre" Kermit Roosevelt, The Overseas Targets: War Report of the OSS, p.113.
91 "Sent long letter to Joe B." Hall Diary. (WC#36)
92 "Holiday today special food—pasta!" Hall Diary. (WC#36)
92 "All marmalade should have been shipped by this time" Hall Diary. (WC#36)

- 255 -

CHAPTER 16: WEAVING THE WEB

93 "Through Foppa, Schiffer was able to" The source of the Schiffer's testimony as well as other German characters in the book stems largely from voluminous and thorough depositions gathered from them by former SS criminal police officer Schoster, who was working for the allies to build war crimes case #36. In their own words the SS tell the story of the final days of the war and Steven Hall's story in their captivity. Schiffer Deposition. (WC#36)

94 "Professor Coleselli was arrested" Christina Roy Deposition. (WC#36)

94 "American captain" Schiffer Deposition. (WC#36)

94 "machine room" Christina Roy Deposition. (WC#36)

94 "I carried out the arrests in the following manner" Schiffer Deposition. (WC#36)

95 "It was Dr. Longon's" Schiffer Deposition. (WC#36)

95 "intensively interrogated," "Friggo," "chief enemy agents," "allowed him to escape," "declared himself ready" Schiffer Deposition. (WC#36)

95 "Longon recognized Mario immediately," "American captain," "execute the death sentence," "I made a suggestion that either the arteries of the Dr. Longon be cut open" Schiffer Depostion. (WC#36)

CHAPTER 17: LA MONTANARA

97 "I finally picked up a bunch of ex-noncoms" Hall Letter. (WC#36, MERCURY, MATERAZZI)

98 "I had my suspicions," "it was just another icicle shop," "they suffered from influenza, dysentery," "maybe in a month we can start work again," "they did not want to quit" Hall Letter. (WC#36, MERCURY, MATERAZZI)

98 "La Montanara" Hall Letter but confirmed through Italian sources.

99 "An hour later" Hall Diary. (WC#36)

99 "We got mortars" Hall Letter. (WC#36, MERCURY, MATERAZZI)

CHAPTER 18: A LOVER'S CHRISTMAS

100 "Steve passed Christmas with me" The original countess's letters given to the author by Albert Materazzi. (MATERAZZI)

101 "So with the local Hitlerites" Hall Letter. (WC#36, MATERAZZI, MERCURY)

101 "one man job" Hall Diary.

101 "[Steve possessed] a great depression" Countess Letter. (MATERAZZI)

CHAPTER 19: TACOMA

103 "Stand in the door, hook up" Chappell Interview. (OH)

104 "Chappell's mission was to first link up with Hall" Tacoma Report. (TACOMA)

104 "Rambo" Interview with Partisan. (OH)

105 "One of the partisans then led us to a rendezvous point" Tacoma Report. (TACOMA)

105 "It was right after Christmas and Chappell reminded me of Santa Claus" Interview with Cangelosi. (OH)

105 "good listener" Interview with Cangelosi. (OH)

105 "[He] had so much courage and he seemed fearless." Chappell Interview. (OH)

106 "He was exciting to watch" Interview with Cangelosi. (OH)

106 "We slept here that day" Tacoma Report. (TACOMA)

106 "rat race where we were hunted every day" Interview with Cangelosi. (OH)

106 "We all moved into a house midway between San Antonio and Trichiana." Tacoma Report. (TACOMA)

CHAPTER 20: MESSAGES IN BOTTLES

107 "literally as hard as boards" Hall Diary. (WC#36)

107 "den in Andrich" Hall Letter. (WC#36, MERCURY, MATERAZZI)

107 "nothing to do but listen to [his] mustache grow" Hall Diary. (WC#36)

108 "If I ever get out of the mess" Hall Letter. (WC#36, MERCURY, MATERAZZI)

109 "The fascist secret police" Hall Letter. (MATERAZZI and WC#36)

110 "This plays in my favor" Hall Letter. (MATERAZZI and WC#36)

110 "Have upstairs room" Kermit Roosevelt, The Overseas Targets: War Report of the OSS), p. 113. This is an official history of the OSS produced by President Roosevelt's son, Kermit and other former OSS personnel shortly after the war. The study remained classified for decades, and is now available in the National Archives.

110 "there was one police officer whose loyalties we never really knew." Italian Partisan and expert interview. (OH)

111 "the American who's been here five months that no one can catch" Hall Letter. (WC#36, MERCURY, MATERAZZI)

111 "Base requests Cortina R.R. cut" Aztec Radio File. (AZTEC)

111 "Haze, clear at night" Hall Diary. (WC#36)

CHAPTER 21: JOURNEY TO CORTINA

112 "My first job was to get to Cortina and Steve Hall" Chappell Interview. (OH), Tacoma Report. (TACOMA)

112 "Chappell's first attempt to reach Hall involved a coffin" Cangelosi Interview. (OH)

113 "We planned to start moving northward to join Captain Hall" Tacoma Report. (TACOMA), (OH)

113 "I need two German soldiers I can trust" Tacoma Report. (TACOMA), (OH)

113 "widely spaced teeth," "Bobbie," "housework," "We were sent here to be guides" Tacoma Report. (TACOMA)

114 "We must get rid of Bobbie and Fred," "What's up Cap'n," "We're going to get rid of the Austrians," "I don't trust you. I'm sending you back" Chappell Interview. (OH), Silsby Interview. (OH)

114 "The shoes were worth 75 to 150 dollars" Chappell Interview. (OH), Tacoma Report. (TACOMA)

114 "I heard reports that after Howard killed the Austrian" Materazzi Interview. (OH)

115 "During the three weeks we made arrangements" Tacoma Report. (TACOMA)

115 "I devised a plan to dress in civilian clothes" Tacoma Report. (TACOMA)

CHAPTER 22: AGAINST ALL ODDS

116 "This is the opportunity I have been waiting for" Tacoma File Sworn Statement Chappell on Hall. (TACOMA and WC#36)

116 "Dear Steve, I have learned that you are moving today" Countess Letter. (MATERAZZI)

118 "presentiment of misfortune" Countess Letter. (MATERAZZI)

118 "Howling wind and frigid snow " Hall's last days in Chappell Report on Hall. (TACOMA)

119 "compassion toward," "Sono stuffo di quest vita" Chappell Report on Hall. (TACOMA and WC#36)

119 "antifascist" Italian Expert. (OH)

120 "the AGO card of Hall and he (Tell) identified him as the Hall of the OSS," "to liberate [him], but Hall was sent to Bolzano instead" Chappell Report on Hall. (WC#36 and TACOMA)

120 "the utmost kindness and consideration," "the wine flowed rather freely," "animated and cheerful conversation," "told him that they would meet at Cortina for the skiing season at war's end" Hollingshead Report. (WC#36)

CHAPTER 23: DISAPPOINTMENT

122 "The icy weather sharpened his thoughts as he reflected" Chappell Interview. (OH)
123 "Joe Benucci loved women" Cangelosi Interview. (OH)
123 "had a ten-thousand-dollar price tag on his head" Aztec Report. (AZTEC)
124 "The partisans carried me down the mountain" Aztec Report. (AZTEC) and Benucci quoted from "Operation Aztec" by Richard Kelly, Blue Book Magazine, New York, 1946.
124 "eating five meals a day, drank dozens of eggnogs," "The God-damned Americans," "You had to be there to understand it" Chappell Interview. (OH)
125 "command" Tacoma and Aztec Mission Report. (TACOMA). (AZTEC)
125 "Due to the many fascists and German garrisons in the area" Aztec Report. (AZTEC)
125 "When we arrived, the commander of the Piave Brigade" Tacoma Report. (TACOMA)
126 "council of war," "[The leader] said if the Germans came in force, we would fight" Tacoma Report. (TACOMA)
126 "without becoming helplessly bogged down in the snow" Tacoma Report. (TACOMA and OH)
126 "They started coming about 0730 hours" Tacoma Report. (TACOMA)
127 "The Alpini were armed to the teeth with nearly every conceivable weapon except tanks and flowers" Captain Paul Brietsche, Bitterroot Report, SOE operative who worked behind the lines in the Belluno area. (MATERAZZI)
127 "They took flight and fled without firing a shot," "Before we knew it, we were the only ones left" Tacoma Report. (TACOMA and OH)
127 "We committed the action known as getting the hell out" Tacoma Report. (TACOMA)
128 "Cherbro a pistol for self-defense" Chappell Interview. (OH)
128 "We started out to reinforce the partisans" Tacoma Report. (TACOMA)
129 "Chappell was infuriated, as he had not realized up until then this type of thing was possible" Bitterroot Report. (MATERAZZI)

129 "entirely finished with all of Benucci's partisans," "take over" Bitterroot Report. (MATERAZZI)

129 "[Benucci] gave me lots of promises and for a few days I was satisfied" Bitterroot Report. (MATERAZZI)

CHAPTER 24: CAUGHT IN THE WEB

131 "relished" SS Deposition. (WC#36)

131 "I'm an American soldier, you can't force me to make any specific declarations" Roy Deposition. (WC#36)

131 "You're an enemy agent, not a soldier," "I am wearing the uniform of a US soldier and am not required to disclose anything more" Schiffer and Roy Deposition. (WC#36)

132 "Hall was a terrorist" Schiffer Deposition. (WC#36)

132 "prisoners of honor" Roy Deposition. (WC#36)

132 "It occurred to me at that moment that Captain Hall might be the American" Schiffer Deposition. (WC#36)

133 "in most cases, this procedure alone sufficed to make the delinquent confess," "suspending," "Usually," "the poles of the induction machine were applied to the cheeks of those who were hanging from the swing or were suspended from the ladder" Schiffer Report. (WC#36)

133 "the American authorities by wireless to immediately to stop the bombing of Bolzano" Roy Deposition. (WC#36)

133 "stooped" Schoster Interview. (WC#36)

CHAPTER 25: LOVER'S LAMENT

134 "When Steve disappeared, no one knew it" Countess Letter. (MATERAZZI)

134 "Hall captured by Nazis" Aztec Radio File. (AZTEC)

135 "Arrangements for an exchange were undertaken through Switzerland" Dulles Report to OSS Headquarters in Italy via radio message. (MATERAZZI)

CHAPTER 26: RESCUE

136 "rescuing distressed allied airmen and ex-prisoners-of-war" OG History. (TACOMA)

137 "Buckhardt [sic] will bring 100,000 lire from Air Corps to be used in caring for pilots" Tacoma Radio File. (TACOMA)

137 "The most popular plan had been to walk to Yugoslavia" Tacoma Report. (TACOMA)

137 "On February 12 we found an excellent landing strip, and we immediately worked to prepare the strip for landings" Tacoma Radio File. (TACOMA)

138 "Men working hard to clear strip" Tacoma Radio File. (TACOMA)

139 "2 locomotives destroyed" Tacoma Summary of Operations, February 15, 1945. (TACOMA)

140 "[The packages] were placed everywhere, quite often just hidden where they would do more harm" Tacoma Report. (TACOMA)

140 "Traffic held up most of the night of Feb. 19" Tacoma Radio File. (TACOMA)

140 "V" Tacoma Report. (TACOMA)

141 "Buchardt, Delaini just missed fires, Ciccone burnt pants" Tacoma Radio File. (TACOMA)

141 "Hello kid, how about a bottle of good wine?" Tacoma Report. (TACOMA)

CHAPTER 27: THE HANGMAN'S NOOSE

142 "the influence of strong drink" Schoster Deposition. (WC#36)

142 "Are you ready to carry out the execution?"Andergassen Stortz Deposition. (WC#36)

142 "I was determined to let Roderick Hall be executed" Schiffer Deposition. (WC#36)

143 "I think that Andergassen then brought a laundry line about as thick as the little finger." Schiffer Deposition. (WC#36)

144 "political unreliability" Pittschieler Depostion. (WC#36)

145 "Andergassen and Stortz roughly threw the body into the coffin," See whether he's dead or not," "I came to the conclusion that the death had taken place approximately six hours previously," "He's dead" Pittschieler Deposition. (WC#36)

145 "a state-less individual named Holl" Materazzi Interim Report on Hall. (WC#36)

145 "Resurrecturis Cemetery in Bolzano" Materazzi Report. (WC#36)

145 "safe keeping," "received this report with a smile" Schiffer Deposition. (WC#36)

CHAPTER 28: A CRY FOR HELP

146 "Germans were to give an answer in three days if they would accept the proposition for exchange," "through Switzerland" Hollingshead Report. (WC#36)

"Then, at last, I told everyone of the capture of Steve by the Germans, and I pleaded that someone should go make the negotiations" Countess Letter. (MATERAZZI)

146 "had no details on Captain Hall and needed more information" Radio Message from Dulles to OSS Italy. (MATERAZZI)

CHAPTER 29: PITCHED BATTLES

148 "About a hundred fascists are moving on our position!" Chappell Interview. (OH)

148 "Bruno," "where shoes on your feet were a luxury," "my war" Bruno Letter to the author September 2007

148 "fire eater," "fight to the last men and to the last shot" Bitterroot Report. (MATERAZZI)

148 "compare favourably with any commander in a regular army" Bitterroot Report. (MATERAZZI)

149 "As we faced south, there was a sharp rocky decline to the plain below." Tacoma Report. (TACOMA)

149 "Hold your fire," "Open fire!" Chappell Interview. (OH)

149 "They met our dreadful resistance" Paride Brunetti, "The Collaberation with the 'Tacoma' Mission," GLI Americani E La Guerra Di Liberazione in Italia, published by Presidenza Del Consiglio Dei Ministri Departimento Per L'Inforamazione I L'Eeditoria. (published Venezia, 1994)

150 "The effect was devastating and the fascists were at once completely demoralized" Tacoma Report. (TACOMA)

150 "Fabrega began to duel with the two enemy guns, which ended by him driving both gun crews to cover" Tacoma Report Fabrega OSC Citation. (TACOMA)

150 "That day there was a massacre..." Bruno Letter to the author, September 2007

151 "Silsby had to stretch the antenna, and while he worked, he was under direct automatic fire" Tacoma Report. (TACOMA)

151 "Am in trouble." Tacoma Radio File. (TACOMA)

151 "we were fighting for Italy's honor" Bruno letter to the author, September 2007

152 "Fabrega, Delaini, Brownie, and myself started out with personal weapons, one bazooka, and two BARs to try to set up an ambush" Tacoma Report. (TACOMA)

CHAPTER 30: MANHUNT

153 "Tedeschi, Tedeschi, San Antonio!" Tacoma Report, Aztec Report. (TACOMA and AZTEC)

153 "Bury the radio!" Chappell Interview. (OH)

153 "Put the rest of the equipment in the caves." Tacoma Report. (TACOMA)

154 "There's a woman pointing out to a German officer our exact location." Tacoma Report, Chappell Interview. (TACOMA and OH)

154 "cleaning up all organized resistance in the entire zone" Tacoma Report. (TACOMA)

154 "it was nearly impossible to escape from the trap," "We moved very rapidly down a steep bank, most of us falling a good part of the way." Tacoma Report. (TACOMA) Chappell Interview. (OH)

155 "Here again, he displayed amazing coolness and confidence" Tacoma Report. (TACOMA)

155 "All this time he kept up his fire with the BAR, making himself a perfect target for Jerry" Tacoma Report. (TACOMA)

155 "Buchhardt and Silsby seemed very tired," "They were running like hell, but getting nowhere," "Captain, they're going to get us" Tacoma Report. (TACOMA)

156 "Now, get the hell out of here! I will cover you!," "If we are caught, you can still get a message back about us." Chappell Interview. (OH)

156 "apparently unconscious" Tacoma Report. (TACOMA)

156 "Kamerad" Tacoma Report. (TACOMA)

156 "fell down, and couldn't get up" Chappell Report. (OH)

157 "It was impossible to move him so I surrendered" Tacoma Report. (TACOMA)

157 "I could not move more than a few inches, and so I brought up my knees" Tacoma Report. (TACOMA)

157 "There's a German behind you!" Tacoma Report. (TACOMA)

158 "I dived into this cavity, pulled as much snow as possible around me, and curled up." Tacoma Report. (TACOMA)

159 "leapt back at the sight," "Follow me" Ciccone Letter to Materazzi. (MATERAZZI)

159 "I heard no voices for a couple of minutes," "The Germans came up the ditch and walked along the top of both sides…" Ciccone Letter to Materazzi. (MATERAZZI)

160 "Kamerad!," "Captain, get out of here. Don't stay with me" Tacoma Report. (TACOMA)

160 "Raus!" Tacoma Report. (TACOMA)

160 "The war is almost over; let us go and I will give you five thousand dollars," "The war is almost over; your house has probably been destroyed" Chappell Interview. (OH)

160 "Yodel-ay-he-hoo! Yodel-ay-he-hoo!," "Each time he did so, I would yodel too." Tacoma Report. (TACOMA) Chappell Interview. (OH)

161 "I insulted the German grenades in general, while praising our own." "Drop your weapon." Chappell Interview. (OH)

161 "He did not realize at first what it was, until I threatened to shoot." Tacoma Report. (TACOMA)

162 "We all knew about the steel meat hooks at Bolzano." Chappell Interview. (OH)

162 "We need to make a break for it soon" "I told Silsby, when we reached the house, to make a break through the stable and I would go through around the house." Tacoma Report. (TACOMA) Chappell Interview. (OH)

162 "racehorse," "He was too far away to jump him in the condition I was in but it did take his mind off Chappell." Tacoma Report. (TACOMA)

162 "I thought I was dead" Tacoma Report. (TACOMA) Silsby Interview. (OH)

163 "I stopped rather stupidly, turned around and walked down the road in the direction we had been going and the guard followed," "The enemy kept firing at me and got as close as about twenty yards from me." Tacoma Report. (TACOMA)

CHAPTER 31: HIDING

164 "One of them ricocheted and hit me in the calf of my left leg." Chappell Interview. (OH)

164 "SS officer had cut off his hands and gouged out his two eyes." Tacoma Report. (TACOMA)

165 "…His death was a serious blow to me, even in death I would like to think of him as being whole…" Chappell Letter to Brownie's sister, 1990. (MATERAZZI)

165 "All day long the enemy passed up and down before the house where the men were hiding," "Should I pull it?," "No, I said" Silsby Interview. (OH)

167 "Sit tight" Chappell Interview. (OH)

167 "They assured me that the Germans would never find this place." Tacoma Report. (TACOMA)

168 "A patrol of about thirty Germans passed by the stable, seemingly neglecting to search it," "The civilians started running out and I saw two go down and

a few others were hit," "I estimated that there were about seventy, although that figure is purely a guess" Tacoma Report. (TACOMA) Chappell Interview. (OH)

168 "You suddenly grab his pistol wrist, bend over, give just the right quick pull and he goes rolling over your shoulder, dazed, on the ground," "It appeared impossible to hide from them," "as though I were a member of the German search party," "as if I were billeted there," "Sitting by the fireplace were an old woman and two young girls, spinning wool by hand" Tacoma Report. (TACOMA) Chappell Interview. (OH)

CHAPTER 32: CAPTURED

170 "I was treated decently by these troops. They were mostly youngsters of 17 and 18." Silsby Interview. (OH)

170 "They applied electric wires to my tongue and ears," "and tried many other savage methods, such as beating me unexpectedly from somewhere in the circle they formed around me," "room of thirty or so partisans" Tacoma Report. (TACOMA)

171 "They brought in two of our partisans they had captured —Porthos and Victor" Chappell Interview. (OH)

171 "ten-thousand lice," "They tortured Fabrega," "They know you're the radio operator," "The old boy could speak broken English." Tacoma Report. (TACOMA)

172 "They seemed very stupid and the story was this," "Why are you in Europe?" Tacoma Report. (TACOMA)

173 "Sorry for what happened. The men will punished," "I continued the same story as told in Belluno until they confronted me with the messages and said they dealt with several OSS teams" Tacoma Report. (TACOMA)

174 "They asked me where the base was. I told them Bari. Also when we dropped, where we operated, and what type of work we did." Tacoma Report. (TACOMA) Silsby Interview. (OH)

174 "Now's our time," "I'll give you a chance to escape. I'll open the door and we'll both run into the hills and join the partisans." Tacoma Report. (TACOMA)

CHAPTER 33: ON THE RUN

175 "Hopping into a creek, I [waded through] the water for about two miles [...] The snow was too deep to walk on. The I ducked into a hole and stayed there until dark." Tacoma Report. (TACOMA)

176 "They hid me in a stable and the following morning, I was mighty happy when they brought in Sgt. Ciccone." Tacoma Report. (TACOMA)

176 "Because he was afraid the Germans would come searching," "It was dark by now," "and I took the road, being very careful, since I did not know whether the Germans had left the town yet." Tacoma Report. (TACOMA)

CHAPTER 34: CAMP

179 "stocky, fat North German," "merely carried out the orders of his superiors," "Hilde" Internee testimony and Tito Deposition. (WC#36)

179 "enjoyed striking male and female prisoners with a whip" Court Testimony. (WC#36)

179 "like a eunuch," "repulsive" Internee Testimony. (WC#36)

180 "jumper's camp" Tacoma Report. (TACOMA)

180 "female without feelings" Schoster Report. (WC#36)

181 "camp for special prisoners," "How can that be done in these circumstances? I shall kill them," "It was the same routine each time." Schiffer Deposition. (WC#36)

181 "How can that be done," "It came to light they," Schiffer Deposition. (WC#36)

181 "Around this time" Schiffer Deposition. (WC#36)

182 "We compelled the three" Storz Deposition. (WC#36)

182 "Trouble with the car" Storz Deposition. (WC#36)

182 "The order for shooting" Storz Deposition. (WC#36)

182 "Good, you did the job" Schiffer Deposition. (WC#36)

182 "Received this report" Schiffer Deposition. (WC#36)

182 "In order to make the escort" Schiffer Deposition. (WC#36)

183 "I want your full report" Andergassen Deposition. (WC#36)

183 "Do I have to go or do" Schiffer Deposition. (WC#36)

183 "It was only in the late" Schiffer Deposition. (WC#36)

183 "One can only assume" Schiffer Deposition. (WC#36)

183 "It was the same routine" Silsby Interview. (OH) Tacoma Report. (Tacoma)

184 "Almost every night while I was there I heard the screaming in adjoining cells in the cell block." Internee Testimony. (WC#36)

CHAPTER 35: REGROUPING

185 "When I was sure he was," "But I didn't have time" Chappell Interview. (OH) Tacoma Report. (TACOMA)

NOTES

186 "We were so happy" Tacoma Report. (TACOMA)

186 "He would not permit" Tacoma Report. (TACOMA)

186 "When Bruno arrived" Chappell Interview. (TACOMA)

187 "On February 7 Toni" Portland Mission Report, National Archives, RG 226, Entry 190, Box 174.

187 "[Gigi's] commander [Toni] almost" Tacoma Mission Report. (TACOMA)

187 "Howard Wheeler Chappel" Tacoma Radio File. (TACOMA)

188 "They were apparently trying to secure" Tacoma Report. (TACOMA)

189 "They were the kind of days that were" Chappell Interview. (OH)

189 "The hole was about 150 yards" Ciccone Interview. (OH)

CHAPTER 36: BLOW THE BRIDGE

190 "Our nearest explosives were" Tacoma Report. (TACOMA) Chappell Interview. (OH)

191 "There were two dozen of us" Chappell Interview. (OH)

191 "Two of the guards scampered to the middle" Chappell Interview. (OH) Tacoma Report. (TACOMA)

191 "two armored cars" Tacoma Radio File. (TACOMA)

191 "I inserted some Composition" Tacoma Report. (TACOMA)
Chappell's Silver Star citation which could be for the Medal of Honor is located in RG 226, Entry 92A, Folder 2239.

192 "Full of disappointment," "more determined to blow it" Chappell Interview. (OH)

192 "I figured the Germans would guess," "The next night planes lit" Tacoma Report. (TACOMA)

CHAPTER 37: THE TRIAL

193 "A beautiful scarf" Rosanna Vedana Colleselli "A Courier for the Aztec Mission" OSS E LA Restenza Italiana, p. 339. The book is a compilation of written accounts in the words of participants who fought behind the lines.

195 "Rafael Da Val" CIC post-war report. (MATERAZZI)

195 "It was not easy" Rosanna Vendana Colleselli, p. 339.

195 "[The trial] was such an obvious" Tacoma Report. (TACOMA)

195 "Declaration: …. American missions" The original document resides in the archives of ISBREC in Belluno. The proceedings of the trial are also archived at the Institute.

CHAPTER 38: TICKET TO RIDE

197 "My main worry," "was that the German" Tacoma Report. (TACOMA)
197 "Alpine Redoubt" The Redoubt was more myth than reality and the Germans continued to feed the Allies propaganda fortifications were under construction.
198 "I kept one hand close to my .45" Ciccone Interview. (OH)
198 "Chappell was a monster" Author interview with Mario. (OH)
199 "Halt! papers" IBID and Chappell Interview. (OH)
199 "Our hearts went into our mouths" Chappell Interview. (OH)
199 "As we heard the driver" Tacoma Report. (TACOMA)
199 "When we passed," "Halt," "Take off the tarp," "We lay as still as death," "We could hear the creak of," "The boxes have to come off" Chappell Interview. (OH)
200 "Verdammter Regen" Tacoma Report. (TACOMA) Chappell Interview. (OH) Mario Interview. (OH)
200 "We could hear" Chappell Interview. (OH)
200 "By the time" Chappell Interview. (OH)
200 "Ettore was quite" Ciccone Interview. (OH)
200 "It was the first" Ibid
200 "They brought down a large cask" Ibid
201 "I don't have any right" Ibid
201 "As we moved down the road," "all types of civilians" Tacoma Report. (TACOMA) Chappell Interview. (OH)
201 "It soon became apparent" Ibid
201 "sanitarium" Ibid
201 "A large German force" Tacoma Radio File. (TACOMA)

CHAPTER 39: AMBUSH

203 "Allies have reached the Piave" Tacoma Radio File. (TACOMA)
203 "Impassable" as for most of the book, the author walked the battle space.
204 "We moved down the road" Tacoma Report. (TACOMA)
204 "Two skinny kids" Ciccone Interview. (OH)
204 "We we pinned the Germans down" Tacoma Report. (TACOMA)
205 "The area was littered" Ciccone Interview. (OH)
205 "Looking down" Chappell Interview. (OH)
205 "If you do not permit" Chappell Interview. (OH) Tacoma Report. (TACOMA)
205 "If any of the civilians" Ibid
205 "Ettore wouldn't budge" Ibid
206 "I'm going down there" Ciccone Interview. (OH)

206 "Get in" Ibid

206 "I want to know" Ibid

206 "What can I do for you," "Go right in" Ibid and Chappell Interview. (OH)

206 "All they could do is kill me" Ciccone Interview. (OH)

206 "I couldn't take him" Chappell Interview. (OH)

207 "I couldn't keep my eyes off him" Ibid and Tacoma Report. (TACOMA)

207 "remembered all the partisans" Chappell Interview. (OH)

207 "What are your terms" Ibid and Tacoma Report. (TACOMA)

207 "There are none" Ibid

207 "customary pleasing," "would be killed" Ibid

207 "If a single civilian is harmed" Ibid

207 "Heim" See Tacoma Report. (Tacoma) and Schneider, Wolfgang: Tigers in Combat I. (Stackpole Books, Mechanicsburg, PA,) 2000. pp. 193-205. The book contains a fine summary of unit's combat actions.

208 "We would like nothing better than," "we are placing ourselves" Tacoma Report. (TACOMA)

208 "Before I agree to surrender" Ibid

208 "Captain Howard Chappell of the OSS" Ibid

208 "I've often heard" Ibid and Chappell Interview. (OH)

208 "Chappell would treat" Ibid

209 "This you can be completely sure of" Ibid

209 "reformed into" Ibid

209 "How old are you" Ciccone Interview. (OH)

209 "No" Ciccone Interview. (OH)

209 "very disturbed" Italian oral history with the women who owned the house. (OH)

210 "businessman" Ciccone Interview. (OH)

210 "We became quite friendly and even joked" Tacoma Report. (TACOMA)

210 "Of course we treated them well," "they tortured Fabrega," "Go back and build a better Germany" Chappell Interview. (OH), Tacoma Report. (TACOMA)

CHAPTER 40: SCHIFFER'S RUN

All quotes from this chapter come from Christa Roy and August Schiffer depositions. (WC#36)

CHAPTER 41: FREEDOM

214 "You are to be removed to Innsbruck" Tacoma Report. (TACOMA)

214 "Half a dozen pistols" Ibid

214 "Organized" Ibid

214 "permission" Ibid

214 "he interceded" Ibid

215 "a thousand more" Ibid

215 "supposedly a stopover" Ibid

215 "They heard we were using" Ibid

215 "We saw a patrol of Germans" Ibid

215 "the building was under the protection" Ibid

CHAPTER 42: CHAPPELL'S WAR

216 "Two battalions," "Have about 1,800 prisoners" Tacoma Radio File. (TACOMA)

216 "Am moving to Cortina" Ibid

217 "Use your influence" Ibid

217 "The central telephone" Ibid

218 "OSS Switzerland" O'Donnell, Operatives, Spies and Saboteurs, p. 299–300. Sunrise-Crossword Operation by Allen Dulles: RG 226, Entry 190C, Boxes 25–30.

218 "for about ten kilometers" Tacoma Radio File. (TACOMA)

219 "I told him they" Tacoma Report. (TACOMA)

219 "looked more like a partisan" Tacoma Report. (TACOMA) Chappell Interview. (OH)

219 "Why are you not saluting" Ciccone Interview. (OH)

220 "What the hell are you" Ibid

220 "Get out of this office" Ibid

221 "Chuck, you're going for a little drive." Ibid

221 "A receipt found in the archives" Tacoma File. (TACOMA)

221 "I'm a West Point officer" Materazzi Interview. (OH)

221 "one official close to the story opined" Italian expert on OSS missions interview. (OH)

CHAPTER 43: TRAPPED

All quotes from Schiffer come from the Schiffer deposition. Information on Schiffer's capture comes from the Deadwood File (RG 226, Entry 124, Box 26), and an oral history interview with OSS agent Fred Mayer, a major figure in the author's next book.

CHAPTER 44: VENDETTA

223 "the previous day two SS officers visited the grave" Materazzi Report on the death of Hall. (WC#36)

223 "Vendetta" Materazzi Interview. (OH)

225 "Stateless," "Holl" Hall death certificate located in the Bolzano archives. (MATERAZZI and WC#36)

225 "Major De Michel" Schoster Report. (WC#36) Schoster describes how De Michel contracted him to track down Hall's killers.

225 "After the arrival" Countess letter. (MATERAZZI)

226 "I lost my best friend" Interview with E. Lukitsch. (OH)

226 "Schoster" "Were purely in the field" See the Schoster Report which gives a detailed bio of the German detective. (WC#36)

226 "Knowledge of the German" Schoster Report. (OH)

227 "Cardiac Paralysis" Hall death Certificate. (WC#36) Pittschieler Deposition. (WC#36)

228 "Brother in the field" Chappell Report on Hall, also see Chappell's officer handwritten notes. (WC#36 and MATERAZZI)

228 "Mr. Fabrega!" Chappell interview. (OH)

228 "Chuck, look who I got." Ciccone Interview. (OH)

228 "It's so good to see you," "Give me your .45" Ciccone Interview. (OH); also, Materazzi recalls Chappell discussing the incident. (OH)

229 "All three of my brigades prepared for parade…I was taking him to Feltre when he tried to escape and was killed." Tacoma Radio File. (TACOMA)

230 "Turning in prisoners" Tacoma Report, and Tacoma Radio File. (TACOMA)

230 "Tell, former aid to Hall and later traitor killed night of April 17. (sic)" [date likely May 17] Tacoma Radio File. (TACOMA)

230 "I practically had to threaten him" Materazzi Interview. (OH)

231 "Donovan wants you to be prepared to give" Tacoma Radio File. (TACOMA)

231 "He said goodbye to the countess" Chappell Interview. (OH)

CHAPTER 45: WAR CRIMES CASE #36

233 "CIC agents" see capture documents. (WC#36)

CHAPTER 46: ON THE LAM

234 "I knew…that in the case" Schiffer Deposition. (WC#36)

CHAPTER 48: ATONEMENT

237 "Escape either to Rome" Glenn Infield, *Skorzeny Hitler's Commando* (New York: St. Martins Press, 1981), 155.
238 "Apparently, Miss Roy is willing to tell everything" Schoster Report. (WC#36)
238 "Not guilty" Court papers. (WC#36)
239 "In the submitted case" Storz. (WC#36)

CHAPTER 49: FULL CIRCLE

241 "your son was a hero," "I know" Chappell Interview. (OH)
241 "Columbia Road" Letter found in OSS post-war archives.

CHAPTER 50: SUNRISE

242 "Captain Steve Hall from Washington" plaque found embedded in larch tree located in front of the countess's house.
242 "Sixty shots" "which bears at its heart" Countess Letter. (MATERAZZI)

INDEX